Contents

8	Willy Messerschmitt
22	Genesis of a legend – 109 design and development
28	Into service and into battle – The 109A to D
34	The 109s in combat
38	Firepower and performance – The 109E
40	Production – The key to success
48	Lithe and light – The 109F
52	Gustav – Too much of a good thing
56	Kurfurst – Production priorities
58	Erich Hartmann

Your favourite magazine, now on your favourite tablet

Search for **Aviation Classics** on the Apple App Store or Google play. Download the **FREE** app with one **FREE** issue included!

http://bit.ly/ACtablet

74	'Toni' – The carrier 109
92	Dead ends and desperate designs
98	Inside the 109
106	Czech Mules and Spanish Pigeons
118	The 109 abroad
126	Survivors

The Messerschmitt Bf 109 of the EADS Heritage Flight being flown by Cassidian test pilot Klaus Plaza. This aircraft was restored to Bf 109G-4 standard from an HA-1112 airframe. **Joe Rimensberger**

Editor: Tim Callaway
editor@aviationclassics.co.uk
Publisher: Dan Savage
Contributors: Lord Michael Ashcroft KCMG, Norm DeWitt, Col. Douglas C Dildy, Keith Draycott, Julian Humphries, Maurice McElroy, Klaus Plaza, Constance Redgrave, Joe Rimensberger, Clive Rowley, Dan Sharp, Warren Thompson, Adam Tooby

Designer: Charlotte Pearson
Reprographics: Jonathan Schofield

Group production editor: Tim Hartley

Divisional advertising manager: Sandra Fisher
sfisher@mortons.co.uk
Advertising sales executive: Stuart Yule
syule@mortons.co.uk
01507 529465

Subscription manager: Paul Deacon
Circulation manager: Steve O'Hara
Marketing manager: Charlotte Park
Production manager: Craig Lamb
Publishing director: Dan Savage
Commercial director: Nigel Hole
Business development director: Terry Clark
Managing director: Brian Hill

Editorial address: Aviation Classics
Mortons Media Group Ltd
PO Box 99
Horncastle
Lincs LN9 6JR

Website: www.aviationclassics.co.uk

Customer services, back issues and subscriptions: 01507 529529
(24 hour answerphone)
help@classicmagazines.co.uk
www.classicmagazines.co.uk

Archive enquiries: Jane Skayman
jskayman@mortons.co.uk
01507 529423

Distribution: COMAG
Tavistock Road, West Drayton,
Middlesex UB7 7QE
01895 433800

Printed: William Gibbons and Sons, Wolverhampton

© 2012 Mortons Media Group Ltd.
All rights reserved.
No part of this publication may be reproduced or transmitted in any form or by any means, electronic or mechanical, including photocopying, recording, or any information storage retrieval system without prior permission in writing from the publisher
ISBN No 978-1-906167-65-3

The leader of the pack

Now this one really is a problem. I have had difficulties with this page before, as anyone who reads it knows, but nothing quite like this. Not only is this aircraft an icon, an astounding piece of engineering that is matched in longevity only by the Supermarine Spitfire, it is also a symbol for the darkest empire to ever throw its shadow across the globe. As Cassadian test pilot Klaus Plaza and photographer Constance Redgrave so simply and eloquently put it, it's the bad guy.

How to celebrate a work of genius when it is so tarnished by association? That's the difficulty here. I have been pondering this piece for some time, having talked to many people who flew and maintained this aircraft during my life, all of whom are now dead, I felt that I owed it to the memory of some astounding friends to do these men and their aircraft justice. Two things happened that opened my eyes as to how this could be achieved, the first was that former RAF fighter pilot Squadron Leader Clive Rowley sent in his piece on the remarkable Luftwaffe fighter pilot Erich Hartmann. The second was I overheard a conversation in Berlin.

At the end of his piece, Clive quotes Hartmann directly, who was recorded as saying: "One thing I learned is this: never allow yourself to hate a people because of the actions of a few. Hatred and bigotry destroyed my nation, and millions died. I would hope that most people did not hate Germans because of the Nazis… never hate, it only eats you alive." A remarkable sentiment from a remarkable man, and one which brooks no argument. The second event was while I was leaning on the fence of the static park at the ILA, the Berlin Air Show. I was admiring the superbly maintained Bf 109 which was part of the flying programme, watching the thousands of visitors bypass the modern and powerful jets and make a beeline for the shark in the park.

That's what it looked like, even in the company of the modern combat aircraft, there was something undeniably dangerous in its lithe and elegant form. It formed the centrepiece of the show, of that there is no doubt. An older lady in company with her husband stopped for a long time next to me by the fence, her eyes never leaving the hive of activity around the 109. She turned to her husband and said simply: "How can something so beautiful make me so ashamed and so proud?"

They stayed by the fence not speaking until long after I had left. I do not know who they were, but I do thank her for her illumination. For too long the association with National Socialism has been allowed to taint the memory of a remarkable engineering achievement and a group of brave and dedicated servicemen. In allowing that, we give the evil represented by the Nazis far too much power. I would like to think we have moved on from this and can now acknowledge that a brave man is exactly that, regardless of the insignia on his aircraft or uniform.

The grace, yet sheer force, of a Bf 109 display today should be a fitting memorial to the pilots and engineers who flew and maintained them. While the Nazi regime the Bf 109 was originally built to serve is the most reprehensible in history by any standards, the crews who operated the Bf 109 cannot be measured alongside it. Pilots, in fact aviators the world over, mostly had little time for politics, they are drawn into the service by their love of flying, proud to serve their country and brave in that service. If I may wax poetic a moment, I think W B Yeats said it best:

Nor law, nor duty bade me fight,
Nor public men, nor cheering crowds,
A lonely impulse of delight
Drove to this tumult in the clouds;

That is what I hope I have captured in this magazine, a combination of the genius behind the aircraft and the dedication of those that flew it, free of the shadow of the past.

As ever, I have been assisted in this end by a great many talented and knowledgeable people, but I would particularly like to thank three great fighter pilots, all now turned writers. Colonel Douglas C Dildy of the USAF, Squadron Leader Clive Rowley, former commander of the Battle of Britain Memorial Flight, and Cassadian Test Pilot Klaus Plaza. An American, an Englishman and a German, all working together to record history accurately and fairly. Now that's a world I can live in with pride.

All best,
Tim

"Never was so much owed by so many to so few"
LANCASTER BOMBER
Exclusive 70th Anniversary Masterpiece Clock

Handcrafted Avro Lancaster Bomber sculpture with bronze-tone finish

•

Showcasing the 617 Squadron motto 'Après Moi, Le Déluge'

•

Clock and thermometer inspired by the Lancaster's authentic cockpit instruments

Expertly handpainted for precision detail

MEASURES OVER 6 INCHES IN HEIGHT

Includes a fascinating FREE FACT CARD!

AVRO LANCASTER FACT CARD
Role: Heavy bomber
Introduced: 1942
Retired: 1963 (Canada)
Number built: 7,377
Crew: 7 - pilot, flight engineer, navigator, bomb aimer, operator, mid-upper and rear gunners
Length: 69 ft 5 in (21.18 m)
Height: 19 ft 7 in (5.97 m)
Powerplant: 4x Rolls-Royce Merlin XX V12 engines, 1,280 hp (954 kW) each
Maximum speed: 240 kn (280 mph, 450 km/h) at 15,000 ft (5,600 m)
Guns: 8x 0.303 in (7.7 mm) Browning machine guns in three turrets, with variations
Bombs: Maximum normal bomb load of 14,000 lb (6,300kg) or 22,000 lb Grand Slam with modifications to bomb bay.

Fearlessly led by Wing Commander Guy Gibson, the battle-ready Lancaster Bombers of 617 Squadron thundered through the night skies high above enemy territory, courageously embarking on the most daring raid of WWII – Operation Chastise. Soaring into the annals of military history as the iconic Dambusters, the valiant heroes of Britain's Bomber Command symbolised the hopes of the Allied nations, each determined to defeat the formidable threat of oppression...

Now you can proudly commemorate the landmark 70th anniversary of the mighty Lancaster Bomber – a true icon of the skies and one of the most successful night bombers of WWII – with a first-of-a-kind collectable treasure. The Lancaster Bomber Masterpiece Clock is a market-first edition, exclusive to The Bradford Exchange.

Clock shown smaller than actual size of 6.4 inches (16.2 cm) in height, 5.9 inches (15.2 cm) in depth and 9.4 inches (24 cm) in width (including plane).

Pay tribute to WWII's most successful night bomber with a unique mastercrafted tribute

- Market-first sculpture honouring the fearless Lancaster pilot Wing Commander Guy Gibson's iconic aircraft, flown during his command of the famed 'Dambusters' 617 Squadron, throughout Operation Chastise
- Authentically mastercrafted with a gleaming bronze-tone finish – reminiscent of stunning museum-quality treasures
- Mounted on a richly grained and polished wooden base with a precision Quartz movement clock and indoor thermometer – both inspired by authentic instruments from the Lancaster's cockpit
- Clock face inscribed with the stirring 617 Squadron motto of 'Après Moi, Le Déluge' (After Me, The Flood) – a striking reminder of the bomber's contribution to the acclaimed 'Dambusters' raids

Celebrate a Landmark Anniversary – order yours today!

This anniversary edition is a one-of-a-kind tribute to WWII's most celebrated squadrons and bombers. Arriving with a Certificate of Authenticity and FREE Fact Card, this fine masterpiece is yours for just 4 interest-free instalments of only £24.99 – that's £99.96 – (plus £9.99 P&H), backed by our famous 365-day guarantee. You need pay nothing now – to reserve your edition, simply complete and return your Reservation Application today!

Offer applies to UK only and is subject to availability. Full Terms and Conditions are available on request. The Bradford Group, 1 Castle Yard, Richmond, Surrey TW10 6TF.

Fastest way to order: www.bradford.co.uk
In the search box, please enter 426-B3949.01
Quote reference code P291621

DON'T MISS OUT THIS CHRISTMAS
PAY NOTHING NOW

THE BRADFORD EXCHANGE
RESERVATION APPLICATION
Please Respond Promptly
To: The Bradford Exchange, PO Box 653, Stoke-on-Trent ST4 4RA

YES! Please reserve ___(Qty) of the *70th Anniversary Lancaster Bomber Masterpiece Clock* for me as described in this advertisement. I need PAY NOTHING NOW!

Certificate of Authenticity and 365-day Money-back Guarantee

Name (Mr/Mrs/Miss/Ms) _____ (PLEASE PRINT)

Address _____

_____

Postcode _____ Telephone _____

Email Address _____

From time to time The Bradford Exchange may allow carefully screened companies to contact you. If you do not wish to receive such offers, please tick box ☐

Order Ref: P291621

Wilhelm Emil 'Willy' Messerschmitt photographed in 1958.
Bundesarchiv

The Messerschmitt family in Bamberg. Wilhelm is standing on the right of the group, behind his elder brother Ferdinand. **Editor's collection**

Willy Messerschmitt
– designer, engineer, organiser and visionary genius
From the Harth S3 to the Bf 108

Stories abound about the legend that is Willy Messerschmitt. His devotion to lightweight airframe construction, his single-minded focus on the engineering problems of aviation and his ability to come up with complete solutions to a given problem in a short time are just a few of these. His career stretched from glider experiments in 1913 to the Panavia Tornado and the foundation of Airbus.

Wilhelm Emil 'Willy' Messerschmitt was born on June 26, 1898, the son of Ferdinand Baptist Messerschmitt, in the thriving industrial and financial city of Frankfurt am Main. At the time, his father wanted to become an engineer and had studied mechanics in Zurich, but with his elder brother's emigration to the United States, Ferdinand was called back to Bamberg in 1906 to take over the family's wine merchant business from his ailing father. While he attended school in Bamberg, the young Willy Messerschmitt was influenced by two of his uncles, one a painter, the other a surveyor, developing an artistic sense of style and design which would come to fruition in later life.

An avid reader, the young man devoured books and articles relating to science and technology, as well as becoming something of a musician. This combination of interests in art and technology were instrumental in shaping Messerschmitt's mind, until two events were to coalesce these diverse elements into a single passion. In 1908, he witnessed the Zeppelin airship Bodensee fly at Friedrichshafen, the following year he visited the International Aviation Exhibition in Frankfurt am Main. Now aged 12, Messerschmitt began building and flying model aircraft, both rubber powered and glider designs based on available plans, but producing his first original design, a radically simple monoplane model in 1910. His father was delighted by his son's ambition and interest, and sent him to Bamberg Secondary School.

The first aircraft built by Messerschmitt, Friedrich Harth's S5 glider. **Editor's collection**

HARTH AND HIS GLIDERS
Also based in Bamberg was the municipal government architect Friedrich Harth who, with a team of assistants, had been experimenting with full sized gliders using the Ludwager Kulm, a small, flat topped hill just north of Bamberg, as a launching site. In September 1913, the 15-year-old Willy Messerschmitt joined this group, just in time to assist Harth with his experiments on the S3, his third glider design. In 1914, the group moved its base of operations to Heidelstein near Oberelsbach on the Rhön and Messerschmitt began to assist with the construction of the S4, the first full sized aircraft he was to work on. Just as they were finishing this move, on August 1, 1914, the First World War began, and a few days later the entire group, except the 16-year-old Messerschmitt, were called up for military service. Messerschmitt, who by this time was considered a valued colleague by Harth despite his relative youth, set up his own workshop on his parents' property in Bamberg, taking anything useful he could gather from the facilities abandoned by the group.

Using designs, sketches, notes and advice in letters and postcards from Harth, Messerschmitt constructed a new glider, the S5, which used a few parts from the abandoned S4, completing the aircraft on August 24, 1915. It must be noted that Messerschmitt achieved all this around his school work and preparations for his entrance exams to college, an astounding effort for a 17-year-old. Harth returned to Bamberg on leave in late August, and he and Messerschmitt took the new glider to the Rhön site with the assistance of a French prisoner of war who had been assigned to work for the Messerschmitt family wine business. Harth made several flights in the new glider between September 1 and 12, ➤

MESSERSCHMITT DESIGNS FROM THE M21 TO THE M36

Designation	Year	Role and type	No. built	Notes
M21	1928	Two seat open cockpit biplane trainer.	2	Ordered by the RVM in two versions with different engines. Mixed wood and metal construction.
M22	1930	Twin engined two seat open cockpit biplane.	1	Intended by Messerschmitt as a bomber and his first twin engined aircraft, the RWM saw the M22 as a night fighter and reconnaissance aircraft. Prototype crashed on October 14, 1930, after test pilot flew an unauthorised loop. Project cancelled.
M23a	1928	Two seat open cockpit low wing monoplane trainer.	13	All wooden construction trainer ordered in small numbers by French and German flying clubs.
M23b	1929	Two seat open cockpit low wing monoplane trainer.	70	Developed low drag version of the M23a with a rounded rear fuselage and monospar wing, also available as a floatplane.
M23c	1930	Two seat enclosed cockpit low wing monoplane trainer and tourer.	11	Built for the 1930 Challenge International de Tourisme, developed from the 23b with an enclosed cockpit and improved aerodynamics and wheel brakes.
M24	1928	Ten seat enclosed cabin and cockpit single engined high wing monoplane airliner.	4	All metal design. Two versions, the 24a and 24b, were built with different engines. Intended to carry eight passengers or 1000kg load over 500km. Evaluated by the RVM as a radio aircraft, mailplane and photo survey platform in both land and seaplane forms.
M18c	1929	Survey aircraft development of the M18 airliner.	2	Armstrong Siddeley Lynx powered all metal design, one supplied to Switzerland, the second to Portugal.
M18d	1929	Eight seat development of the M18 airliner.	9	All metal design, stretched fuselage version of the M18 which improved handling and allowed two extra passengers to be carried.
M25	1929	Single seat high wing aerobatic aircraft.	0	Competition aircraft intended for Ernst Udet. Cancelled after Udet bought Curtiss aircraft instead.
M26	1929	Three seat high speed commuter monoplane.	1	Two M26s ordered as high speed commuter aircraft for two passengers by the Eastern Aircraft Corporation in the US. Stock market crash in the US caused the project to be cancelled.
M27	1930	Two seat open cockpit low wing monoplane trainer.	12	Produced in two versions with different engines as a flying school trainer.
M28	1931	Two seat enclosed cockpit high speed mailplane.	1	Built at the request of the RVM and intended for use by the German Postal Service.
M29	1931	Two seat tandem enclosed cockpit high speed tourer and sport aircraft.	6	Built for the 1930 Challenge International de Tourisme, first use of single strut cantilever undercarriage and wing flaps on a Messerschmitt design.
M30	1929	Design study.	0	A design study on behalf of the RVM to examine the costs of producing a version of the M26 out of the light metal alloy Electron.
M31	1932	Two seat tandem open cockpit trainer and sport aircraft.	1	An attempt to produce a cost effective yet high performance trainer using a low powered engine and advanced aerodynamics.
M32	1932	Two seat tandem open cockpit biplane trainer.	0	A design study into producing a simple basic trainer. Not developed.
M33	1932	Two seat tandem open cockpit kit sport aircraft.	1	Only built in mock up form, the 'Volksflugzeug' was intended to be built and flown from a kit by aviation enthusiasts.
M34	1932	Very long range monoplane design study.	0	A study into very low drag airframe design to maximise range.
M35	1932	Two seat tandem open cockpit trainer, aerobatic and sport aircraft.	15	Radial engined but streamlined and efficient, the M35 would recover from a spin just by letting go of the controls, so balanced was its handling. Seen as the logical stepping stone to the Bf 108.
M36	1934	Eight seat single engined high wing enclosed cabin and cockpit airliner.	1	Single example built then assembled by ICAR in Romania. Used by airline LARES from 1936 to 1938.

An in flight view of the BFW works at Augsburg in 1926. **Editor's collection**

Nordbayerische Verkehsflug, Theo Croneiss' airline, operated M17s, 18s, 23s and 24s as seen here at Nuremberg in 1928. **Editor's collection**

of existing aircraft over the next three years. The workload on the design department at Messerschmitt was so great that a separate project department was formed to handle the extra work in 1927. This new department was initially run by Kurt Tank, later to become the designer of the Focke-Wulf Fw 190. This prodigious output of Messerschmitt's fertile mind resulted in a wide range of types, from sport aircraft to airliners and they are listed in the table here. The new aircraft began to take on a distinctive Messerschmitt 'look' as Willy, as he was now widely known, refined his thinking regarding lightweight and simple construction. As can be seen from the list, several of the new types were highly successful for both the designer and manufacturer. While doing all of this, Messerschmitt also became a pilot, gaining his A then B licence in 1929 under instructor Otto Brindlinger, who was later to become BFW's operations director.

Just as the new joint company between Messerschmitt and BFW was getting into its stride building the M20, disaster struck. On October 6, 1930, eight people were killed when an M20b crashed near Dresden on a flight to Vienna. This was followed by a second crash on April 4, 1931, when M20b D-1928 crashed on a charter flight to Görlitz. The crew were killed and four of the eight passengers, all Reichswehr officers, were injured. The first crash was thought to be caused by downdraughts, but the second crash caused the M20 to be grounded while the cause was investigated. It was discovered that the maximum safe load stated in the official general specifications for the M20 was inaccurate, and this official figure had been adhered too. Messerschmitt was blameless in this inaccuracy, but DLH cancelled the deliveries of the 10 M20s under construction and demanded the return of its money.

The director of DLH at the time was Erhard Milch, who had already turned against Messerschmitt and his aircraft as a result of the death of his friend Hans Hackmack and used the crashes as the reason for the cancellation and demand for recompense. This enmity was to have a serious effect on Messerschmitt later, as Milch became the state secretary of the newly formed Reichsluftfahrtministerium (RLM or Reich Aviation Ministry) and one of the founding generals of the Luftwaffe responsible for aircraft acquisition, but more of that later.

The immediate effect of the crashes and the cancelled M20 order was that BFW, which had become a wholly privately owned company in 1928, declared bankruptcy on June 1, 1931. Messerschmitt resurrected his old company, Messerschmitt Flugzeugbau GmbH, to continue his design work, which had lain dormant as his personnel had effectively become the BFW design department. As he owned many of the designs and patents, separate to and independent of BFW, Messerschmitt and his company weathered the financial storm.

He raised start up capital and began rehiring a number of BFW workers who had been laid off so small scale production could continue. By 1933 a solution to BFW's ailments had been found. A court settlement was arrived at with the firm's creditors which was ratified on April 27, the company restarting work on May 1. Steadily, Messerschmitt's firm was reabsorbed into the manufacturer, regaining the position it had held previously as design and project director. Lastly, with the required modifications to the M20 complete (the aircraft had literally been sitting on the airfield at Augsburg), deliveries of the aircraft began again to DLH, which was to use them with great success until 1943.

NATIONAL SOCIALISM CHANGES THE INDUSTRY

Also in 1933, on January 30, Adolph Hitler became chancellor of Germany and rapidly centralised power into the hands of the National Socialist German Workers' Party (NSDAP). The utterly reprehensible ➤

The 25m span wing of the M20 was of single spar D-box construction. These are aircraft waiting to be delivered to DLH while investigations were conducted into the loss of two aircraft in crashes. **Editor's collection**

An M20b of Lufthansa. These aircraft were still in service in 1943, being extremely well built and tremendously efficient. **Editor's collection**

Messerschmitt's great friend and supporter, Theo Croneiss, with an M23a. **Editor's collection**

activities of both Hitler and the party have been thoroughly documented and largely fall outside the scope of this narrative, but I would like to clear up one point regarding Messerschmitt and his motivations. Too often I have seen the man and his aircraft associated with the Nazis in a way that suggests that he was more involved than just as an aircraft manufacturer. I do not believe, nor have I ever believed, that Willy Messerschmitt was a supporter of the NSDAP or the government, if you can call it that, of Adolph Hitler.

In fact, Messerschmitt was initially to suffer at the hands of the regime, as will be detailed. My long research into this remarkable gentleman has underlined his abiding passion to be aviation, pure and simple. From his early days of building model aircraft, a hobby I can identify with; creating extraordinary aircraft and advancing the cause of aviation were his only ambitions, and yes, a financially successful company was a necessary part of that goal. That the aircraft he created were of service to his country was a matter of pride, not because he supported the Nazis, but because he was German.

He was developing aircraft a long time before the NSDAP came to power. His focus was extraordinary; his ability to take a complex problem and solve it over the course of a weekend is a matter of record. For example, when the development of the butterfly tail for testing on the Bf 109 was giving Ludwig Bölkow of the project department several weeks of problems in 1941, Messerschmitt asked him for his documents and some of the drawings and told him he would think about it on Sunday. On Monday, he handed Bölkow 28 pieces of drafting paper, on which were such detailed drawings and structural analysis that no further work was needed, other than a draughtsman to complete the full size construction drawings. The completed tailplane design went to the workshop just two days later. A similar story exists about Messerschmitt solving the problem of the undercarriage of the VJ 101 in 1961 with equal aplomb. The VJ 101 was a supersonic vertical take off and landing jet fighter programme which the Bölkow, Heinkel and Messerschmitt companies developed together for the West German government, but was cancelled in 1968 in the face of rising costs. The fact that Messerschmitt maintained his focus and his capacity for engineering innovation for such a long and distinguished career is proof of my point I believe. Like Sydney Camm and other great designers of their generation, these men had little time for politics or politicians, they suffered them as necessary adjuncts to their life's work, as customers only, they did not embrace them or their beliefs, their focus and workload did not allow it.

With the coming to power of the National Socialists, the aviation departments of the German government were reorganised, the RLM being formed in April 1933 with Hermann Göring as its head. In May, the army's Department of Military Aviation was transferred to the RLM, with the Luftwaffe being officially founded on February 26, 1935. The restrictions on German military aviation placed by the Versailles Treaty were now being completely ignored and the infrastructure was being grown to support the new independent air service. Thousands of aircraft would be required, and the German aviation industry was in no real shape to supply them. To oversee this expansion, the RLM was initially divided into two departments, one civil and one military. As the workload rapidly grew, this was subdivided again in September into military

The M23b was also supplied to Romania, as seen here, and a further 15 were built under licence by ICAR. **Editor's collection**

Inside the BFW workshop in 1930 showing an M18c, M20, M22, several M23s and an M26 from the cancelled American order. **Editor's collection**

This M29 was fitted with a seven-cylinder Siemens Sh 14 radial engine. **Editor's collection**

(Luftkommandoamt or LA), civil (Allgemeines Luftamt or LB), technical (Technisches Amt, LC or C-amt, in charge of research and development), construction (Luftwaffenverwaltungsamt or LD), training and staffing (Luftwaffenpersonalamt or LP) and lastly a central command (Zentralabteilung or ZA). A logistics department (Luftzeugmeister or LZM) was added in 1934. These departments began contracting directly with the manufacturers for aircraft production and directing future development by issuing requirement specifications. The RLM also encouraged the expansion of the existing companies and the establishment of new factories and manufacturing facilities.

MILCH AND OTHER PROBLEMS

Initially, this reorganisation and expansion was a very bad thing for BFW and Messerschmitt. The Staatsekretär (State Secretary) for Aviation, answering only to Hermann Goring, was, as previously mentioned, the petty and dangerously ambitious Erhard Milch. Milch was initially responsible for civil and military aircraft development and acquisition, and used his position to settle a few scores with his enemies. First to suffer his wrath was the socialist and pacifist Hugo Junkers, who was forced to give up his patents and companies to the RLM, including the rights to the Ju 52 transport aircraft. Junkers was threatened with imprisonment and placed under house arrest, so acquiesced. Junkers died on February 3, 1935, aged 76. Messerschmitt was next. First, Milch ignored his company when placing orders for new commercial aircraft to expand DLH. He then forced BFW to build other manufacturers' aircraft under licence, such as the Heinkel He 45c and 50. This was a double blow for Messerschmitt. Firstly, Ernst Heinkel had attempted to smear his reputation during the flying competitions of the 1920s as they were in direct competition and Heinkel considered Messerschmitt a 'young upstart'. Secondly, all of the licence built aircraft types were a mix of wooden and metal structures and Messerschmitt was now embracing all metal construction. New staff and engineers were required to build what became nearly 400 other manufacturers' aircraft between 1934 and 1937, which initially caused problems, but also caused an expansion in the workforce just in time for when it would be needed most.

The elegant M35 seen over Augsburg in 1933. **Editor's collection**

Messerschmitt was not a man to take such a challenge lying down; if Germany would not buy his aircraft, he would seek customers abroad. Since Romanian firm ICAR had already produced the M23b under licence, Messerschmitt already had strong business contacts there. He designed the M36, an eight seat single engined high wing transport aircraft powered by a 360hp 10-cylinder Armstrong Siddeley Serval radial engine. ➤

Willy Messerschmitt (left) and his great friend Theo Croneiss in 1929. **Editor's collection**

The sole example of the M36, seen here in Romania, where it served with the airline LARES from 1936 to 1938. **Editor's collection**

A single example was built, assembled by ICAR and used by Romanian airline LARES between 1936 and 1938. Messerschmitt had also learned a great deal about the practicalities of business, an extension of his extraordinary abilities as an organiser, not just a designer and engineer. He had developed his own contacts within the new German hierarchy, and began to lobby them on behalf of his company.

It may be remembered that Theo Croneiss, Messerschmitt's long time friend, test pilot and airline customer, was also a friend of Hermann Göring and Rudolph Hess and exerted influence on Messerschmitt's behalf. Croneiss had become the chairman of the board of BFW in 1933 and had also been given responsibility for developing the aircraft industry in Bavaria by the RLM, so was able to help Messerschmitt directly through his official office. Messerschmitt also had his own friend at court, Ernst Udet, the First World War flying ace and one of the most famous pilots in Germany, indeed the world, at the time. In 1933, Udet, widely respected as a pilot and innovator, had joined the NSDAP at the insistence of Göring and had begun to influence aircraft design policy through his work at the RLM. Udet was promoted to Oberst (Colonel) and put in charge of the Technisches Amt of the RLM in 1936, becoming responsible for aviation research and development. Effectively, Udet's interventions ended Messerschmitt's problems with the new government, a situation helped by the fact he had just produced two aircraft which would seal his reputation and make his company indispensable.

THE BF 108

By 1933, Messerschmitt had developed a world class team at his company. Robert Lusser, a competition pilot and former design employee at Klemm and Heinkel, was now head of the project department, and Richard Bauer, who had been with BFW since 1929, was leading the design department and Hubert Bauer, another BFW veteran, was in charge of prototype production. The four men were all perfectionists, which made for a stormy but ultimately effective working relationship. The aircraft they combined to produce is still regarded as a pinnacle of modern light aircraft, in terms of both handling and performance. It all started with a late decision by the RLM to enter the 1934 Challenge International de Tourisme, a Fédération Aéronautique Internationale (FAI) competition for touring aircraft in three parts, a technical trial, a trans-European rally and a speed trial.

Poland had won the 1932 Challenge so it was the host nation in 1934. In September 1933, the RLM issued contracts to Messerschmitt, Fieseler and Klemm to build six prototypes of new four seat touring aircraft designs. Known by Messerschmitt as the M37 but given the designation Bf 108 by the RLM, the company had just nine months to develop, design and build the new type. It would need to be fast yet capable of slow flight for the

The remarkably clean and simple lines of the Bf 108A. Note the three bladed propeller fitted before the variable pitch unit became standard. **Editor's collection**

landing competitions, able to fold to pass through a gate 4.5m wide and 3.5m high and long ranged for the rally section of the challenge. What was required was a culmination of everything Messerschmitt had learned about aircraft engineering and design to that date, and was intended from the outset to form the basis of the future commercial design ethos of the company.

The wing used Messerschmitt's single spar D-box design with a full metal stressed skin. This included large Fowler flaps, flaperons and Handley Page leading edge slats, all lift enhancing devices to allow the aircraft as wide a speed range as possible. Messerschmitt traded the licence for the British Handley Page slats for the patent rights for his single spar wing design in the UK. The wing could be quickly and easily folded against the fuselage by loosening the connector bolts in the centre section. The fuselage was a metal monocoque built in two halves made up of sequential sections of tapering cross-section, forming a light but extremely strong and capacious shell that was reinforced internally with riveted stringers. Flush rivets were used throughout the aircraft to minimise drag. The landing gear was fully retractable, only the third German aircraft to be so equipped, consisting of a pair of cantilever oleo shock struts to the main

Messerschmitt publicity photograph of a Bf 108 over the Alps. Famous pilots used the superb Bf 108 to set new records for distance and altitude. **Warren Thompson**

A close up of the simple mechanical worm gear that retracts the main undercarriage on the Bf 108. **Constance Redgrave**

The leading edge Handley Page slats in the extended position. The use of high lift devices contributed to the Bf 108's excellent performance and speed range. Constance Redgrave

The spacious and simple cockpit of the Bf 108 was luxuriously finished even by modern standards. **Constance Redgrave**

The rear fuselage of the Bf 108 consists of sections of monocoque metal skin of tapering cross section, flush riveted to reduce drag. **Constance Redgrave**

wheels that retracted by means of a simple mechanical worm gear and a fixed castoring tailwheel. Pneumatic brakes were operated by a lever on the control column and a warning system of lights and a horn operated automatically if the engine was throttled back with the undercarriage still in the up position. Lastly, in an emergency, the glazed roof of the cabin could be completely jettisoned to allow a speedy exit by all four occupants. Not an outstanding or earthshaking design by any means, but incorporating all of the advances in aviation to that point in a simple and low drag, lightweight way.

CHALLENGE AND RECORDS

The Bf 108 V1, the prototype, was built with a wooden wing to test the validity of the design, and was followed by five more all metal Bf 108As, the last of which made its first flight on July 28, 1934, exactly one month before the challenge was due to start. There was a sudden stop to the development when the RLM test pilot was killed when flying Bf 108 V1, but it was determined he had hit a tree and flight testing resumed. Four of the five remaining Bf 108As were entered into the competition, achieving fifth, sixth and 16th places overall piloted by Theo Osterkamp, Werner Junck and Carl Francke respectively. Otto Brindlinger, Messerschmitt's flying instructor, was forced to withdraw from the competition when he went off course during the speed trial. Theo Osterkamp in Bf 108A D-IMUT achieved the highest recorded speed in the challenge when he averaged 291kph over a 300km course.

This success was just the start for the delightful tourer. On August 13, 1935, record breaking aviator Elly Beinhorn 'borrowed' Bf 108A D-IJES from Messerschmitt to fly from Gleiwitz to Istanbul to Berlin, a distance of 3570km which she covered in just 13 and a half hours. She named her aircraft 'Taifun' (Typhoon) for the record breaking flight, a name that was to be adopted generally for the Bf 108. The publicity from Beinhorn's flight assisted Messerschmitt in advertising the speed and prodigious fuel load of the tourer, and also enabled Beinhorn to attract funding for her later flights, including a 34,000km flight to India and back between April and June 1939.

When combined with its success in the Challenge and the highly regarded handling of the type, the Taifun's achievements attracted an order from the RLM for a training and liaison version for the Luftwaffe. ➤

This side view of the Bf 108 reveals where the later 109 got many of its distinctive lines from. **Constance Redgrave**

A pair of Bf 108s in flight at the 2012 ILA Berlin Air Show. The handling of the gem of an aircraft means it is still much sought after today. **Constance Redgrave**

The Bf 108B had a modified wing of 30cm greater span, with normal ailerons and simplified leading edge slats. The fuselage fuel tank was increased to 220 litres, giving the Bf 108B a 1000km still air range. The engine was standardised on the 240hp Argus As 10C, fitted with a variable pitch propeller, and many other detail changes were made before the new model began rolling down the production lines in 1936, initially at Augsburg, but production was moved to the new Messerschmitt Regensburg factory in 1938. Aside from the Luftwaffe order, over 100 Bf 108Bs were exported the world over, as far afield as Japan and Brazil, for civilian owners, airlines and air forces.

The Bf 108B was followed by two of the record breaking C model, fitted with a more powerful 270hp Hirth HM 508C engine. These were used to set a variety of climb and altitude records in the late 1930s. The Bf 108D followed in 1941, with a variety of modifications to the rudder and electrical system, as well as the ability to be tropicalised for operations in North Africa. With the wartime pressure for combat aircraft taking up all of the production capacity at Messerschmitt, Bf 108D production was moved to Paris at the Société Nationale de Constructions Aéronautiques du Nord (SNCAN) factory at Les Mureaux in February 1942. Production continued until the war's end, when Nord took over the factories and continued to produce the Bf 108 as the Nord 1000 Pingouin. Two Renault engined versions, the Nord 1001 and 1002, and two Potez engined versions, the 1003 and the 1004, were produced and served as liaison and training aircraft with the French armed forces.

To complete the story of the Bf 108, two more developments must be mentioned. The first was requested by the RLM in 1941 as a study into an enlarged nosewheel undercarriage version of the design with a range of 1300km. Known as the Me 208, a modified Bf 108 was tested with a nosewheel in October 1942 and the whole project was handed over to SNCAN for development. The first of two prototypes flew in July 1943, the Me 208 being cancelled by the RLM shortly afterwards in the face of Allied bombing and a need for consolidation of their aircraft production programmes. After the German forces withdrew from Paris, the surviving prototype was redesignated the Nord 1101 Noralpha and a new version was proposed with a 240hp Renault 6Q engine. Over 200 production examples of the Nord 1101 Ramier were produced for the French armed forces, serving into the early 1960s as a communications and liaison aircraft. One aircraft was produced as the Nord 1104 with a Potez engine, and two more were modified to be powered by the Turbomeca Astazou turboprop in 1959 as the Nord-Astazou 1110.

Lastly, postwar interest in the Bf 108, particularly from civilian owners, prompted Messerschmitt to study producing a new version of the aircraft between 1951 and 1955, but interest was limited and the project did not progress beyond drawing stage. This concept was resurrected with a six seat version proposed in 1973 as the Bf 108F, Messerschmitt reworking the design himself. A company, Taifun Flugzeugbau, was

Messerschmitt at his desk with Rakan Kokothaki, the commercial director of BFW, examining a model of the aircraft they were about to develop from the ideas that came together in the Bf 108. **Warren Thompson**

established to produce it, but finances were not forthcoming and the project again came to nought. These postwar developments show just how right Messerschmitt got the original design. Many light aircraft have been built since the Bf 108, but few have surpassed or significantly improved upon its performance. As a light training and touring aircraft, the Bf 108 remains a pinnacle of design.

To return to 1934, the Bf 108 had just flown for the first time, and Messerschmitt was standing on the edge of a level of success he could never have imagined even a year previously. Through the rapid and inspired work that resulted in the Bf 108, his company was ready to produce all metal monocoque designs of low drag and light weight, just at the time the RLM was interested in clandestinely acquiring 'high speed mail planes' and 'single seat courier aircraft', euphemisms for the bombers and fighters that the new Luftwaffe would require to become a fighting force. The next Messerschmitt aircraft was to become the most produced fighter aircraft of all time, its RLM designation following on from the Bf 108. The Bf 109 was about to take shape. ■

Words: Tim Callaway

A Nord 1101 Ramier painted to represent an Me 208, the larger nosewheel development of the Bf 108. **Constance Redgrave**

CLASSIC aviation

 from Ian Allan PUBLISHING

Me163 Rocket Interceptor Vol 2
Stephen Ransom and Hans-Hermann Cammann
Hardback • 303 x 226mm
978 1 903223 13 0 • £35.00

Me 262 Volume 2
J. Richard Smith & Eddie J. Creek
Hardback • 303 x 226mm
978 0 952686 73 6 • £35.00

Me 262 Volume 3
J. Richard Smith & Eddie J. Creek
Hardback • 303 x 226mm
978 1 903223 00 0 • £35.00

Messerschmitt Bf110 C, D & E
John Vasco and Fernando Estanislau
Hardback • 303 x 226mm
978 1 903223 89 5 • £35.00

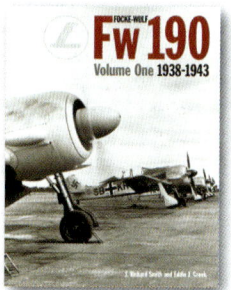

Focke Wulf Fw 190 Vol 1 1938-1943
J. Richard Smith & Eddie J. Creek
Hardback • 303 x 226mm
978 1 906537 29 6 • £50.00

NEW

Focke Wulf Fw 190 Vol 2 1943-1944
J. Richard Smith & Eddie J. Creek
Hardback • 303 x 226mm
978 1 906537 30 2 • £50.00

AVAILABLE NOW
- From our website at www.ianallanpublishing.com
- From our Mail Order Hotline on 0844 245 6944
- From our bookshops in London, Cardiff, Birmingham and Manchester

Join us...

Binoculars UK
www.binoculars-uk.co.uk

The largest selection of optics in the UK!

Please visit our website to see our full range of Binoculars, Digital Cameras, Monoculars, Night Vision equipment, Spotting Scopes, Tripods and much more.

Enter the discount code 'ACLASSIC' and get
5% DISCOUNT
off our already low prices!

For Sales & Advice 01253 300600

TRANSPORT STORE

18 Nasmyth Court,
Livingston, EH54 5EG, UK
Tel: +44 (0) 1506 441023
sales@transportstore.com

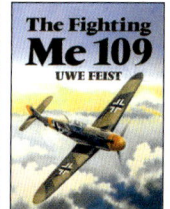   

Aviation books from the UK and world-wide
www.transportstore.com
The largest web stock available to browse using our simple and unique categorisation

  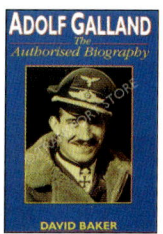 

Immediate availability and purchase with secure payment online
Telephone enquiries and orders welcome
Collections purchased

DETAILING THE FIGHTER

A triumphant Messerschmitt returned to his factory and began discussions with Robert Lusser, who was then head of the projects department. A great deal of the experience gained from the Bf 108 development went into the new fighter, as well as the culmination of all Messerschmitt's knowledge and experience in building simple, lightweight structures. This had a number of dramatic effects on the fighter design, keeping it small and light yet structurally very simple, as many components had more than one function within the structure because of the way the loads were distributed within it. This made for an airframe that was extremely strong, but keeping the structure small and simple also meant the fighter would be easy to build, requiring relatively few man hours, and easy to maintain, especially in the field.

On March 1, 1934, the National Socialists officially stated their intention to maintain their own military forces and the Luftwaffe was revealed to the world, even though it had really been in existence since May 15, 1933, when all the sport and military aviation organisations in Germany had been merged. In March 1934, Robert Lusser began discussions about the engine for the new aircraft with the Luftwaffe elements of the RLM as well as the armament and the ancillary equipment required, such as the radio and Dräger oxygen system. Two engines were considered applicable, the 610hp Jumo 210A and the 750hp BMW 116, both of which were 20 litre V12s and were liquid-cooled. Three armament variations were considered, the first being a single MG C30 20mm cannon firing through a hollow propeller shaft, the second being a pair of MG 17 7.9mm mounted on top of the engine and firing through the propeller arc, the last being a combination of both. The original fighter requirement had also called for a small bomb load to be able to be carried internally in the rear fuselage, but this was dispensed with shortly after the design stage began.

The Messerschmitt Bf 109 V1 prototype was registered D-IABI and given the infamous national marking of National Socialist Germany. **Editor's collection**

Interestingly, another of the original requirements was for the wings to be able to fold for storage and transportation. This was to produce the only really detrimental characteristic of the new design and a factor that would plague Bf 109 pilots throughout its career. The ability to fold the wings meant that the main undercarriage was designed from the outset to be attached to the lower fuselage structural members. These also supported the engine and cockpit as well as being the attachment point for the wing, as part of the multi-function structural member philosophy of the design. Using the narrow fuselage as the undercarriage attachment point made for a very narrow track between the main wheels. This gave the Bf 109 tricky handling on the ground, particularly on take off or landing, and was never solved as it was such an integral part of the fuselage structure and design. However, this feature also had two major advantages. Since the undercarriage was attached to the fuselage, the wing could be removed, or major maintenance or repairs carried out, without the need for jacks or other lifting devices. Secondly, the shock forces of landing were transmitted directly to the toughest part of the airframe, the centre section, and not via the wings as with some other types.

Messerschmitt Bf 109 V5 prototype, D-IEKS, was the pattern aircraft for the production Bf 109B-1 variant of the fighter. **Editor's collection**

FIRST FLIGHT

With the project defined by these discussions, detail design work started in August 1934 under the direction of Richard Bauer who headed the design department at the time. A major problem was encountered for the initial prototype when it was apparent that neither of the engines projected for use in the fighter would be ready for some time. A single Heinkel He 70 had been supplied to Rolls-Royce for use as an engine testbed for the Kestrel, and since the RLM had been at some pains to foster good relations with Britain and

Willi Stor of the DVL in discussion about the Bf 109 with the great First World War fighter ace Ernst Udet and Willy Messerschmitt. **Editor's collection**

CLASSIC aviation

from Ian Allan PUBLISHING

Me163 Rocket Interceptor Vol 2
Stephen Ransom and Hans-Hermann Cammann
Hardback • 303 x 226mm
978 1 903223 13 0 • £35.00

Me 262 Volume 2
J. Richard Smith & Eddie J. Creek
Hardback • 303 x 226mm
978 0 952686 73 6 • £35.00

Me 262 Volume 3
J. Richard Smith & Eddie J. Creek
Hardback • 303 x 226mm
978 1 903223 00 0 • £35.00

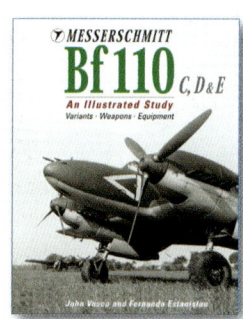

Messerschmitt Bf110 C, D & E
John Vasco and Fernando Estanislau
Hardback • 303 x 226mm
978 1 903223 89 5 • £35.00

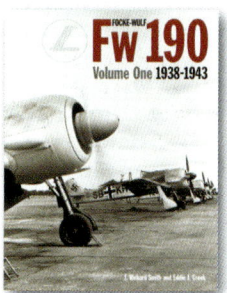

Focke Wulf Fw 190 Vol 1 1938-1943
J. Richard Smith & Eddie J. Creek
Hardback • 303 x 226mm
978 1 906537 29 6 • £50.00

Focke Wulf Fw 190 Vol 2 1943-1944
J. Richard Smith & Eddie J. Creek
Hardback • 303 x 226mm
978 1 906537 30 2 • £50.00

AVAILABLE NOW
- From our website at www.ianallanpublishing.com
- From our Mail Order Hotline on 0844 245 6944
- From our bookshops in London, Cardiff, Birmingham and Manchester

Join us...

Binoculars UK
www.binoculars-uk.co.uk
The largest selection of optics in the UK!

Please visit our website to see our full range of Binoculars, Digital Cameras, Monoculars, Night Vision equipment, Spotting Scopes, Tripods and much more.

Enter the discount code 'ACLASSIC' and get
5% DISCOUNT
off our already low prices!

For Sales & Advice 01253 300600

TRANSPORT STORE

18 Nasmyth Court,
Livingston, EH54 5EG, UK
Tel: +44 (0) 1506 441023
sales@transportstore.com

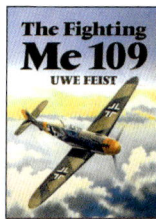   

Aviation books from the UK and world-wide
www.transportstore.com
The largest web stock available to browse using our simple and unique categorisation

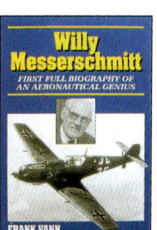  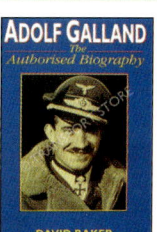 

Immediate availability and purchase with secure payment online
Telephone enquiries and orders welcome
Collections purchased

Genesis of a legend

The Bf 109 design and development

Messerschmitt's Bf 109 must rank among the best Second World War fighters for two reasons. Firstly would be its performance, even at the end of the conflict it could outclimb any Allied fighter, but secondly, it was the most produced fighter aircraft in aviation history with 33,984 of all versions built.

The Reichswehrministerium (State Defence Ministry or RWM) had been founded in October 1919 to oversee the minimal land defence forces allowed to Germany by the Versailles Treaty that ended the First World War. In April 1933, the aviation departments of the Reichsverkehrsministerium (RVM or Reich Transport Ministry) were separated to form the Reichsluftfahrtministerium (RLM or Reich Aviation Ministry) which was responsible for civil aviation and, along with the RWM, the initially clandestine development of a military air force later known as the Luftwaffe. The military elements of this organisation did not initially affect Messerschmitt. The only military project it was asked to produce was the aborted M22 twin engined biplane night fighter and reconnaissance aircraft of 1930. This lack of interest in Messerschmitt as a provider of military aircraft was almost entirely due to the enmity of Erhard Milch, the state secretary of aviation, who blamed Messerschmitt for the death of his friend, test pilot Hans Hackmack in the crash of the M20 prototype in 1928.

What changed the way Messerschmitt was viewed by officialdom were three unrelated but significant events. Firstly, Messerschmitt's friend and former First World War fighter pilot Ernst Udet had joined the RLM and eventually became the head of research and development, allowing Messerschmitt to enter design competitions for military aircraft. Secondly, Messerschmitt's friend and supporter Theo Croneiss, now chairman of BFW, had been made responsible for the development of the whole aviation industry based in Bavaria. In this role, Croneiss had received a letter on October 20, 1933, from the Minister of Aviation, Hermann Göring, which told him the Government required the development of a first rate commercial airliner and single seat high speed courier aircraft, in reality a bomber and a fighter, and that large contracts would be placed to supply these. Naturally, Croneiss discussed this with Messerschmitt, so he was aware that the wind of change was blowing as regards official policy. Lastly, Messerschmitt had produced the superb Bf 108 four seat tourer for the 1934 Challenge International de Tourisme. Its success in the contest and its subsequent use by famous pilots to break records and make long distance flights attracted the attention of the RLM, which wanted a high performance trainer and liaison aircraft for the Luftwaffe.

The Messerschmitt Bf 109 V1 prototype seen during an engine run. The bulges on the top of the wings are to accommodate the oversize tyres as the intended ones were not ready in time for the test flight programme. **Editor's collection**

NEW FIGHTERS AND CONTRACTS

This official requirement for a new fighter was only issued by the RLM to the big three established factories, Heinkel, Arado and Focke-Wulf in December 1933. The aircraft was to have a speed in excess of 400kph and be able to reach an altitude of 6000m (20,000ft), as well as having good manoeuvrability and spin recovery characteristics. These produced three

Wind tunnel testing a full size Bf 109E-3 in 1941. The wind tunnel was part of the facilities provided to aircraft designers by the RLM, Messerschmitt using it extensively throughout the development of the Bf 109 and its variants. **Editor's collection**

very different fighters, the Arado Ar 80 being a low wing design with a fixed undercarriage. Focke-Wulf produced the Fw 159, a parasol winged aircraft fitted with a complicated and troublesome retractable undercarriage and based on their earlier Fw 56 Stösser trainer, while Heinkel designed the He 112, initially an open cockpit aircraft.

Messerschmitt was not invited to take part in the competition. Instead, in 1933, the Technisches Amt (research and development section) of the RLM sent Messerschmitt a stiffly worded letter regarding his company designing and building the M36 for Romania, and asking how he could allow his team to work on foreign projects when other matters were pressing. He was called to the RLM headquarters in Berlin to explain himself, and while there was told that if he wanted to enter the fighter competition his design would be considered for contract. What happened next is as much a testament to Messerschmitt's character as anything else. He took the official requirements for the fighter and studied them in detail, returning to Berlin to tell the RLM that the fighter described in the documents stood little chance of intercepting and shooting down a modern bomber.

Therefore he was not interested in the competition as written as the aircraft produced would be pointless. The nerve of the man in dealing with the National Socialist hierarchy was breathtaking. Both his nerve and sincerity impressed the commander of the RLM at the time, the intelligent and knowledgeable Generaleutenant Walther Wever, who issued Messerschmitt what was essentially a separate contract to produce a fighter to his own specifications in February 1934. This almost entirely new project was known as the Verfolgungsjäger (Pursuit Fighter or VJ) and given the designation Bf 109. ➤

Messerschmitt Bf 109 23

DETAILING THE FIGHTER

A triumphant Messerschmitt returned to his factory and began discussions with Robert Lusser, who was then head of the projects department. A great deal of the experience gained from the Bf 108 development went into the new fighter, as well as the culmination of all Messerschmitt's knowledge and experience in building simple, lightweight structures. This had a number of dramatic effects on the fighter design, keeping it small and light yet structurally very simple, as many components had more than one function within the structure because of the way the loads were distributed within it. This made for an airframe that was extremely strong, but keeping the structure small and simple also meant the fighter would be easy to build, requiring relatively few man hours, and easy to maintain, especially in the field.

On March 1, 1934, the National Socialists officially stated their intention to maintain their own military forces and the Luftwaffe was revealed to the world, even though it had really been in existence since May 15, 1933, when all the sport and military aviation organisations in Germany had been merged. In March 1934, Robert Lusser began discussions about the engine for the new aircraft with the Luftwaffe elements of the RLM as well as the armament and the ancillary equipment required, such as the radio and Dräger oxygen system. Two engines were considered applicable, the 610hp Jumo 210A and the 750hp BMW 116, both of which were 20 litre V12s and were liquid-cooled. Three armament variations were considered, the first being a single MG C30 20mm cannon firing through a hollow

The Messerschmitt Bf 109 V1 prototype was registered D-IABI and given the infamous national marking of National Socialist Germany. **Editor's collection**

propeller shaft, the second being a pair of MG 17 7.9mm mounted on top of the engine and firing through the propeller arc, the last being a combination of both. The original fighter requirement had also called for a small bomb load to be able to be carried internally in the rear fuselage, but this was dispensed with shortly after the design stage began.

Interestingly, another of the original requirements was for the wings to be able to fold for storage and transportation. This was to produce the only really detrimental characteristic of the new design and a factor that would plague Bf 109 pilots throughout its career. The ability to fold the wings meant that the main undercarriage was designed from the outset to be attached to the lower fuselage structural members. These also supported the engine and cockpit as well as being the attachment point for the wing, as part of the multi-function structural member philosophy of the design. Using the narrow fuselage as the undercarriage attachment point made for a very narrow track between the main wheels. This gave the Bf 109 tricky handling on the ground, particularly on take off or landing, and was never solved as it was such an integral part of the fuselage structure and design. However, this feature also had two major advantages. Since the undercarriage was attached to the fuselage, the wing could be removed, or major maintenance or repairs carried out, without the need for jacks or other lifting devices. Secondly, the shock forces of landing were transmitted directly to the toughest part of the airframe, the centre section, and not via the wings as with some other types.

FIRST FLIGHT

With the project defined by these discussions, detail design work started in August 1934 under the direction of Richard Bauer who headed the design department at the time. A major problem was encountered for the initial prototype when it was apparent that neither of the engines projected for use in the fighter would be ready for some time. A single Heinkel He 70 had been supplied to Rolls-Royce for use as an engine testbed for the Kestrel, and since the RLM had been at some pains to foster good relations with Britain and

Messerschmitt Bf 109 V5 prototype, D-IEKS, was the pattern aircraft for the production Bf 109B-1 variant of the fighter. **Editor's collection**

Willi Stor of the DVL in discussion about the Bf 109 with the great First World War fighter ace Ernst Udet and Willy Messerschmitt. **Editor's collection**

The Messerschmitt Bf 109 V3 prototype, D-IOQY, first flew in June 1936 with a Jumo 210A engine. **Keith Draycott**

Dr Hermann Wurster of the DVL was an extraordinary pilot and engineer, seen here discussing the handling of the Bf 109 with Willy Messerschmitt. **Editor's collection**

Messerschmitt Bf 109 V3 prototype, D-IOQY, a rare view in flight. **Editor's collection**

A close up of the Jumo 210A installation in one of the early prototypes with a fixed pitch propeller. **Editor's collection**

the Royal Air Force, a deal was struck for the supply of four Rolls-Royce Kestrel engines in return for the aircraft. The Kestrel VI was a 695hp V12 of similar size and layout to the intended Jumo and BMW products. These were given to Arado, Heinkel and Messerschmitt to allow test flying to take place with the minimum of delay to the new aircraft programmes. Construction of the Bf 109 V1 prototype was delayed only for as long as it took to modify the engine bearers and nose to accept the new engine. On May 28, 1935, after only 15 months from the time the contract had been issued, test pilot Hans-Dietrich Knoetzsch took the Bf 109 V1 D-IABI, into the air for the first time.

The first flight went well, with Knoetzsch reportedly delighted with the handling of the new machine. Only one small problem was encountered with the mechanical retraction system of the undercarriage, which was rectified post flight. Testing continued until the summer, when Knoetzsch had a landing accident in the prototype, the damage from which took several months to repair.

COMPARISONS AND TRIALS

However, the second prototype, Bf 109 V2 D-IILU, made its first flight on December 12, 1935, powered by the Jumo 210A engine. At this point, the Deutsche Versuchsanstalt für Luftfahrt (German Research Institute for Aviation or DVL) took over the test flying programme. The man placed in charge of the programme in January 1935 was DVL test pilot Dr Hermann Wurster, who proved to be a real asset to Messerschmitt. His flying skills were of the highest order, as were his understanding of aerodynamics and engineering. Wurster flew the acceptance flight trial at the RLM's Erprobungsstelle (Test and evaluation site or E-Stelle) at Travemünde, in front of a examination commission from the RLM and Luftwaffe. As part of this flight, on top of the standard manoeuvres required by the trial, Wurster flew two spins, one to the right for 21 turns and to the left for 17, all with the aircraft at its maximum tail-heavy setting and also made a vertical dive from 7500m (25,000 ft) to almost ground level. Reliable and easy spin recovery was an important part of the RLM's safety requirement for unpressurised aircraft intended for high altitude operations in case of incapacitation of the pilot through anoxia. The dive was intended to exhibit structural strength, as many senior officers, Ernst Udet among them, still considered monoplanes unsuited for the stresses of combat. It is widely considered that Wurster's flight demonstration of the qualities of the Bf 109 were instrumental in convincing the RLM to order the fighter. ➤

Messerschmitt Bf 109 25

Two views of the Bf 109 V7 prototype D-IJHA. This aircraft was one of five Bf 109s that took part in the Sixth International Flightmeeting at Dubendorf military airfield near Zurich in Switzerland in July 1937. **Editor's collection**

A Bf 109B-1 delivered to the E-stelle at Rechlin, just North of Berlin, for evaluation and testing. **Editor's collection**

The Messerschmitt Bf 109 V11 prototype seen after a landing accident. Handling the aircraft on the ground was to be tricky for its entire history. **Editor's collection**

The Bf 109's thin monoplane wing made some doubt its strength, but Messerschmitt's single spar and monocoque D-box leading edge as seen here were incredibly tough. **Editor's collection**

The competitive flight trials between the Bf 109 and He 112 took place between February 26 and March 2, 1936, and were carried out using the V2 prototype. Initially, the centre's test pilots were distrustful of the Bf 109 for a number of reasons. Its steep, nose-high, attitude on the ground, made taxiing the aircraft difficult unless the pilot zig-zagged to see down either side of the nose in turn. The wing loading was higher than types the centre had previously tested and it was thought this would cause handling difficulties. The cockpit canopy hinged open to the right, and could not be opened in flight except when jettisoned in an emergency, and lastly it was thought the automatic leading edge slats would cause handling problems in high-G manoeuvres.

As flying time was accumulated, all of these negative points were quickly forgotten as the pilots were delighted with the handling of the prototype. They learned to handle the aircraft on the ground and slowly got used to the enclosed cockpit. The high wing loading did not prove a problem but the slats did, causing instability if they deployed in tight turns, which could cause aiming problems in combat. However the speed, rate of climb and carefree handling bestowed by the strong airframe put this problem into perspective, as on the whole the Bf 109 was a real fighter pilot's aircraft. While at the test centre, Wurster also had the

The architects of success, from the left, Theo Croneiss, chairman of BFW, Hubert Bauer, in charge of prototype production for Messerschmitt, Rudolph Hess, the deputy leader of the National Socialist Party and Willy Messerschmitt. Hess was a regular visitor to Augsburg, Messerschmitt had learned the hard way about having friends in high places. **Editor's collection**

Bf 109 V6, D-IHHB, seen here with tufts of wool stuck to the wing to examine the airflow, with the cameras used to film the wool while the aircraft was in flight are sitting on the tailplane. **Editor's collection**

chance to fly the He 112, and found it to lack the Bf 109's handling in aerobatics and stalls, as well as being slower and heavier on the controls. While the test flying was going on, the centre's chief test pilot had to bale out of one of the He 112's when it had refused to recover from a spin, which did not bode well for the rival design. Both Ernst Udet, whose opinion of combat aircraft carried enormous weight in the RLM as he had been a very successful First World War fighter pilot, and the General der Jagdflieger (General of Fighters) Ritter von Greim both flew the Bf 109 and confirmed Wurster's opinion of the type's superb handling.

PRODUCTION BEGINS

Given the universal approval the Bf 109 received from the German military flying community at all levels, the decision by the RLM to place production orders for the Bf 109 on March 12 came as no surprise. The second Bf 109 prototype was followed into the air by the third, Bf 109 V3, in June 1936, again with the Jumo 210A engine. Five more prototypes were flying by the end of the year, all of these aircraft being fitted with a pair of MG 17 7.9mm machine guns in the upper nose, firing through the propeller arc, so armament tests could also be flown. The later prototypes were powered by more powerful versions of the Jumo 210, the B, C and D series engines which increased the power to 720hp. In August 1936, the Bf 109 was officially introduced to the public when the Bf 109 V1 prototype took part in the opening ceremony of the Berlin Olympic Games. By December 1936, the first six Bf 109B-1 production standard aircraft were finished, and the orders called for the construction of 654 more between 1937 and 1938.

Even though the Messerschmitt factory at Augsburg was being massively expanded, it was quickly realised that this would be insufficient, as the Bf 108 production line was under way and the twin engined Bf 110 heavy fighter was about to enter production. This potential production hiatus caused the decision mentioned in the previous article to build an additional Messerschmitt factory at Regensburg. However, even this massive expansion to meet the demand would not be enough, so the RLM arranged licence production for the Bf 109 with other German companies. AGO, Arado, Erla, Fieseler and Focke-Wulf all agreed to build the fighter, with the blueprints, jigs and tools all being supplied by Messerschmitt BFW at Augsburg. This licence organisation was put in place so quickly that before the end of 1937 326 Bf 109A-0s and B-1s had been produced by Messerschmitt BFW, Erla and Fieseler.

The way the production of the Bf 109 was handled is a part of the secret of its success and massive production numbers, and will be covered later in this magazine. Suffice to say that the production methods laid out for the aircraft were typical of Messerschmitt, his organisation skills being as important to the company as his engineering and design abilities. With the first aircraft rolling down the production lines, a legend was being born.

■ *Words: Tim Callaway*

The ability to build Bf 109s quickly was part of the type's great success, its simplicity of construction meant that it was equally easy to maintain in the field. **Editor's collection**

Into service and into action
The Messerschmitt Bf 109A, B, C and D

Two views of 6-2, the Bf 109 V3 in Spanish Civil War markings. This aircraft was sometimes referred to as a Bf 109A, adding to the confusion. Note the large undercarriage housing bulge on the wing in the second photograph, and the one piece side to the front canopy.
Editor's collection

By the beginning of 1937, the Bf 109 production lines were well established, official testing and evaluation was building experience with the fighter and the first examples were entering squadron service. All of this was providing feedback regarding the design to Messerschmitt, and the aircraft began to evolve.

There is a great deal of confusion over the first four versions of the Bf 109 to enter service with the Luftwaffe, largely due to the aircraft being in a state of flux. Modifications and improvements were added to the production line as they occurred, causing a number of differing models to appear concurrently or out of sequence. It quickly became apparent that in the Bf 109 the Luftwaffe had a world beating fighter, but shortcomings with power and armament were highlighted by the test and evaluation E-Stelle units and by the pilots who first took the Bf 109 into combat over Spain. These evaluation comments and the operational feedback caused Messerschmitt to re-examine several facets of his fighter, and in solving the problems the company rapidly created a range of prototypes and sub variants of the four basic models. For simplicity I will take the individual versions in alphabetical rather than chronological order, as with some of these aircraft the picture is obscure enough without complicating matters unnecessarily.

THE BF 109A
The A model, or Anton as it was known from the German phonetic alphabet of the time, started with the Bf 109 V4 prototype which first flew in August 1936. This was never really a set version of the Bf 109, rather a combination of aircraft with differing engines and experimental armament combinations which can be regarded as an extension of the

The cockpit of what is purported to be 6-15, the Bf 109A-0 forced down on November 11, 1937, by fuel starvation and sent to the Soviet Union for analysis. Note the early spade grip on the control column and the central brake lever. **Editor's collection**

Messerschmitt Bf 109 V3, D-IOQY in flight. This aircraft was the basis for the A models and features a cut down spinner for use with an engine mounted MG 17 machine gun, the single piece side to the front canopy and the pronounced overwing bulge to clear the oversize tyres on the retracted undercarriage. This aircraft was one of the four prototypes sent to Spain. **Editor's collection**

One of the 41 Bf 109B-1s supplied to the Condor Legion. Note the fixed pitch propeller. The baptism of fire in Spain would change the Bf 109 into a world class fighter. **Editor's collection**

V series of prototypes. The Bf 109 V4 and at least half the A model aircraft had a 640hp Jumo 210D engine which was driving a two bladed simple fixed pitch propeller. The armament initially consisted of just the upper cowling mounted pair of MG 17 7.9mm machine guns, but this was being found to be too little firepower by the pilots already operating the Bf 109B version in the Luftwaffe's Condor Legion fighting in the Spanish Civil War.

Since other fighters of the day, such as the British Spitfire and Hurricane, were already armed with eight .303in machine guns, increasing the firepower of the Bf 109 became a priority. Firstly, a third MG 17 was fitted firing through the hollow propeller shaft which became designated the Bf 109A-0. During the limited production run, the more powerful 670hp Jumo 210D engine became available, so this was fitted on the production lines, but not all of the new aircraft received the additional machine gun. Experiments with the armament continued, with the engine mounted machine gun being replaced with a single MG C30 20mm cannon on several of the prototypes and at least four of the production Bf 109Bs, which according to some sources were later redesignated as the Bf 109A-1, despite the majority of them being based on a later model. Problems were encountered with both the engine mounted machine gun and the cannon, not least in terms of vibration when either were fired. This could be so severe as to damage the engine, or at least to make aiming a question of luck.

Providing adequate cooling to the weapons was also problematic, as a consequence ammunition feed and breech jams were frequent. The overall layout of the Bf 109A was not fixed, the aircraft were relatively individual in having differing oil cooler shapes and locations as the ideal cooling solution was sought. The change in engine during production caused the nose cowling shape to be modified several times along with the oil cooler modifications, and additional cooling vents and slats were added or deleted to suit the armament of the individual aircraft. It is known that 16 of these early development aircraft were sent to Spain, where the solution to the oil cooling and armament problems were most pressing.

It can be said that these aircraft served as operational experimental development fighters, as much of the performance data collected in Spain was fed back into the development team at Messerschmitt to improve the breed still further. One of the Bf 109A-0s made a forced landing and was captured by the Republicans on November 11, 1937. This aircraft was later transferred to the Soviet Union for analysis and was found to have the equipment for a variable pitch propeller that was becoming standard on the Bf 109B-1s by this time, but still had the simple fixed pitch propeller fitted. Altogether only 22 of this much modified machine were produced, 23 if you count the Bf 109 V4 prototype.

BF 109B

This aircraft was actually the first variant of the Bf 109 to enter full scale series production, the first six of the type actually being produced by the end of 1936. The aircraft was standardised on the 670hp Jumo 210D engine with a fixed pitch propeller and the twin cowling mounted machine guns and was known as the Bf 109B-1 or Berta. The propeller was replaced by a two-bladed variable pitch unit produced by Messerschmitt early in the production run which was retro-fitted to a number of the earlier aircraft. The aircraft with the new propellers were unofficially referred to as the B-2 in Luftwaffe units. The combination of engine and propeller gave the Bf 109B-1 a maximum speed of 289mph (465kph). Several of the B-1s were also fitted with the MG 17 firing through the propeller shaft, but the vibration and overheating problems still caused these weapons to be more trouble than they were worth. Altogether, 41 Bf 109B-1s were supplied to the Condor Legion for ➤

Two Messerschmitt publicity photographs of an early production Bf 109B-1 in flight. Note the large coolant radiator under the nose and how clean the wings look without the radiators required by the later DB 600 series engine. **Editor's collection**

A rear view of a Bf 109B-1 showing the three wire radio antenna, one of the identification features of this type. **Editor's collection**

A very rare colour photograph of a Bf 109B-1 being the centre of attention for a group of Hitler Youth, obviously on a visit to a Luftwaffe station in 1938. **Editor's collection**

operations in Spain in 1937. There, the Bf 109B-1s were used to replace the earlier biplane fighters Germany had supplied, such as the Heinkel He 51 and Arado Ar 68.

The Condor Legion had been officially formed on November 7, 1936, and at its peak consisted of 12 fighter, bomber and reconnaissance units. It was organised into three Gruppen or Groups, the bombers in Kampfgruppe 88 (KG88), the fighters in Jagdgruppe 88 (JG88) and the reconnaissance aircraft in Aufklärungsgruppe 88. There were also anti-aircraft and ground support troops attached to the Legion, as well as a detachment of tanks. Initially there were three fighter staffels (the equivalent of a squadron), which later rose to four, being designated 1.J/88 to 4.J/88. Also in theatre was VJ/88, a test and evaluation staffel, which was there to record comparative fighter performance and make recommendations regarding future developments by actually flying the fighters in combat.

The new fighter quickly established air superiority for the Nationalists, because, despite the shortcomings of its limited armament, the Bf 109B completely outperformed the Polikarpov I-15 and was a match for the I-16 fighter supplied by the Soviet Union to the Republicans. The monoplane I-16 was manoeuvrable, and if an attempt was made to engage one in a turning dogfight it could be a dangerous opponent, but the Bf 109B met it on equal terms. The first three Bf 109B-1s arrived in Spain on March 14, 1937 and were allocated to 2.J/88. On April 6, 1937, Oberleutenant Günther Lützow shot down an I-15, claiming the Bf 109's first official victory. These were not the first Bf 109s in theatre, four of the prototypes, the Bf 109 V3 to V6 had also been sent to

Throughout its career and in every version, the Bf 109 was popular with maintenance personnel for its ease of access to vital systems. Here, a Bf 109B-1 undergoes an engine run with the large cowlings removed. **Editor's collection**

VJ/88 of the Condor Legion in December 1936 to begin evaluation of the fighter under combat conditions. However, by the end of 1937, the new version of the I-16, the Type 10, had been delivered to the Republicans and was superior to the Bf 109B in climb rate, turning circle and firepower.

By the summer of 1938, 1.J/88 and 2.J/88 only had 11 aircraft left between them. Losses were mounting, and the Bf 109 needed to be improved, rapidly. The combat deficiencies being encountered by the Condor Legion were partly solved by the introduction of a few of the Bf 109C model, but the solution to the new Republican fighters was not to be found until the introduction of the Bf 109D in June 1938. In the interim, new tactics were developed to overcome the I-16 Type 10s advantages. Fighter tactics from the First World War were revised completely to suit the performance of modern aircraft. The pilots who were flying these aircraft would later become household names in Germany, and later the world, including as they did young pilots like Werner Molders, Adolph Galland and Walter Oesau. It was over Spain that these men honed the Luftwaffe into a weapon ready for the Second World War.

It may be said that the Spanish Civil War was used as an operational training ground for the newly developing Luftwaffe, who used the opportunity to test their new equipment and develop their tactics. In the heat and dust of Spain, the aircraft and its systems were thoroughly tested by the conditions, with cooling, oil, carburettor and undercarriage problems all being reported as well as the lack of armament as already mentioned. All of these problems were gradually overcome, and if the Spanish Civil War was a crucible, the Bf 109 was to be radically changed by its time in it.

The successful introduction of the fighter into service led to more orders being placed, so as previously described, more production lines were opened to meet the demand. Altogether 341 Bf 109Bs were produced, 326 of them in 1937 alone, at the Messerschmitt, Erla and Fieseler factories, the latter two building the aircraft under an RLM organised licence.

As the later models of the Bf 109 came into service, the B series aircraft were relegated to secondary duties, such as with 1 Jagdfliegerschule or fighter pilot's school, seen here in 1939. **Editor's collection**

Like the Bf 109B, the extremely rare Bf 109C-1 ended up in secondary duties with units such as the 1 Jagdfliegerschule once the Bf 109E was in series production. **Editor's collection**

The VDM variable pitch two bladed propeller was standardised on the Bf 109B-1, improving performance over the earlier fixed unit. **Editor's collection**

BF 109C

Only 58 Bf 109Cs were built, all by Messerschmitt at Augsburg, because it was originally intended that this would be the last version of the fighter to use the Jumo engine as the Daimler-Benz DB 600 programme was approaching completion. The development began as a reaction to the calls from Spain for fighters with greater firepower for the Condor Legion and was intended only as a stop gap measure to address these needs. The Bf 109 V8 prototype was produced which had the cowling mounted pair of MG 17s as well as an additional pair mounted one in each wing. However, flight testing of the aircraft revealed that the wing structure would require strengthening to take the extra weight under combat conditions.

At the same time, another prototype, Bf 109 V9 was constructed, with a pair of MG FF 20mm cannons in the wings, with the same result. While work continued on strengthening the wing structure, the 700hp Jumo 210G engine became available and was selected for the new version. This engine had an important advantage over earlier Jumo versions, it was fitted with a direct fuel injection system that meant the engine did not cut out or lose power under negative G. This was an important consideration in combat, as to escape from an enemy you could now just shove the stick forward and dive away, without having to roll and pull for positive G to keep the fuel flowing to the engine. The new engine also increased the maximum speed slightly to 292mph (470kph).

Another improvement resulting from the Condor Legion's experiences was that the main fuel tank was increased in size by an additional 100 litres. The relatively short endurance of the earlier Bf 109s had caused concern in a country as large as Spain and the Bf 109A lost and captured in November 1937 had made a forced landing because he had run out of fuel. For such a small production run, the C model has five different sub types, the first of which was the C-0, the pre-production and test aircraft for testing the new strengthened wing. This was followed by the C-1, which had four MF 17 machine guns. Two were in the cowling with 500 rounds per gun (rpg) and two in the wings with 420rpg, effectively doubling the firepower of the earlier versions of the fighter. Five of these aircraft were sent to Spain in April 1938 and replaced some of the lost aircraft of 3.J/88, receiving the unit codes 6-46 to 6-50 making them relatively easy to identify among the different types used by the Condor Legion.

Of the last three variants of the C model, or Caesar as it was known, little is known. The C-2 was intended to have the engine mounted MG 17, bringing the gun total to a respectable five, but in the light of the experience of other models with engine mounted weapons, it is not certain if any were built or tested, if they were it was in very small numbers. The C-3 ➤

Rearming a Bf 109C-1 of JG51 at Friedrichshafen in 1939, note the large doors to the wing mounted guns for ease of access. **Editor's collection**

A Bf 109C-1 ready for inspection. Note the oil cooler under the port wing and the stub exhausts from the fuel injected Jumo 210G. **Editor's collection**

Bf 109D-1s of 11.(Nacht)/JG2 seen here in Norway in the spring of 1940. Night fighter units were the last to operate the Bf 109D. **Editor's collection**

One thing that was common on all the early Bf 109s was the starting mechanism, a crank handle to turn a flywheel up to speed before the pilot released a clutch to turn the engine over. Operating this required some muscle, and could be quite dangerous in wet or icy conditions as the mainwheel was the only place to stand as demonstrated on this Bf 109D-1. **Editor's collection**

was to have the wing mounted MG 17s replaced with a pair of MG FF 20mm cannons, but none were ever built. Lastly, the C-4 was to have the four MG 17s of the C-1, but added a "motorkanone", an engine mounted MG FF cannon. Again, this version was planned but never produced.

BF 109D

With the introduction of the Bf 109D, or Dora, the production of the Bf 109 really got into full stride. Altogether 647 of this version were produced, being built by AGO, Arado, Erla, Fieseler and Focke-Wulf, only the four Bf 109D-0 pre-production aircraft being built by Messerschmitt. The Dora had an incredibly short service life for such a mass produced fighter. Production began at the end of 1937 and by August 1938 the Dora made up nearly half of the 643 front line fighter strength of the Luftwaffe. By October nearly 600 Bf 109D-1s were in service, but when the Second World War began in September 1939, only 235 aircraft remained, these being fully replaced in the day fighter units by November. A few Bf 109D-1s remained in service with night fighter units

A row of brand new Messerschmitt Bf 109D-1s are seen here outside the Focke-Wulf factory where they were built. Focke-Wulf was just one of the five companies building the Bf 109 under licence. **Editor's collection**

until early 1940, but these too were quickly retired as the Bf 109E took ascendancy.

The Bf 109D was intended to be the first version of the fighter to be fitted with the DB 600 series engine from Daimler-Benz. Four prototypes, the Bf 109 V10 to V13 were built, using Bf 109B airframes as testbeds for the

DB 600A which offered significant performance increases for the fighter. The DB 601A followed soon after the DB 600, and since it offered a direct fuel injection system the new version was chosen for the Bf 109 and the V aircraft were fitted with them. The DB 600 series had a troubled development, with delay after delay dogging the promising engine, so it quickly became apparent it would not be ready to be fitted to the Bf 109D. Interestingly, despite the success of the fuel injected 700hp Jumo 210G in the Bf 109C model, the Jumo 210D was chosen to replace the delayed DB 600 in the Bf 109D. This was a carburetted engine which produced 670hp and had been fitted to the Bf 109B. Other than that, the Bf 109D-1 airframe was fitted with the same strengthened wing and four machine gun armament of the Bf 109C-1 which it resembled in most respects. The Bf 109D-2 had an additional engine mounted MG 17, but as before, this installation cause many problems and was not adopted for production. The last variant, the Bf 109D-3, saw the wing mounted MG 17s replaced with MG FF 20mm cannons, giving the fighter the much needed firepower it had previously lacked.

The highest scoring Luftwaffe pilot of the Spanish Civil War was Hauptmann Werner Molders of 3.J/88 with 14 victories. This is Molders' Bf 109D-1, named 'Luchs' or Lynx, as Molders was reputed to have the eyes of one. It was Molders who developed the 'Schwarm' or 'Finger Four' formation tactics for Luftwaffe fighters. **Editor's collection**

6-56, one of the 36 Bf 109D-1s supplied to the Condor Legion in Spain. **Keith Draycott**

In June 1938, 36 Bf 109D-1s were sent to Spain, where they proved to be a match for the I-16 Type 10, returning air superiority to the Nationalists. These began to be replaced by the DB 601 engined Bf 109E at the end of 1938, but by then the air war had been won even though the fighting did not end until April 1 the following year. The Bf 109D was also the first version of the fighter to attract foreign orders. The Swiss Air Force ordered 10 in 1939, several of which were still in use as trainers for the rest of the Swiss Bf 109 fleet as late as 1949. Three ex-Luftwaffe aircraft were supplied clandestinely to Hungary, prior to sufficient Bf 109Es being available, to act as trainers to ready the Hungarian air force to operate the type. The Bf 109D had been a stop gap while the Daimler-Benz engine development was finished, and when it was ready it would produce what was widely considered to be the best handling variant of the fighter, the Bf 109E, which will be covered later in this magazine.

RECORD BF 109BS AND DS

During the development of the Bf 109 as a fighter, time was found to produce a number of unusual racing and competition variants of the early versions of the fighter. As already mentioned, the Bf 109 V13 and V14 had been built using a DB 601A engine, and the Bf 109 V7 was fitted with the fuel injected Jumo 210G. These aircraft and a team of three other Bf 109s attended the Flugmeeting Airshow at Dübenfdorf Airfield near Zurich in July 1937. Ernst Udet was flying the V14, D-ISLU, and was plagued with engine problems, being forced to retire from both the speed race over 200km and the following day's Alpine Circuit. In the latter, his engine seized after losing oil. In the ensuing forced landing, the aircraft was written off, Udet being slightly injured but able to walk away from the wreck.

Dr Hermann Wurster flew the Bf 109 V13, fitted with a specially race prepared 1660hp DB 601R, to capture the world speed record for landplanes in November 1937. **Editor's collection**

However, the V13 and V7 shone in the competition. The 200km speed race was won by Carl Franke from the E-Stelle at Rechlin at an average speed of 254mph (409kph) and the Alpine Circuit was won by Major Seidemann who completed the 367km course in just 56 minutes. Lastly, the three Bf 109B team won the Team Alpine Circuit. This performance was what prompted the Swiss Air Force to order the Bf 109D and the new fighter caused an international sensation. A propaganda coup was scored at the event as it was claimed the Bf 109 was fully in service, where at the time only a few staffels were equipped, with several aircraft acting as pilot conversion trainers in other Luftwaffe units.

The redoubtable Dr Hermann Wurster re-enters the Bf 109 story at this point, as the success at Dübendorf had stirred the competitive juices at Messerschmitt. The Bf 109 V13 was fitted with a specially race prepared 1660hp DB 601R fuel injected engine and thoroughly cleaned up, with close fitted cowlings, a new spinner for the three bladed VDM variable pitch propeller and a rounded off cockpit canopy. The pitot tube and radio mast were removed, and any gaps in the airframe were taped over, the entire aircraft being polished to a high gloss. In this form, Wurster set a new absolute world speed record for landplanes in V13 on November 11, 1937, reaching a speed of 379.38mph (610.55kph). This was the first time the record had been held by Germany and was a real coup for Messerschmitt. The following year Heinkel took the record in a specially prepared He 100, which prompted Messerschmitt to develop the Me 209 which is described later in this magazine.

You may have noted that the designation changed to Me for the 209. This is because on July 11, 1938, Messerschmitt was allowed to buy out BFW, reconstituting the two companies as Messerschmitt AG and becoming chairman and managing director. From this date, new designs and proposals were given the prefix Me by the RLM, all older designs retaining their Bf prefix. ■ *Words: Tim Callaway*

The Messerschmitt Bf 109D-1s and a single C-3 of I./ZG 2 are seen here at Gross-Stein airfield in August 1939. The C and D models of the Bf 109 would all have left service within a year of this image being taken. **Bundesarchiv**

The 109 in combat:

The story from the other side...

I have had a half-century-long interest in bravery in general, and gallantry medals in particular. I collect decorations awarded to British, Commonwealth and occasionally other Allied servicemen. Yet, as I write in my new book Heroes of the Skies, for me the concept of bravery is not, and never will be, limited to just one side in a battle or conflict.

The author, Lord Michael Ashcroft, KCMG. **Jon Enoch**

German pilots, including those flying the famous Messerschmitt Bf 109s faced similar trials and tribulations in the air to their British and Allied counterparts, and repeatedly showed outstanding courage in combat. However, my new book tells the stories of those men who flew against the Bf 109 pilots. Here are two excerpts from Heroes of the Skies…

PILOT OFFICER (LATER FLIGHT LIEUTENANT) GEORGE GRIBBLE DFC

George Gribble served with 54 Squadron and, as a pilot officer, flew Spitfires during the Battle of Britain when he was in constant combat with Bf 109s.

On May 24, 1940, Gribble and his squadron were involved in a heavy combat with the Luftwaffe over the Dunkirk-Calais sector. Gribble destroyed a Bf 109 after firing 1700 rounds from a range of 250 yards. He later recalled: "I saw my tracer crossing into his aircraft while he was on his back. He just fell into the ground…" However, Gribble's Spitfire was badly damaged the following day when his squadron was jumped by about a dozen Bf 109s. Gribble carried out a forced landing on a beach near Dunkirk where he removed his radio equipment from the cockpit before finding passage home on a steamer bound for Dover.

Gribble's DFC was announced on August 13, 1940, when his citation stated: "Pilot Officer Gribble has led his section, and recently his flight, in a courageous and determined manner… this officer has personally destroyed three Messerschmitt 109s, and damaged many others."

On August 16, Gribble damaged a Bf 109 east of RAF Hornchurch, Essex. "I managed to get in a long burst (10 seconds), opening at 300 yards and closing to 200 yards range. Smoke began to pour out of the machine and it went into a dive," he wrote. Two days later Gribble acted as blue leader in 'B' Flight, and destroyed another Bf 109.

By early November 1940, Gribble's confirmed score stood at six and one shared enemy aircraft destroyed. However, while on a bomber escort sortie on June 4, 1941, Gribble was seen leading his section against two Bf 109s when his Spitfire was suddenly 'bounced' by further enemy fighters.

Gribble was heard to say over his radio: "Engine cut, baling out." A fellow pilot saw his parachute going down into the sea, some 12 miles off the English coast. Boats quickly reached the spot where Gribble hit the water but the pilot could not be found and he was presumed dead, just two weeks before his 22nd birthday.

In a letter to Gribble's mother dated June 9, the squadron's CO wrote: "George was an exceptional pilot and leader and also a very keen officer. He was also very entertaining in the mess and most loved by all of us. The whole squadron will miss a very gallant and brave gentleman for a very long time to come…"

SERGEANT (LATER SQUADRON LEADER) JAMES LACEY DFM AND BAR

James 'Ginger' Lacey was quite simply one of the greatest fighter aces of the Second World War, including being the second highest scoring British fighter pilot of the Battle of Britain. By the end of the war, he was credited with 28 enemy aircraft destroyed, five 'probables' and nine damaged. Many of Lacey's most memorable dogfights during the Battle of Britain were with pilots of Bf 109s.

While based in Le Mans and serving as a sergeant with 501 (County of Gloucester) Squadron, Lacey had a close call after a combat with a Bf 109 over Le Mans on June 9, 1940, when, after a forced landing, his aircraft was thrown on to its back. As blood streamed

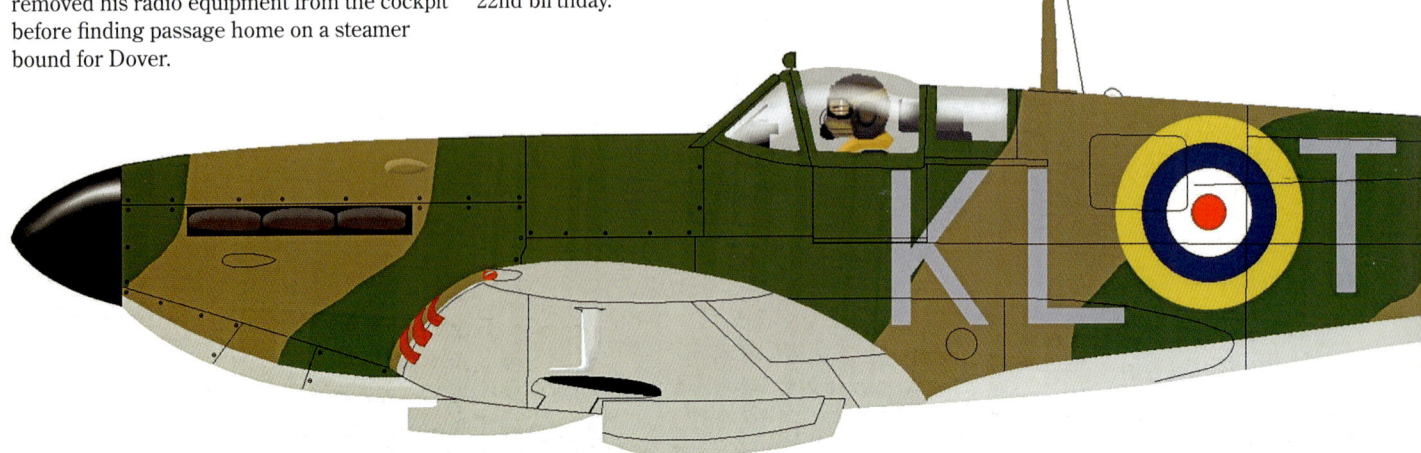

Flight Lieutenant George Gribble DFC. **Author's Collection**

James 'Ginger' Lacey DFM and Bar pictured later in the war in the cockpit of a Spitfire. **Editor's Collection**

A Hawker Hurricane Mk.I of 501 Squadron. **Keith Draycott**

HEROES OF THE SKIES BY MICHAEL ASHCROFT

The book is published in hardback by Headline and costs £20 (RRP). It is available now from all good bookshops or online at Amazon. All author's royalties are being donated to the RAF Benevolent Fund, the custodian of the new Bomber Command Memorial.

The book is published in conjunction with a six part Channel 5 documentary series. The author is a Conservative peer, international businessman and philanthropist.

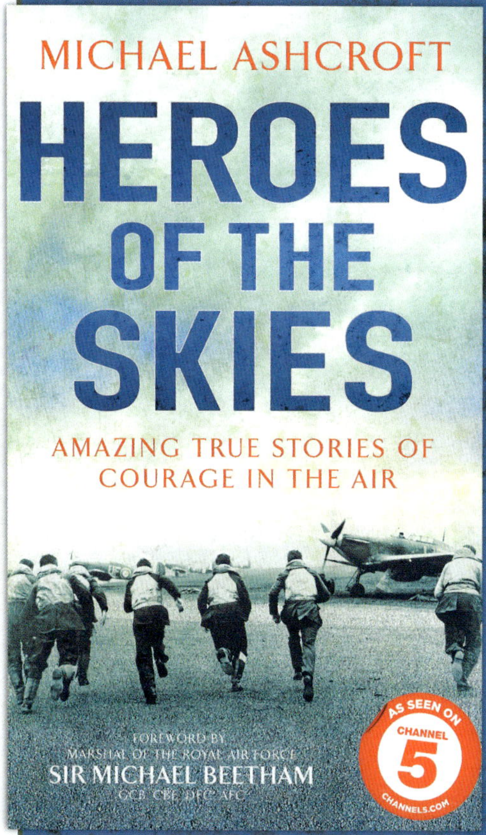

down his face from a cut, water and petrol fumes filled the cockpit. Lacey managed to kick out the Perspex canopy. However, overwhelmed by fumes he passed out, still in the cockpit, but he was saved by French peasants who cut him free and took him for medical treatment.

However, he enjoyed better luck on July 20, 1940, when his squadron was scrambled and ordered to defend a convoy off Jersey. After flying out over Portland Bill, they saw a horde of Junkers Ju 87 bombers, with Messerschmitt escorts, and went into battle.

> "GRIBBLE'S SPITFIRE WAS BADLY DAMAGED WHEN HIS SQUADRON WAS JUMPED BY ABOUT A DOZEN BF 109S. HE CARRIED OUT A FORCED LANDING ON A BEACH NEAR DUNKIRK BEFORE REMOVING HIS RADIO GEAR AND FINDING PASSAGE HOME ON A STEAMER BOUND FOR DOVER."

After Lacey spotted a Bf 109 turn towards him, he broke hard and, after several decreasing inward turns, put a burst into the fuselage. He then followed the stricken aircraft down to finish it off.

Next he successfully engaged a Bf 109 which was crossing his path at 90°. As Lacey turned for a second attack, he saw that Flying Officer 'Pan' Cox was on the enemy's tail, finishing it off. Lacey put in no claim for the second 'kill' allowing his comrade his first victory.

Lacey was awarded the DFM in August 1940 and a bar to his decoration in November of the same year. He survived the war and, after becoming a flying instructor, he was appointed in 1968 as a technical adviser on the film, Battle of Britain. Lacey died on May 30, 1989, aged 72. ■ *Words: Lord Ashcroft, KCMG*

A Supermarine Spitfire Mk.Ia of 54 Squadron. **Keith Draycott**

CHECK SIX

During the Battle of Britain, on August 15, 1940, Major Adolph 'Dolfo' Galland was the Gruppenkommandeur of III./Jagdgeschwader 26 (JG26) based at Caffiers flying the Bf 109E, while New Zealander Flight Lieutenant 'Al' Deere was a Spitfire Mk.I pilot with 54 Squadron. The two met over the Channel on that day, the fight progressing to low level with Deere eventually forced to bail out of his badly damaged aircraft between Folkestone and Dover. At the time, Deere had shot down 17 enemy aircraft, this dogfight was Galland's 22nd victory.

Firepower and performance
The Messerschmitt Bf 109E

The early models of the Bf 109 were limited by two things, power and firepower, both of which they lacked. The Bf 109E or Emil was to address both of these and turn the aircraft into a world class fighter.

As already mentioned, four Bf 109B airframes had been used to create the Bf 109 V10 to V13 prototypes in 1937, fitted with pre-production test versions of the Daimler-Benz DB 600 and 601A engines. The latter engine was the fully fuel injected version that became available as the test programme was being run. It had been intended that the Bf 109D would use the engine, but development problems delayed the production of the new powerplant which was not available in large numbers until 1938. Fitting the new engine required a redesign of the forward fuselage and cooling systems of the Bf 109. The oil cooler was much larger and could no longer be housed in the small fairing under the port wing as had been the case with the Jumo powered fighters.

It was moved to directly under the engine and enclosed in a fairing in the lower cowling. This included a rear flap that could be opened and closed by the pilot to maintain oil temperature at the optimum. The large coolant radiator had been in this position, so also had to move. It was split into two and placed in aerodynamic fairings under the rear of each wing, close inboard to the fuselage. Again, controllable flaps were fitted to the rear of these fairings to allow the coolant temperature to be maintained. Lastly, the DB601A was a supercharged engine, which required an air intake to be positioned on the port side of the cowling. A dozen designs were tested to decide the best aerodynamic shape for this to minimise drag.

WEIGHT AND BALANCE
The new engine increased the empty weight by 490kg to 2610kg. The undercarriage and its attachment points had to be strengthened to take the additional load and the 1100hp now acting on the airframe through the new VDM three bladed variable pitch propeller.

44 Bf 109E-1s were sent to Spain as part of the Condor Legion but saw little combat there. **Editor's collection**

Maximum speed rose from the 460kph of the D model to 570kph for the Bf 109E. The strengthened wing for the Bf 109C and D, with its capacity to take wing mounted armament, was found to be more than sufficient so the wing modifications were limited to the new radiators. Two more prototypes were built and fitted with a variety of armament, Bf 109 V14 had two cowling mounted MG 17 machine guns and a pair of MG FF 20mm cannon mounted in the wings. V15 had only the two machine guns. In comparative trials, the V14 armament was selected as the new standard for the fighter beginning with the E-3 variant.

The first models of the Bf 109E had the same armament as the Bf 109D, four MG 17 machine guns, two in the wings and two in the cowling. A pre-production batch of 10 Bf 109E-0s were ordered and produced in 1938, these aircraft were for service trials as the factories were gearing up to produce the new model. Three factories were involved in building the Bf 109E initially, Messerschmitt's two at Augsburg and Regensburg, and the Wiener Neustädter Flugzuegwerke (WNF) in Weiner Neustadt, an independent manufacturing facility. Luftwaffe units began to receive the Bf 109E in 1938, and as production increased, the Regensburg factory also produced the fighter for overseas customers who had been impressed by the Bf 109 at the Flugmeeting Airshow at Dübenfdorf Airfield near Zurich in July 1937. These included Bulgaria, Hungary, Spain, Switzerland and Yugoslavia.

It soon became apparent that the new engine had improved the already sparkling performance of the Bf 109 but there were still some concerns over the handling, as the early elevators could produce very high stick forces in pitch and the rudder could run out of control authority at low speeds, especially against the increased torque of the engine.

INTO BATTLE
In December 1938, the first of 44 Luftwaffe Bf 109Es began deploying to Spain for operations with the Condor Legion, but by then the air fighting was almost over and they saw little combat. By the time the Second World War started in September 1939, nearly all of the

A Bf 109E-4 Trop with the extended sand filter on the supercharger air intake to prevent ingestion of sand or dust. **Editor's collection**

Lithe & light
The Messerschmitt Bf 109F

The experience of flying the Bf 109E against the RAF in the Battle of Britain had highlighted the shortcomings of the design in combat. As a result of the feedback from operational units, Willy Messerschmitt was to radically alter the aerodynamics of the fighter.

The development of the Bf 109F or Friedrich can be said to have begun as early as December 1939, when work began on four prototypes aimed at improving the manoeuvrability of the aircraft. Bf 109 V21 and V22 were a pair of Bf 109E-1 airframes fitted with pre-production versions of a new engine, the 1350hp DB 601E, and had their wings clipped by 2ft (61cm) to improve the roll rate. The shorter wing was found to have a detrimental effect on the handling, especially at low speed, so V23 was built with the new engine and extended rounded wingtips. One more prototype, the V24 was also built, this having the short wing but a new egg shaped supercharger air intake which extended further into the airflow and proved very efficient.

CLEANING UP THE AIRFLOW
Elements of these four prototypes were brought together to produce what many people describe as the best handling of the Bf 109 series. The Bf 109F was a delight in all respects, the aerodynamic enhancements removing many if not all of the problems encountered with the earlier versions. These improvements were many, and started with a completely redesigned nose. A smaller, 9ft 8.5in (3m) diameter VDM propeller was fitted, made of light alloy to reduce weight. This was an electrically controlled variable pitch unit fitted with an automatic constant speed control unit with a manual backup. This reduced the cockpit workload as the pilot no longer had to adjust the propeller in any way. A larger spinner was fitted to this which blended back into a completely redesigned nose cowling, producing a very smooth nose profile. The oil cooler fairing was redesigned to provide improved airflow over the oil radiator and to reduce drag. More streamlined ejector exhausts were designed, which not only reduced drag, but also added a degree of propulsion from the exhaust gases. The supercharger air intake from the V24 was adopted as it offered better airflow for reduced drag. The rest of the fuselage remained relatively unchanged, the only real difference being the deletion of the lower forward cockpit windows and the addition of more armour plate to the cockpit and fuel tank.

The major improvements to the Bf 109F occurred in the wings and tailplane. The most obvious feature on the wings was the new rounded wingtips which actually reduced the wing area slightly even though the span was increased, but offered superior aerodynamic qualities. The thickness to chord ratio of the new wing was also reduced, making it aerodynamically slicker, and improved shorter but wider leading edge slats were fitted. The simple ailerons of the early models were replaced with balanced Frise ailerons, which eliminated adverse yaw with roll, reducing the rudder input in turns, which improved the turn rate. To fit in the thinner wing, new coolant radiators had to be designed with thinner, lower drag fairings.

A close up of the nose of a Bf 109F-4 Trop in the Western Desert, showing the extended tropical filter with its forward doors in the closed position. **Editor's collection**

The Bf 109 V24 prototype with the 1350hp DB 601E engine showing the clipped wings and protruding supercharger intake. **Editor's collection**

High over the Western Desert, a pair of Curtiss P-40B Tomahawks of 112 Squadron RAF are intercepted by Unteroffizier Franz Schwaiger in his Messerschmitt Bf 109F-4 Trop. Officially known as Yellow Three of 6 Staffel from II Gruppe of Jagdgeschwader 3 (6./JG3), Schwaiger named his 109F Gisela. Based at Castel Benito in Libya in February 1942, the unit spent most of the war on the Eastern Front, where Schwaiger achieved 56 of his total of 67 victories.

Desert Duel

A 250kg bomb is attached to the under fuselage rack, a feature only introduced at the factory on the E model of the Bf 109.

An image which we think is supposed to show Willy Messerschmitt congratulating a test pilot of a Bf 109 given the narrative nature of the images up to this point, but actually shows Willy Messerschmitt congratulating Chief Messerschmitt Test Pilot FlugKapitan Fritz Wendel on capturing the World Speed Record at 469.22mph (756kph) on April 26, 1939, in the Me 209.

The finished product of the line in flight. The Bf 109E was considered by many to be the most well mannered of the series, the perfect balance of power and weight.

Although heavily retouched, the final image shows that the Bf 109E was already in action, with the Condor Legion in Spain.

The wing spar, as already mentioned, was a single I-beam spar forming a torsionally rigid D-box with the ribs and monocoque skin to the leading edge. This meant the spar was positioned further aft than was the norm, which allowed the mainwheels to retract without hindrance. Any wing mounted weapons could be attached to the front of the spar, avoiding the necessity of cutting holes in it and weakening it. The fact that the undercarriage was attached to the fuselage and not the spar simplified the structure as the wings did not need to be able to absorb take off and landing loads. Lastly, the coolant radiators, oil cooler, fuel tank and battery could all be accessed easily through their own access doors. In short, the aircraft was an engineer's delight, simple, light and easy to maintain.

These photographs from the very early days at Messerschmitt show the layout for the production line, the construction of sub-assemblies and much of the individual parts that went into what many believe was the finest model of the Bf 109, the 109E, which began production in 1938. By the time that production got fully cranked up, the factories were enormous and for them to produce more than 30,000 airframes was a tribute to German industry and ingenuity. These images were taken out of Germany at the war's end by an engineer (now deceased) who had worked for Messerschmitt. We believe they formed the basis for an illustrated brochure or company commemorative publication celebrating the production of the Bf 109 from metal to in service. They lay packed away in a trunk from 1945 until 1976 when they were given to Warren Thompson. This is the first time they have been published since then and *Aviation Classics* would like to thank Warren for his generosity in providing them. ■ *Words: Tim Callaway and Warren Thompson. Pictures: Warren Thompson*

A pair of the MG 17 machine guns are fitted to the top of the engine bay on the production line.

Likewise, the wing team fits the wing mounted weapons after the wings have been attached to the fuselage.

Once the aircraft is almost complete, the weapons are boresighted in the firing bay to ensure accuracy.

Work was often interrupted in the prewar days by VIP tours as the aircraft had become a symbol of the power of National Socialism. Here, Adolph Hitler talks to a boy apprentice, surrounded by Theo Croneiss, Hubert Bauer and Willy Messerschmitt.

Right: Willy Messerschmitt (right) explains a technical point to Adolph Hitler and Ernst Udet.

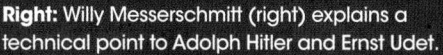

Once complete, the Bf 109s were towed by tractor to the separate aircraft paint shop.

With painting complete the final technical inspections and checks were carried out on the systems. Here the engine is inspected while an undercarriage retraction test is being run.

Once the technical inspections were complete, the aircraft were handed off to the flight test department for pre-delivery test flying.

The finished product in service. Here armourers prepare ammunition for the fuselage MG 17 machine guns.

The Daimler-Benz engines were supplied with cradle lugs attached to keep them steady in their crates. These were removed and the engine bearers for the Bf 109 were added in the Messerschmitt engine shop.

Inside the cockpit, attaching the armament and radio switches to the control column. The instrument panels were constructed separately and fitted into the cockpit complete with instruments, cabling and pressure feeds.

Attaching the engine fuel, cooling and oil systems and their attendant controls. The cabling and pressure feeds for the instruments are as yet unconnected, hanging over the side of the fuselage.

An inspector checks the engine bay control, fuel and oil feed fittings.

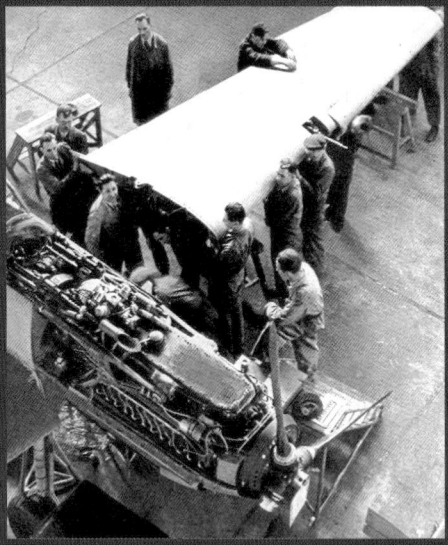
Another advantage of the Bf 109's lightweight construction was that major subassemblies could be manhandled into place by small teams. Here a team prepares to attach a wing.

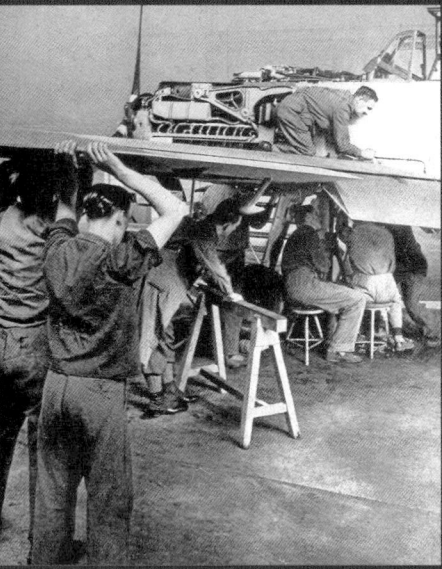
The wing attachment team lines up the wing accurately so the connecting bolts can be fitted.

Messerschmitt built its own variable pitch propellers for some models of the Bf 109. Here, a batch of very early F-model propellers are in various stages of construction.

With the propeller and forward fixed cowling mounted on the airframe, the upper cowling fitted.

In a separate workshop, an armaments technician checks one of the MG 17 7.9mm machine guns prior to fitting it to the aircraft.

The forward engine cowling and gun trays being formed on a jig, again from simple shaped parts riveted together.

The finished rear fuselages were given a protective coat of primer inside and a coat of primer and base paint colour outside, as well as the large national markings.

The engine team fitting a Daimler-Benz DB 601 to the forward fuselage. Note the fuselage is now standing on its own mainwheels, making handling the growing aircraft much simpler.

The rear fuselages then had the tailplanes, forward bulkheads for the cockpit and engine bay and the cockpit internal structure added. The next step was to add the main undercarriage.

minimum number of large parts, the Bf 109 required less riveting and welding than most of the German aircraft of the day, certainly a great deal less than its rival, the He 112. This also meant that less equipment was required on the factory floor, making for a cleaner and more efficient working environment. All of this had significant advantages when it came to licence production too, as the licence companies needed only minimum equipment and jigs to be supplied in order to start work. This was why 33,984 Messerschmitt Bf 109s were produced between 1936 and 1954, a figure including those aircraft built by other countries after the war and 13,633 more than next comparable fighter of the day, the Supermarine Spitfire.

From the outset, the Bf 109 was designed with ease of maintenance in mind, particularly in the field. To this end, the engine, weapons and other systems were all mounted behind large easy access panels.

The engine cowlings were large and could be removed quickly in three pieces. The engine was mounted on a pair of Y shaped bearers which attached to the main firewall, which itself formed the stress centre of the aircraft. A single piece forging was attached to the firewall which in turn attached to the wing spars, and two brackets from the firewall also formed the main undercarriage attachment points and the lower mounts for the engine. Therefore the stresses imposed on the Bf 109 by the engine, in flight or on the ground were absorbed in just three pieces of multi-function metal. The engine bearers could be released from their attachment points by eight quick release bolts and the control connectors, fuel, oil and coolant pipes were all grouped together, all with joints at the firewall. All of the electrical connectors were also in a junction box on the firewall, the practical upshot of which is that a small crew could change the engine on a Bf 109 in just minutes, not hours. ➤

The wing structure under construction. The single spar was relatively far back on the wing, making for a large and strong D-box leading edge.

Sheet metal being bent in presses to form the few curves on the design, such as the wing, tailplane and fin leading edge, the wing joint fillet and the rear fuselage.

Flush riveters at work fixing the skin to the wing structure.

The rear fuselage after the sections had been joined and the battery hatch cut. The external bracing is a jig to allow the internal strengthening and attachment structure to be accurately placed.

The rear fuselage sections were supplied whole, the rear fuselage battery access hatch had to be cut into them once complete.

Production, the key to success

A rare photo journey down the Messerschmitt production lines

The performance of the Bf 109 in the air was only part of its success story. The design of the internal structure was fundamental to the legend in two ways, firstly it allowed the fighter to be built rapidly and in very large numbers and secondly, it allowed aircraft to be maintained and repaired in the field in poor conditions and with the minimum of equipment.

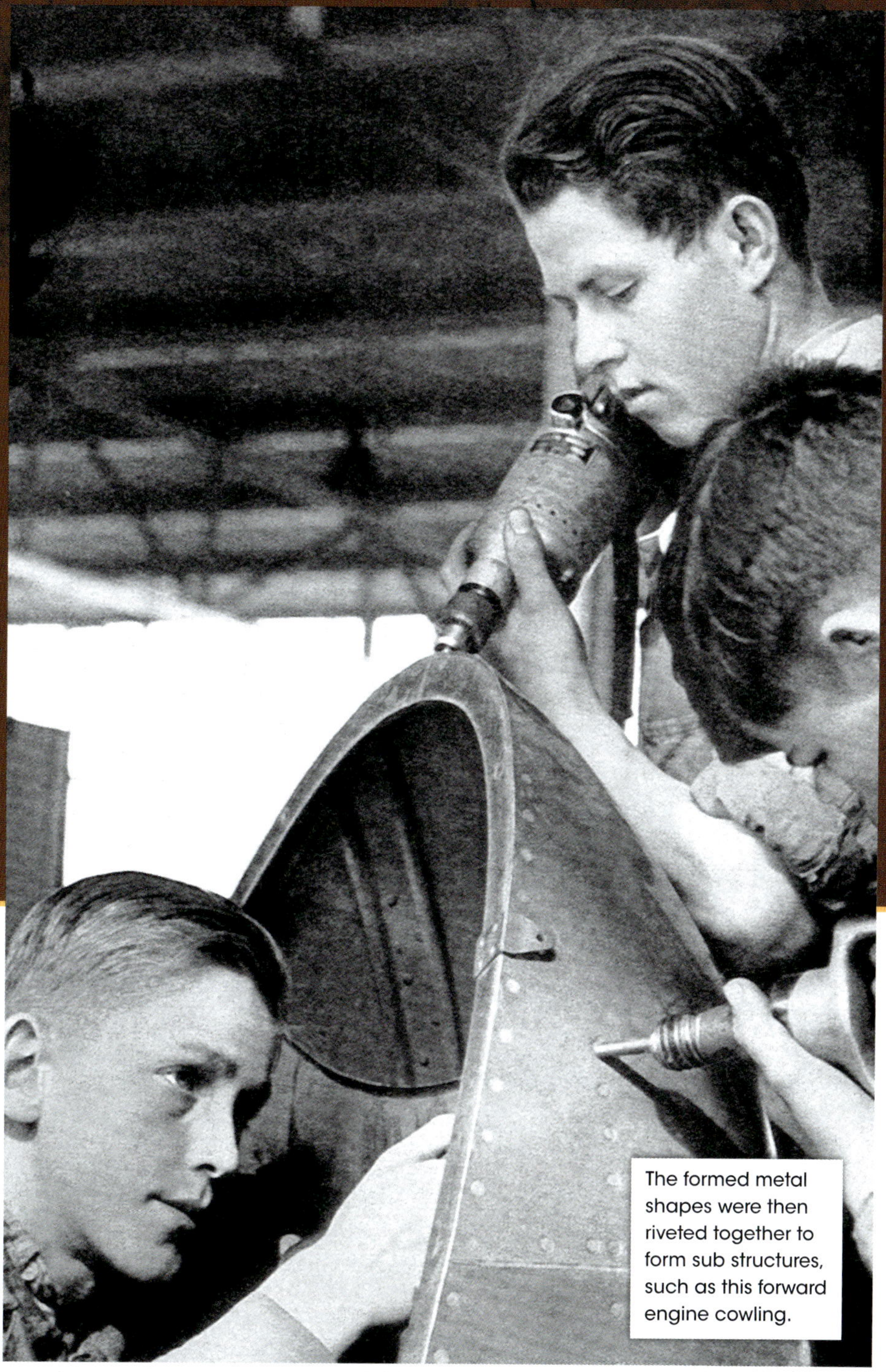

The formed metal shapes were then riveted together to form sub structures, such as this forward engine cowling.

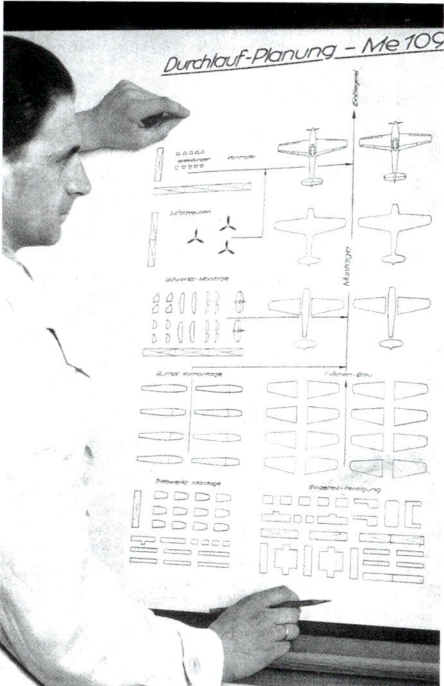

A flow chart of the factory floor for building Bf 109s shows exactly how the work was broken down and how the discreet parts came together and in what order.

How this simple and lightweight design was arrived at has been covered earlier in this magazine, how the production was managed to produce it in such numbers has not. This article is intended as a photo journey into the Messerschmitt factory at Augsburg, to show how a typical Bf 109 production line went together. The simplified construction of the aircraft also meant when it came to the production line, no specialist skills were required of the work force, most of the tasks in building a Bf 109 were straightforward. Items like the wing with its simple shape, the fuselage and tailplane could be brought together without the need for large numbers of cradles or jacks as the main undercarriage attached to the fuselage, so even before the wings and engine were fitted, the fuselage could be easily moved round the factory on its own wheels by only one or two men.

Given that as much of the structure as possible was contiguous, made from the ➤

The inside of the RAF Museum's Bf 109E-3 cockpit, showing the offset Revi C/12C gunsight. **Editor's collection**

BF 109E VARIANTS

Type	Sub type	Total built	Notes
Bf 109E-0		10	Pre-production order with 4 x MG 17 machine gun armament.
Bf 109E-1		1073	Production equivalent of E-0 with Revi gunsight.
	Bf 109E-1/B	110	Fighter bomber version of E-1 with centreline ETC500 bomb rack for 1 × 250kg/550lb bomb and DB 601Aa engine.
Bf 109E-2		Unknown, small numbers	Wing mounted MG 17s replaced with MG FF 20mm cannon and a motorkanone, an engine mounted MG FF. In service with II./JG27 in August 1940, the engine cannon again not a successful fit.
Bf 109E-3		1193	As per the Bf 109E-2, but without the engine mounted cannon.
	Bf 109E-3a	83	Export version of the E-3.
Bf 109E-4		250	Improved armour plate, centre section structure and clear vision square canopy. MG FF/M cannons with high explosive rounds fitted.
	Bf 109E-4/B	211	Fighter bomber version of E-4 with centreline ETC500 bomb rack for 1 × 250kg/550lb bomb and DB 601Aa engine.
	Bf 109E-4 Trop	65	Tropicalised E-4 for service in North Africa.
	Bf 109E-4/N	15	As the E-4 but with the 1175hp high altitude DB 601N engine.
	Bf 109E-4/BN	20	Fighter bomber version of the E-4/N with the DB 601N engine and ETC500 bomb rack.
Bf 109E-5		29	Reconnaissance version of the E-3 with cameras and only the two cowling mounted MG 17 machine guns.
Bf 109E-6		9	Reconnaissance version of the E-4/N with cameras and only the two cowling mounted MG 17 machine guns.
Bf 109E-7		438	As the E-4 but with the 300 litre drop tank or bomb rack installation.
	Bf 109E-7/N		As the E-4/N but with the E-7 drop tank installation.
	Bf 109E-7/NZ		As the E-4/N but with a GM-1 nitrous oxide boost system.
	Bf 109E-7/U2		As the E-7 but with additional armour for ground attack missions.
Bf 109E-8		9	Long range version of the E-1 with drop tank and four MG 17 machine guns.
Bf 109E-9		16	Long range reconnaissance version of the E-7/N with cameras, drop tank and only the two cowling mounted MG 17 machine guns.

Luftwaffe's day fighter units were equipped with the Bf 109E, and by the spring of 1940 only the Bf 109E variants were in service, all the earlier models being retired to secondary duties such as training. Feedback from the operational units was acted on rapidly by Messerschmitt, causing the nimble Bf 109E to be produced in no fewer than 19 types and sub types which are listed here.

During the initial assaults into Poland, Scandinavia and Western Europe, the Bf 109E proved superior to its opposition, even the new French Morane Saulnier MS 406 and Dewoitine D 520 fighters. Some modifications were made to the aircraft from these early engagements, such as the addition of more armour to the cockpit and fuel tank, but it was only when the Battle of Britain began in July 1940 that the fighter met its first really equal opponents, the Spitfires and Hurricanes of the RAF. Having said that, the Hurricane lacked the Bf 109's high altitude performance and the Spitfire still did not have fuel injection, so there were areas of the flight envelope where the Bf 109 still had the advantage.

What limited the aircraft in the Battle of Britain more than any other factor was its short range. This had an effect on mission planning, as often the fighters had to fly straight to and from the more distant targets which meant the bombers did too, removing any chance of the element of surprise. It also affected pilot performance. Flying with one eye on the fuel gauge was no way to go into combat. This was addressed in August 1940 by the introduction of the Bf 109E-7, which could carry a 300 litre drop tank on a centreline rack. This had been adapted from the earlier fighter bomber versions, the attachment points on the centre section could take either the tank or the ETC500 bomb rack. The original airframe design, with its single piece forged centre section, proved easy to adapt to take the additional loads.

Just over 3500 Bf 109Es of all versions were built, remaining in front line service from late 1938 to early 1941. It began to be replaced by the Bf 109F in October 1941, a number of the new type taking part in the final days of the Battle of Britain. ■ *Words: Tim Callaway*

The older rounded canopy on the Bf 109E-3, with a non-standard rear view mirror. Compare this with the flat canopy on the E-4 Trop image to the left. **Editor's collection**

Rearming the motorkanone, the engine mounted MG 151/20 20mm cannon on a Bf 109F-4. **Editor's collection**

BF 109F VARIANTS

Type	Sub type	Total built	Notes
Bf 109F-0		8	Pre-production order from Bf 109E airframes fitted with the 1,175hp DB601N engine, two MG 17 machine guns and a motorkanone, the 20 mm MG FF/M cannon.
Bf 109F-1		208	As the F-0, the first production version.
Bf 109F-2		1,384	Fitted with two MG 17 cowling mounted machine guns and a motorkanone, the 15 mm MG 151 cannon.
	Bf 109F-2 Trop		A tropicalised version with the extended supercharger air intake and other refinements supplied as a field kit.
	Bf 109F-2/Z	0	As the F-2 but with a GM-1 nitrous oxide boost for use as a high altitude fighter, cancelled.
Bf 109F-3		15	As the F-1 but with the 1,350hp DB601E engine.
Bf 109F-4		481	As the F-2 but with the 1,350hp DB601E engine and the motorkanone upgraded to an MG 151/20 20mm cannon.
	Bf 109F-4 Trop	576	A tropicalised version with the extended supercharger air intake.
	Bf 109F-4/R1	240	As the F-4 but able to carry two MG 151/20 20mm cannons in underwing pods.
	Bf 109F-4/Z	544	As the F-4 but with a GM-1 nitrous oxide boost system for use as a high altitude fighter.
Bf 109F-5		1	Reconnaissance version of the F-4 with cameras and only the two cowling mounted MG 17 machine guns.
Bf 109F-6		0	Planned but not built as the Bf 109G was in production.

The inlet and outlet flaps to these were controlled by a new automatic regulator system, again reducing the cockpit workload. This was governed by a thermostat, which would always give the most efficient cooling for the lowest possible drag. The exhaust from the radiators passed through the inner flaps, which were split to allow the upper half to act as the rear cooling governor. The lower half of this acted as a normal aerodynamic flap, increasing lift and drag at reduced speeds for landing. Later in the development of the Bf 109F, valves were added to the system to enable the pilot to shut off one radiator in the case of it being damaged, therefore preventing all the coolant from draining from the system. All armament was deleted from the wing, however strongpoints were later built in to enable the carriage of underwing weapons when greater firepower was required.

BALANCING THE TAIL

As previously mentioned, the elevators and rudder of the earlier models and their control effectiveness had been a cause of concern in some aspects of the flight envelope. The Bf 109F solved this in a particularly elegant way. Instead of the symmetrical fin originally fitted, the fin on the F was given an airfoil section. This meant it produced a lifting force in flight, pushing the tail to the left. This helped counteract the torque force from the engine and propeller, and increased the efficiency of the rudder as a control surface enormously. As a result, the need to apply right rudder on take off was reduced, thus saving stress on the undercarriage. It also meant that sudden applications of power from low speed, such as when forced to abort a landing, became rather less stressful for the pilot than they had been, as the rolling movement created by the sudden torque was much easier to control. ➤

Oberleutenant Heinrich Krafft in his Bf 109F-4 of III./JG51, shown here in the winter camouflage adopted for the Russian front. **Editor's collection**

Groundcrew replenishing the oil on a Bf 109F-4 using a hand pump. Conditions on forward airfields could be primitive, and any transport was welcome. **Editor's collection**

The rudder on the F model was actually reduced in size because of this improvement in effectiveness, again reducing weight and drag. The tailplane was also improved, moving forward and down from its original position which improved the elevator effectiveness and reduced the stick forces to a degree. The stronger tailplane also lost its external bracing struts, which had been a feature of the early Bf 109s, again reducing weight and drag. Lastly, the main undercarriage legs were raked further forward, which lowered the nose slightly and made the ground handling of the aircraft a little easier, but this was a question of degree rather than a tremendous improvement. The result of all these improvements was that the Bf 109 was suddenly a great deal easier to fly, had a much reduced cockpit workload and much improved handling. It was also faster, capable of 382mph (615kph) and longer ranged. The increase in range from 745 miles (1200km) for the Bf 109E to 1060 miles (1700km) was due to three reasons. The improved aerodynamic efficiency of the type certainly helped, as did the addition of another 100 litres capacity to the main fuel tank, but mostly the new versions of the Daimler-Benz engines were much more fuel efficient despite their increase in power.

FEWER GUNS AND FRACTURES

One of the major changes to the Bf 109F was the reduction in the number of guns on the aircraft from four to three. This was initially met with scepticism by the fighter community, but the concentration of firepower in the nose of the aircraft gave it a greater punch and the pilots were steadily won round, especially when they flew the improved fighter. Initially the Bf 109F was fitted with the two MG 17 machine guns in the upper cowling and the MG FF/M motorkanone firing through the propeller hub, but as production continued several other combinations of weapons were fitted, including the ability to fit underwing cannons in pods.

Groundcrew cleaning the motorkanone of a Bf 109F-4 of JG54. Makeshift stands and equipment were the order of the day on the Russian front. **Editor's collection**

In all, nine types and sub types of the Bf 109F were produced, as listed in the table here. When the first Bf 109Fs entered service in small numbers in October 1940 towards the end of the Battle of Britain, two major problems were encountered with the modified airframe. Firstly, the skin on the upper wings would wrinkle, and sometimes fracture, causing the wings to break off. Several pilots, including the commander of JG2, were killed when this happened in combat. Immediate studies showed that reinforcing the spar and thickening the wing skin was sufficient to cure the problem and the modifications were immediately introduced on to the production lines.

Secondly, several early Bf 109F-1s lost their tails, the fuselage structure breaking just in front of the fin. This was found to be caused by harmonic oscillations in the tailplane spar combining in the rear fuselage with vibration from the engine at certain power settings. This caused a vibration at the resonant frequency of the rear fuselage, which then failed. The problem was solved on in-service aircraft by changing the resonant frequency by simply screwing a pair of stiffening plates on to the rear fuselage at the break point. A modification was rapidly included in the production line which added internal stiffening to the structure which had the same effect. Interestingly, Hawker had exactly the same problem with the Typhoon for the same reason, and fixed it the same way, with a set of externally mounted stiffening plates round the rear fuselage.

IN SERVICE

As can be imagined, these failures of the structure in the early Bf 109F caused the type to be viewed with some suspicion by pilots. However, as the improved versions began to reach the staffels in April 1941, the superb handling and performance of the aircraft, and the lack of any more incidents, meant the Friedrich quickly became a great favourite. In total 3457 Bf 109Fs were produced, by Messerschmitt at Regensburg, AGO, Arado, Erla and WNF. The Friedrich was used to counter the RAF's raids into Western Europe, it established air superiority for the Luftwaffe over the Western Desert and it was at the forefront of Operation Barbarossa, the invasion of the Soviet Union. However, the supremacy of the Bf 109F was not to last long. New allied fighters began to match its performance and by the summer of 1942 the type was being replaced by the Focke-Wulf Fw 190 and the next and most produced version of the Bf 109, the G or Gustav. ■ *Words: Tim Callaway*

A very rare surviving Messerschmitt Bf 109F-4 is on display at the Canada Aviation Museum, Ottawa, Ontario, Canada. **A Hunt**

EAGLE OWL

by
Mark Postlethwaite

A Heinkel He219 'Uhu' night fighter brings down an RAF Lancaster over Germany, late 1944. The 'Uhu' or Eagle Owl was one of the best night fighters of the war but thankfully for the men of RAF Bomber Command, only a few hundred examples were built.

The RLM Collection is a unique and ongoing set of aviation art prints dedicated to recording many of the unique aircraft that saw service with the Luftwaffe during WWII. Painted by award winning artist and author Mark Postlethwaite, each subject is meticulously researched to represent actual events and combats that took place during WWII.
Each print is limited to 250 copies + 50 Artist's Proofs and all collectors are given the opportunity to collect the same edition number throughout the series.

Image size 53cm x 34cm
Overall size 59cm x 42cm

Numbers 1-250   £50
50 Artist's proofs   £60
Remarques are available for either edition, just add £120.
All prints signed by the artist.

To order, please visit the website or contact us via the details below.

Mark Postlethwaite, Sidewinder Publishing Ltd, 11 Sheridan Close, Enderby, Leicester, LE19 4QW England.
Tel. 0845 095 0344   email. mark@posart.com   www.posart.com

The Bf 109G-2 Trop in the RAF Museum at Hendon. Note the tropical filter and how much this aircraft resembles the earlier F model. **Julian Humphries**

Too much of a good thing?
The Messerschmitt Bf 109G

With the Bf 109F in production but the DB 601E engine already surpassed, Messerschmitt turned to the next generation of the Daimler-Benz powerplant to create the most produced and varied version of the Bf 109, the G or Gustav.

A Bf 109G-6 undergoing maintenance in the field. Even now with all the development, the aircraft was still engineer friendly. **Editor's Collection**

Improvements in Allied fighter performance spurred on developments in Germany, so when the latest version of the Daimler-Benz V12 engine, the DB 605 of 1475hp, became available, Messerschmitt began a new development of the Bf 109 to take advantage of it. The new model, known as the Bf 109G or Gustav, was intended to create a fully multirole aircraft out of the fighter, albeit in separate versions with specialist equipment. This was to create a vast array of types and sub types of the Gustav, especially when the standard field kits of specialist equipment were added.

These kits, known as Rüstsatz (R), were designed to modify the Bf 109G in the field for a specific role, and could be changed as local military needs dictated, giving the fighter force a new level of flexibility. On top of these, the Umrüst-Bausatz (often shortened to Umbau, designated U), or conversion kits, were intended for use at the factories on the production line or at repair depots where they were applied to existing aircraft. These often fitted a different internal armament or additional boost systems to the engine, so required more facilities than were often available in the field. These kits, when fitted to an aircraft, changed its designation with the addition of an R or a U to the G number, followed by the number of the kit fitted, making Bf 109G designations rather complex. The G remained in production until the end of the war despite the introduction of the later K model and accounted for around two-thirds of all Bf 109s built, about 22,000, although exact figures are difficult to come by, many of the production records being destroyed.

The Revi C/12C gunsight as fitted to a Bf 109G-2. **Editor**

NEW ENGINES, NEW WINGS

The development that started this plethora of variants began when the first pre-production DB 605 engines became available at the end of 1941. The new engine was developed from the DB 601E and included many modifications to make mass production easier. The internal displacement had grown from 33.9 to 35.7 litres, and the compression maximum revolutions had increased from 2600 to 2800rpm. The new engine was 56kg heavier than the DB 601, but produced an additional 125hp that more than offset this. During its development the engine was produced in several increasingly powerful versions, culminating in the final variant, the 2000hp DB 605ASC of 1945. The DB 605 could be fitted with the GM-1 nitrous oxide boost system for improved high altitude performance or the MW-1 water methanol injection system for improved power at low altitude, or indeed both.

These were included in the U2 Umbau kit and fitted at the factory or maintenance and repair units. The supercharger was a superb piece of engineering, being controlled by a barometric hydraulic clutch which automatically adjusted the supercharger rpm and output to allow for the change in external air pressure as the aircraft climbed. This was very advanced for its day, and gave the pilot yet another thing he didn't have to worry about. When fitted to the Bf 109, the automatic coolant control systems from the F model were also used, but the radiator airflow system was modified, eliminating the radiator bypass outlets which had been a feature of the Bf 109F wing.

These automatic engine management systems greatly reduced the cockpit workload and made the Bf 109G a much easier aircraft to operate. This was an important factor at the time because an increasing number of new pilots were being introduced to the type as Luftwaffe losses on all fronts were beginning to mount. All these improvements were made to the engine without much alteration in its external size, meaning the cowling required little in the way of change, the aircraft just ▶

BF 109G VARIANTS

Type	Sub type	Total built	Notes
Bf 109G-0		12	Pre-production order fitted with the 1350hp DB601E engine.
Bf 109G-1		167	Pressurised production version, 1475hp DB605A engine.
	Bf 109G-1/R2		Not a Rüstsatz kit, a high altitude reconnaissance fighter with cameras, armour removed, 300 litre drop tank, and GM-1 boost.
	Bf 109G-1/U2		Not an Umbau kit, a high altitude fighter with GM-1 boost.
Bf 109G-2		1587	As G-1, unpressurised production version.
	Bf 109G-2 Trop		A tropicalised version with the extended supercharger air intake.
	Bf 109G-2/R1		One built, a long range fighter bomber with underwing drop tanks and jettisonable tailwheel to allow a 1,100lb (500kg) bomb to be carried.
	Bf 109G-2/R2		Not a Rüstsatz kit, a reconnaissance fighter with cameras, 300 litre drop tank, and GM-1 boost.
Bf 109G-3		50	As the G-1 but with improved radios.
Bf 109G-4		1246	As G-3, unpressurised production version.
	Bf 109G-4 Trop		A tropicalised version with the extended supercharger air intake.
	Bf 109G-4/R2		Not a Rüstsatz kit, a reconnaissance fighter with cameras and 300 litre drop tank.
	Bf 109G-4/R3		Not a Rüstsatz kit, a long range reconnaissance fighter with cameras and two 300 litre underwing drop tanks.
	Bf 109G-4/U3		Not an Umbau kit, a reconnaissance fighter with cameras.
	Bf 109G-4y		Additional radios to act as a command aircraft.
Bf 109G-5		475	As the G-3 but with two MG 131 13mm machine guns mounted in the cowling.
	Bf 109G-5/U2		Not a Rüstsatz kit, a high altitude fighter with GM-1 boost.
	Bf 109G-5/U2/R2		Not a Rüstsatz kit, a high altitude reconnaissance fighter with cameras, armour removed, 300 litre drop tank, and GM-1 boost.
	Bf 109G-5/AS		A high altitude fighter with the 1435hp DB605AS engine with larger supercharger.
	Bf 109G-5y		Additional radios to act as a command aircraft.
Bf 109G-6		12,000+	As the G-4 but with two MG 131 13mm machine guns mounted in the cowling.
	Bf 109G-6/R2		Not a Rüstsatz kit, a reconnaissance fighter with cameras, 300 litre drop tank, and MW 50 boost.
	Bf 109G-6/R3		Not a Rüstsatz kit, a long range reconnaissance fighter with cameras and two 300 litre underwing drop tanks.
	Bf 109G-6 Trop		A tropicalised version with the extended supercharger air intake.
	Bf 109G-6y		Additional radios to act as a command aircraft.
	Bf 109G-6/AS		A high altitude fighter with the 1435hp DB605AS engine with larger supercharger.
	Bf 109G-6/ASy		A high altitude fighter with the 1435hp DB605AS engine with larger supercharger and additional radios to act as a command aircraft.
	Bf 109G-6N		A night fighter version, usually with the R6 kit and sometimes with FuG 350Z Naxos radar homing system.
Bf 109G-8		Small numbers	Reconnaissance aircraft with a variety of camera installations. Range could be extended with drop tanks and either boost systems could be fitted.
Bf 109G-10		2600+	As G-6 but with 1700hp DB605DM engine, later aircraft fitted with the DB605DB of 1850hp.
	Bf 109G-10/R2		Not a Rüstsatz kit, a reconnaissance fighter with cameras, 300 litre drop tank and MW 50 boost.
	Bf 109G-10/R6		As G-10 but with PKS 12 autopilot.
Bf 109G-12		Small numbers	Conversion of used G-4 and G-6 airframes to two seat trainers fitted with 300 litre drop tank.
Bf 109G-14		5500+	As G-6 but with 1800hp DB605AM engine and MW 50 boost..
	Bf 109G-14/AS		A high altitude fighter with the 1800hp DB605ASM engine with larger supercharger and MW 50 boost.
	Bf 109G-14/ASy		A high altitude fighter with the 1800hp DB605ASM engine with larger supercharger, MW 50 boost and additional radios to act as a command aircraft.
	Bf 109G-14y		Additional radios to act as a command aircraft.
Bf 109G-16		1	Planned ground attack version, one built.

A side view of 'White 8', a Bf 109G-4 of JG27.
Keith Draycott

required rebalancing to take the extra weight. The early pre-production engines revealed two problems. The first was incipient engine fires caused by overheating oil which was soon fixed enabling full production to begin in early 1942. The second problem was one of recurrent low oil pressure, and although many attempts were made to fix this, it continued to crop up throughout the engine's life.

While Daimler-Benz was developing the DB 605, Messerschmitt had been working on the structural problems that plagued the early Bf 109F aircraft so took the opportunity to create a new version of the fighter by permanently fixing these and fitting the new engine. Several other modifications suggested by front line experience were also incorporated. The wing structure was reinforced to allow the carriage of internal or externally mounted weapons. The rear fuselage and tailplane fittings were further modified to fully eliminate the resonance problems encountered in the F. Lightweight alloy armour plate was fitted to the main fuel tank and an internal bulletproof windscreen was included in the fixed front canopy. Otherwise the aircraft was almost identical externally to the Bf 109F, except for two identification points.

The front cowling was modified to provide two additional cooling inlets for the spark plugs, a small scoop appearing on either side of the nose just behind the spinner. The outer edges of the main wheel recesses in the wing were squared off, instead of being round as on earlier models. This was originally intended to allow a second undercarriage door to be fitted, to fully enclose the wheel when in the up position. However, tests showed that the reduced drag these provided was not worth the weight of the door or the complexity of the additional retraction system, so the doors were never fitted, but the recesses remained squared off.

VARIED VARIANTS

By October 1941, the first 12 pre-production aircraft, known as the Bf 109G-0, were under construction. The new engine was not ready in time so these were fitted with DB 601Es for testing and trials. As the production of the DB 605 got into its stride and the oil overheating problem was solved, all of these aircraft were refitted with the new engine which dropped straight into the bearers, being the same size. Production of the new fighter began in earnest in early 1942, with Messerschmitt's factory at Regensburg, Erla and WNF all going over to the new model. The first six versions of the Bf 109G were produced in pairs. The odd numbered variants had pressurised cockpits for high altitude operations, the even numbered aircraft did not. Other than that these paired aircraft types were identical in all respects.

The pressurised cockpit required a stronger canopy with a welded frame, which was standard across all models, pressurised or not, to simplify production. As a result of the complications of a pressurised cockpit system, it was the Bf 109G-2 that was the first into service by several weeks, being supplied to units in Western Europe and North Africa in March 1942. Many of these G-2 aircraft were fitted with the R-6 kit, as detailed in the table here, to increase their firepower against Allied heavy bomber raids. To improve ground handling, the G-3 and G-4 introduced a modified undercarriage with a larger tailwheel and the mainwheels angled so they were nearly vertical on the ground despite the splay of the undercarriage legs. To accommodate the angled wheels, teardrop shaped fairings were introduced into the upper wing surface over the wheel recesses. The development of these first six versions happened in the space of just a year, the G-6 entering service in February 1943.

The BF 109G-6 became the most produced variant of any model of the fighter, with over 12,000 being built. It was intended to be a true multirole aircraft, capable of being fitted with any of the U and R kits and any combination of cannons, bombs and drop tanks. With the G-5 and G-6 came a new tailplane design with a taller fin and larger rudder, this and the tailplane being made of wood to reduce the use of strategic materials and again ease and standardise production, a factor that was becoming increasingly important in the face of the growing Allied heavy bomber raids against German aircraft factories. This new tailplane became a standard feature of the later G-10 and K-4 models of the fighter. The G-5 and G-6 also introduced a new weapon and a new identification feature. The cowling

A Bf 109G-6/R6 with two Mauser 20mm MG 151/20 cannons in underwing pods.
Editor's Collection

A Bf 109G-6/R1 fitted with the ETC 501 bomb rack under the fuselage to carry a 550lb (250kg) bomb. **Editor's Collection**

Bf 109G-6s roll down the production line. This was to be the most produced variant of the fighter, with over 12,000 built. **Bundesarchiv**

A Bf 109G-10 seen after being captured in 1945. The taller wooden fin and rudder and clear vision canopy standard to this model. **Warren Thompson**

RÜSTSATZ (R) AND UMRÜST-BAUSATZ (U) KITS FOR THE BF 109G

Rüstsatz (R) field kits

R1	ETC 501 bomb rack under the fuselage to carry a 550lb (250kg) bomb.
R2	ETC 50 bomb rack under the fuselage, to carry four SC 50 110lb (50kg) bombs.
R3	Schloß 503A-1 rack for one 300 litre drop tank.
R4	Two Rheinmetall-Borsig 30mm MK 108 cannons in underwing pods.
R6	Two Mauser 20mm MG 151/20 cannons in underwing pods.
R7	Direction finding equipment with loop antenna.

Umrüst-Bausatz (U) factory kits

U1	Messerschmitt P6 propeller with reverse pitch. Only fitted to the prototypes.
U2	GM-1 nitrous oxide boost or MW-50 water methanol boost, or both.
U3	Reconnaissance fit with one Rb 50/30 camera or two Rb 12.7/7x9 cameras behind the cockpit and a Robot II camera in the wing, aimed via the gunsight. By September 1943 the G-6/U3 became the G-8 production reconnaissance variant which entered service in early 1944.
U4	A Rheinmetall-Borsig 30mm MK 108 fitted as the motorkanone, the engine-mounted cannon.
U5	As the U4 with two more 30mm MK 108 cannons in underwing pods. Not used.

mounted MG 17s that had been a feature of every model up to the G-6 were finally replaced by a pair of the MG 131 13mm heavy machine guns. The breeches for these were much larger and caused the rear of the cowling and the space ahead of the cockpit to be bulged to accommodate them. These prominent features resulted in these G models receiving the nickname 'die Beule', the Bulge.

LATER MODIFICATIONS

As the engine and armament of the Bf 109G were developed, the cowling again changed shape with extended bulged fairings to accommodate them and the new superchargers coming into service. These new fairings were far more aerodynamically efficient that those of the early G-6 and smoothed the outline of the entire nose. New weapons, such as the BR 21 21cm rocket with its 90lb (40.8kg) warhead, were introduced, as were larger MK 108 30mm cannons, both engine mounted and in pods under the wings. All of these increases in armament and performance were aimed at combating the Allied heavy bomber raids which were starting to disrupt production.

New Allied fighters were also being introduced, and the Bf 109 crews found themselves in an increasingly desperate situation as the war ground on. The last mass produced version of the Bf 109G was the G-14, which was an attempt to thoroughly standardise production which had become fragmented through the vast number of types and sub types. The G-14 had also been produced because of the delays to the G-10 model. These delays were caused by problems with the development of the DB605D engine which produced 1800hp initially and improved later to 2000hp. Many of these later aircraft were fitted with a new canopy, the Erla-Haube clear vision unit, which reduced the heavy framing of the earlier models and improved the pilot's view.

All of the Bf 109G models are listed in the table here, but one final variant deserves a mention, the Bf 109G-12. This was the first attempt to build a two seat trainer version of the fighter by fitting a second cockpit behind the first. A small number of G-4 and G-6 airframes were modified to this standard, the requirement coming from the deteriorating handling of the Bf 109 and the increasing number of landing and ground accidents with the type, especially among new pilots. The Gustav, particularly in its later models, had become a bit of a beast. The increased power, torque and weight made the aircraft faster, but eroded the manoeuvrability and the low speed handling. Spin recovery was still as sharp as ever, but the sparkle had gone out of the little fighter. Through necessity, the rapier had become a bludgeon. These problems were to be partly exacerbated and partly solved by the last of the production models, the Bf 109K. ■

Words: Tim Callaway

Loading cameras and film magazines into the rear fuselage bay of a rare Bf 109G-8. **Editor's Collection**

Production priorities
The Messerschmitt Bf 109K

The last production development of the Bf 109 proved to be the fastest, capable of 440mph (710kph). However, production was to be delayed by the Allied bombing campaign meaning that the Bf 109K was almost too little, too late.

As the tide of the war turned against Germany in 1943, the RLM became concerned with the plethora of types and sub types of the Bf 109 then in service. The maintenance situation was complicated, even getting the right spares could be difficult as there were so many possible combinations of airframe, engine and armament even within a single unit. Walter Göttel, who at the time was in charge of organising the licence production contracts for the Bf 109, estimated that over 1000 detail changes had been incorporated into the fighter since it entered service, and the situation was becoming both costly and critical.

The RLM advised Messerschmitt that the design and production of the fighter was to be rationalised. A new version of the aircraft was to be produced with fewer variants and more commonality of spares and equipment. At the same time, the problems still evident in the aircraft were to be dealt with. Messerschmitt handed the consolidation programme to Ludwig Bölkow in late 1942, who at the time was one of the Augsburg project team. A consolidation team of 140 designers, stress analysts, draughtsmen and engineers was assembled at the Weiner Neustädter Flugzuegwerke (WNF) in Austria who began work early in 1943. By August, the plans and design drawings for the new model, known as the Bf 109K or Kürfurst, were almost complete. On August 13, 1943, the WNF was heavily bombed, and some of the work was lost, as were some of the development team. The project was moved to the Messerschmitt plant at Regensburg, which caused delays, exacerbated by development problems with the Daimler-Benz DB 605D engine. However, the

The tail of a Bf 109K-4, showing the modified fin and rudder and the extended tailwheel leg which did much to improve the ground handling. **Editor's collection**

new design was finally completed in the middle of 1944 with deliveries beginning in October.

While the new fighter was to be produced at Regensburg, initially the WNF and Messerschmitt Augsburg factories were to continue producing the last models of the Bf 109G to avoid to much disruption in the supply of new fighters at this critical time. Since none of the proposed models of the Bf 109K were fitted with pressurised cockpits to keep production simple, all of the model designations were given even numbers. The RLM reviewed the plans, and decided that the first model, the Bf 109K-2, was simply too similar to the Bf 109G-10 to allow the disruption it would cause for no real benefit. Production of the K-4 was approved, and by March 1945, 1593 had been delivered to the Luftwaffe.

Figures for the production after this were lost as the war ended. This was the fastest Bf 109 of the Second World War, with a maximum speed of 440mph (710kph). New propellers were being developed for the aircraft which would have boosted this impressive figure still further, but the war ended before they could be tested. The first aircraft off the production line were powered

Four Bf 109K-4s of JG77 preparing for Operation Bodenplatte on January 1, 1945. **Editor's collection**

A new build Bf 109K-4 awaits delivery. **Editor's collection**

The Revi EZ42 lead computing gyro gunsight could be set to the wingspan of the target aircraft and was intended to be fitted to the Bf 109K, but the war ended before this could be achieved. **Editor's collection**

A Bf 109K-4 of JG77 pictured near the end of 1944. **Editor's collection**

by the 1800hp DB 605DM, but this was only intended as a development version of the engine. After the first few aircraft, it was quickly replaced by the DB 605DB and DC production versions which could produce 2000hp with the MW 50 water methanol boost system. Every Bf 109K produced was fitted with the MW 50 as standard.

The armament was also standardised, as ammunition supplies to the front line units was another of the logistics problems the RLM wished to solve. The 30mm MK 108 motorkanone was fitted firing through the engine and a pair of MG 131 13mm heavy machine guns were mounted in the upper cowling. Having said that, it is known that a number of Bf 109K-4s were fitted with the 20mm MG 151/20 motorkanone, as the MK 108 was prone to jamming. This problem also caused the addition of a pair of Mauser 20mm MG 151/20 cannon in underwing pods as one of the Rüstsatz (R) kits for field use to ensure the K's potency as a bomber interceptor.

With the Bf 109K-4 in full production at Regensburg, a number of other variants were proposed that would eventually replace all of the Bf 109G aircraft then in service. A few of the K-6 version were produced with an additional pair of wing mounted MK 108 cannon, but these proved to have such a deleterious effect on the performance of the aircraft that they were removed from the few built. None of the pilots flying the Bf 109 liked the wing mounted cannons on the later versions of the fighter as they had a dramatic effect on the roll rate of the aircraft, dramatically reducing the fighter's manoeuvrability. Given that they were now encountering the latest Allied fighters such as the Yak 9D, P-51D Mustang and Hawker Tempest, they needed all the manoeuvrability they could get.

The Bf 109K played a major part in the last large scale Luftwaffe operation of the Second World War, Operation Bodenplatte. This was an attack in the early hours of January 1, 1945, by every fighter that could be mustered, 1035 in total, against the Allied airfields in Northern France, Belgium and the Netherlands. Although some damage was done to the Allied tactical air forces, greater harm was done to the Luftwaffe's fighter units, who lost many experienced leaders in the operation. This was to be the swan song of the Bf 109, as in the remaining 17 weeks of the war, fighter units were becoming increasingly short of ammunition, fuel and pilots. In the last year of the war, despite the bombing campaign aimed at the aircraft industry, German aircraft production actually doubled, so aircraft were never the problem. Finding fuel and experienced men to fly them was.

As the Allies advanced and the airfields and then the factories were overrun, the dwindling numbers of fighters and pilots fought an increasingly desperate and hopeless battle. The last Bf 109Ks were on a par with the latest Allied fighters, in fact the Bf 109 had the best climb rate of any fighter of the conflict, but the many novice pilots then in the Luftwaffe were unable to match their opponents in either experience or numbers. Many Bf 109s were burnt on their airfields to prevent their capture, but many fell into the hands of the Allies. On May 8, 1945, the agony was over, but the legend of the Bf 109 was to continue in some very surprising theatres, as will be described later in this magazine. ∎

Words: Tim Callaway

RÜSTSATZ (R) KITS FOR THE BF 109K

These kits were similar to those of the Bf 109G, but few were produced before the war's end.

R1	The ETC 501 or the Schloß 503A bomb rack under the fuselage to carry a 550lb (250kg) or 1100lb (500kg) bomb.
R3	The Schloß 503A-1 rack for one fuselage drop tank (300 litre).
R4	The BSK 16 gun camera fitted in the port wing.
R6	Two Mauser 20mm MG 151/20 cannons in underwing pods.

BF 109K VARIANTS

K-0	Pre-production aircraft, powered by the 1800hp DB 605DM engine with MW 50 water methanol boost.
K-2	An unpressurised version that was so similar to the G-10 that it was not proceeded with to avoid disrupting the production lines.
K-4	About 1650 K-4s were built before the war's end. It was an unpressurised fighter and powered by the DB 605DM, DB or DC engine, ranging from 1800 to 2000hp.
K-6	As K-4 with reinforced wings intended as as a bomber interceptor. Two additional 30mm MK 108 cannons and additional armour were fitted, but so reduced the performance these were removed from the few built.
K-8	Equivalent to the Bf 109G-8, intended as a camera equipped reconnaissance version. None built.
K-10	As K-4 but with the MK 103M engine cannon instead of MK 108. None built.
K-12	Two seat trainer, equivalent to Bf 109G-12. None built.
K-14	Similar to the K-6, this was intended as a high speed interceptor with the DB 605L engine which could produce over 2000hp. Neither the engine or the aircraft were built.

The great Erich Hartmann, pictured as a major. **Editor's collection**

Erich Hartmann
'Der Oberste Experte'

With three decades of experience himself as an RAF fighter pilot, Clive Rowley investigates the use of the Bf 109 on the Eastern Front, the circumstances that produced the most successful fighter pilots the world has ever seen and tells the story of the highest scoring fighter pilot of all time.

NOT A BRILLIANT START…

Leutnant Erich Hartmann, aged 20, flew his first combat mission in a Bf 109G of 7 Staffel, III Gruppe, Jagdgeschwader 52 (JG 52), on October 14, 1942, from Soldatskaya airfield in the Caucasus, on the Russian Front. He flew as wingman to the experienced and highly successful Bf 109 fighter pilot Oberfeldwebel (Master Sergeant or Warrant Officer) Edmund 'Paule' Roßmann. It did not go well.

Patrolling at 12,000ft Roßmann spotted 10 enemy aircraft far below. Calling out the contacts on the radio he started to dive towards them. The fledgling Hartmann could see nothing at first, but followed his leader down. As they levelled off at high speed, Hartmann suddenly spotted two "dark green aircraft" 2000m ahead and slightly higher. Obsessed with the idea of scoring his first kill and entirely forgetting his discipline, he opened his throttle fully and shot past and in front of his leader to get into a firing position. Closing fast, he opened fire at the enemy aircraft at about 300m.

His shots missed completely and he almost collided with his intended victim. Suddenly surrounded by enemy aircraft and separated from his leader as he overshot his target, he pulled up into a cloud layer alone and still at full power. His leader called him on the radio, calmly talking him down out of the cloud, but when Erich emerged into clear sky, much to his eternal embarrassment, he mistook his leader for an enemy aircraft. Roßmann was still talking to him on the radio and trying to join up with him, while Hartmann was calling that he had an unidentified enemy aircraft on his tail, which he was trying to fight off and escape from.

When his leader eventually convinced him that his tail was clear, Hartmann climbed to determine his position. Finding the Elbrus River to his left he started to make his way home, but then, as a result of all the time he had spent at full throttle, a red low fuel warning light illuminated in his cockpit and five minutes later his Daimler-Benz engine spluttered and died as his Bf 109 ran out of fuel. Hartmann was forced to make a wheels-up, 'belly' landing in a field of sunflowers, virtually destroying his aircraft.

Some German Army soldiers drove him the 30km back to his airfield where he had to endure a bawling out from the Gruppenkommandeur of III./JG52, Major Hubertus von Bonnin, and then a lecture from his leader Paule Roßmann about flight discipline and tactics. Young Hartmann had violated just about every commandment in the fighter pilot's 'bible'. As a punishment he was grounded for three days and told to work with the ground crews. He later said: "I felt awful, but it gave me time to think about what I had done." ➤

Oberfeldwebel Edmund 'Paule' Roßmann, who led Hartmann's eventful first combat flight. **Editor's collection**

A Messerschmitt Bf 109G-2 of III/JG52 under maintenance in 1942. **Editor's collection**

Erich Hartmann's last aerial victory was a Yak-9, similar to this Yak-9UM still flying today. **Editor**

... BUT A STRONG FINISH

Just over two and a half years later, at 8.30am on May 8, 1945 – the day that the war in Europe ended – the same Erich Hartmann (now a major) took off from the Czechoslovakian airfield that I/JG52 had retreated to in the face of the advancing Russians. He led his rotte (pair) of late model Bf 109 'Gustavs' over Czechoslovakia on a reconnaissance mission to report the position of the Soviet forces; the first of which they found only 40km away. He also spotted some Russian Yak-9 fighters below, at least one of which appeared to be performing aerobatics over the town of Brno (Brünn), apparently in celebration of the impending Soviet victory. Determined to 'spoil the party' Hartmann struck quickly and ruthlessly.

Diving on the Yaks from 12,000ft he opened fire on one from 60m (200ft) range and the hapless Russian aerobat became his last kill of the war. He decided not to re-attack the other Yaks as he spotted 12 USAAF P-51 Mustangs arriving high overhead. He and his wingman fled at low level through the smoke pall that covered Brno and as they left the two Allied aircraft formations appeared to be fighting each other. Amazingly after his unpromising start, this was Erich Hartmann's 352nd confirmed victory.

All of his kills were achieved flying the Bf 109 and all on the Eastern Front. This score beats those of all other fighter aces of all nations and all other conflicts easily, and leaves him as the ultimate ace of aces, the most successful and probably the greatest fighter pilot of all time.

'EXPERTEN'

The general definition of a fighter ace – a pilot who has scored five kills or more – was not used by the Luftwaffe, which unofficially used the term 'Experte' to describe any experienced pilot of outstanding ability and achievement, regardless of his number of kills. If the Germans had used the Allied definition of five kills, the Jagdwaffe would have been able to boast more than 5000 'aces' by the end of the war. It is a fact that more aerial kills were made with the Bf 109 than any other aircraft of the Second World War and, incredibly, more than 100 Bf 109 pilots – most of whom are practically unknown today – were each credited with the destruction of 100 or more enemy aircraft. Thirteen of these men achieved more than 200 kills, while two scored more than 300 – Erich Hartmann (352 kills) and Gerhard Barkhorn (301 kills).

Altogether, this group of pilots was credited with a total of nearly 15,000 kills. When these scores are compared to those of other nation's top aces in the Second World War they seem even more incredible. Officially, the RAF's top ace of the war was 'Johnny' Johnson with 38 kills (although many believe that South African-born 'Pat' Pattle actually had a higher score with at least 40 kills, possibly as many as 50).

The USAAF ace of aces was Richard Ira Bong who scored 40 kills in his P-38 in the Pacific area of operations (see *Aviation Classics* Issue 14); the top scoring Soviet ace was Ivan Nikitovich Kozhedub with 62 victories and the Japanese top scorer was Hiroyoshi Nishizawa with 87 kills (during the First World War no pilots scored into the hundreds and the top scorer among all the combatants was Manfred von Richthofen, the Red Baron, with 80 kills).

Gerhard Barkhorn, a close friend of Hartmann's and the only other fighter pilot to shoot down more than 300 enemy aircraft, a total of 301. **Editor's collection**

Early Soviet wartime fighters included the Polikarpov I-16 'Rata', outclassed by the Bf 109. **Editor's collection**

> "ALTOGETHER, THIS GROUP OF PILOTS WAS CREDITED WITH A TOTAL OF NEARLY 15,000 KILLS. WHEN THESE SCORES ARE COMPARED TO THOSE OF OTHER NATION'S TOP ACES IN THE SECOND WORLD WAR THEY SEEM EVEN MORE INCREDIBLE"

For Luftwaffe fighter pilots on the Eastern Front pickings were rich and this is where Hartmann and Barkhorn achieved their amazing 300-plus scores. In addition to these two stars, there were seven other Bf 109 pilots who scored more than 200 kills on the Russian Front, a further 66 who achieved more than 100 victories and another 154 who knocked down more than 50 enemy aircraft. How was it that so many Second World War Jagdwaffe pilots scored so prolifically on the Eastern Front and how did Eric Hartmann achieve the barely credible score of 352 kills? Before looking into the personal story of the highest scoring fighter pilot of all time, it is perhaps worth investigating the background to these amazing kill totals, their accuracy and the reasons why they were achieved.

INCREDIBLE SCORES

In the light of postwar research, it is now conceded that over-claiming occurred in every air force and in every theatre of war, usually as a result of genuine confusion in the heat of battle. Many an Allied fighter pilot made a claim against a Bf 109 emitting its usual trail of smoke from its exhausts as it dived away at full throttle, actually unharmed.

The very high level of claims by the German fighter pilots on the Eastern Front seemed to take even the Luftwaffe hierarchy by surprise. It is reported that Reichsmarschall Göring was incredulous and doubted the veracity of the staggering number of kills being claimed by his pilots over Russia. It is interesting to note that early in the war 20 aerial victories were enough to earn a Luftwaffe fighter pilot a Knight's Cross, but by late 1943 a long serving pilot needed more than 100 kills for the same award.

Göring was not the only one who did not believe the claims coming out of Russia in the early days and the Germans set up a strict system to verify all claims. This required written confirmation of each kill, with one or more aerial witnesses to the action, plus, if possible, back-up confirmation, also in writing, from an observer on the ground. Shared kills were not individually allotted to the pilots involved – there were no half kills allocated – instead they were added towards the squadron's score as a whole. The resultant reams of paperwork this strict system engendered meant that it sometimes took a year or more for a pilot's claim to receive official confirmation and sometimes, particularly toward the end of the war, far from over claiming, claims were not formally submitted. ➤

The Polikarpov I-153 'Chaika' was of similar vintage to the I-16 and equally lacking in performance in comparison with the German fighters. **Editor's collection**

The heavy and underpowered wooden Lavochkin-Gorbunov-Gudkov LaGG-3 was known as the 'Lacquered Coffin' to its pilots. **Editor's collection**

Thousands of Allied fighters were sent to Russia to bolster the Soviet Air Force including 2952 Hawker Hurricanes. **Editor's collection**

The US also provided 10,000 fighters, including more than 2000 Curtiss P-40 Tomahawks, such as the one here and the later Kittyhawk. **Editor's collection**

The Yak-9 was comparable to both the Bf 109 and Fw 190 in performance, fast and powerful with a superior turning performance. **Editor**

Hartmann's official score of 352 kills has caused many over the years to disbelieve the statistics. One Soviet historian, Dimitri Khazanov, attempted to prove that Hartmann did not score anywhere near that number of victories, but his politically motivated work has subsequently been discredited. At the height of Hartmann's killing spree with JG52 there was even one pilot in his own wing – Leutnant Friedrich 'Fritz' Obleser (who flew frequently as wingman to Günther Rall and eventually achieved 120 kills himself) – who questioned the number of kills Hartmann was achieving. Hartmann asked Rall to have Obleser transferred to be his wingman for a while and, after seeing him in action, Obleser became convinced of Hartmann's abilities and of his scoring rate. He actually signed off as a witness on a number of Hartmann's kills and the two became friends.

It is quite reasonable to question whether the enormous claim figures by Hartmann and other Luftwaffe fighter pilots on the Eastern Front can be taken seriously. It is not possible to verify every single claim against Soviet loss statistics, but it is a fact that, during 1944, German fighter pilots claimed a total of 8501 Soviet aircraft shot down, while the Soviet loss statistics record 10,400 of their aircraft lost in combat during the year. My personal opinion is that the scores of the German fighter pilots are not grossly inflated or exaggerated and can be accepted as broadly accurate. In truth it doesn't matter whether Hartmann scored exactly 352 kills or whether the real number was below or even above that. The fact remains that he is indisputably the highest scoring fighter pilot in history by a long way.

EASTERN FRONT: 'TURKEY SHOOT'?

Only a select handful of Luftwaffe fighter pilots scored more than 100 kills while fighting against the Allied air forces in the West; by contrast, more than 70 pilots achieved this feat on the Eastern Front. So how and why was it possible to achieve such high scores on the Eastern Front?

Firstly, it must be borne in mind that the Luftwaffe pilots did not fly 'tours' with lengthy rest periods interspersed between periods on operations, as was the practice in Allied air forces. Most German pilots remained on operations in the front line without respite, until they were killed, captured, incapacitated or, perhaps, elevated to a staff position. Pilots of other nations during the Second World War generally flew far fewer sorties than their German counterparts, very few reaching the 500 mark, when many long serving and high scoring Luftwaffe pilots flew two or three times that amount. Erich Hartmann flew more than 1400 operational sorties. The sheer amount of operational flying and length of wartime service with minimal breaks gave the German fighter pilots ample opportunity to achieve large tallies of kills, if they survived for long enough to do so.

The US also supplied more than 4700 Bell P-39 Airacobras, which were used mostly in the ground attack and anti-tank roles. **Editor's collection**

Although an incredibly tough ground attack aircraft, formations of Ilyushin Il-2 Shturmoviks often flew unescorted and proved easy prey for the German fighters. **Editor's collection**

Once the Soviet aircraft industry was reorganised it began producing more effective fighter designs such as the Lavochkin La-5. **Editor's collection**

It is relatively easy to provide explanations for the Luftwaffe pilots' success rates in the early days of the war in the east, immediately after the German invasion of Russia – Operation Barbarossa – which began on June 22, 1941. In the beginning, the Jagdwaffe enjoyed undisputed superiority over the Soviets in all three essentials for survival and success in the air: equipment, training and tactics.

The Bf 109 was vastly superior to the antiquated aircraft designs flown by the Soviet Air Force, such as the barrel shaped Polikarpov I-16 'Rata' ('Ishak' or 'Donkey' to Soviet pilots) of 1934 vintage, the Polikarpov I-153 ('Chaika' or 'Seagull') biplane of similar vintage, or the heavy and underpowered, wooden, Lavochkin-Gorbunov-Gudkov LaGG-3 ('Lacquered Coffin' to its pilots). These and other Soviet aircraft of that time were completely outclassed by the Bf 109, particularly in rate of climb, ceiling and speed (both straight and level and in a dive).

The Bf 109 pilots also had an advantage in hitting power with superior aircraft armament. In addition, the Soviets did not initially have up to date gunsights in their aircraft and many German pilots felt unconcerned if a Soviet pilot got into a shooting position against them as the Russian pilots could not assess how much lead to pull for an accurate shot.

Much has been made of the lend-lease aircraft delivered to the Soviet Union to 'bridge the gap' between the initial shock of Barbarossa and Russian industry gearing up to full production after evacuating its manufacturing plants to safety beyond the Ural mountains. Between 1941 and 1945 the UK supplied a total of 4300 Hurricanes and Spitfires to the Soviets (the latter being particularly unsuited to the primitive conditions at forward landing grounds). After the United States entered the war, it extended the lend-lease scheme to provide direct supply to the Soviets.

Among the aircraft sent were almost 10,000 fighters, including more than 4700 Bell P-39 Airacobras and more than 2000 Curtiss P-40 Tomahawk/Kittyhawks. In common with the Soviets' home-based aircraft production though, this was a case of quantity over quality and although these aircraft brought the Russians valuable gunsight technology, they were still considered inferior to the Bf 109 by the German pilots.

In terms of both training and tactics the Soviets fell significantly short against the Germans. The Stalinist purges of the 1930s had emasculated the Soviet armed forces, draining them of experience and expertise, thoroughly cowing those that remained and stifling initiative. The Soviet pilots were ill prepared and barely trained; few of them had any idea tactically. German pilots' reports are full of accounts of formations of Russian aircraft either sticking rigidly to course and altitude despite being under attack, or milling about chaotically providing easy pickings.

The Soviets focused on ground attack against the German Army tanks and infantry rather than winning air superiority. In addition, their detection, tracking and ground control systems were rudimentary and lacked the benefit of radar. Soviet formations of ground attack aircraft were often sent out without fighter escorts, the slow and low flying Ilyushin Il-2 Shturmoviks, for example, being forced to rely on their heavy armour for survival. Poorly trained and flying mediocre aircraft, the courageous Russian pilots did not have much of a chance against their well trained opponents, flying a significantly superior aircraft and utilizing well honed tactics.

From the very beginning of the campaign in Russia the Luftwaffe was significantly outnumbered; a situation that only got worse as the war drew on. While this was a problem for the German pilots and contributed to their eventual defeat, it also created a target rich environment in which high scores were readily achievable. The Soviets launched wave after wave of aircraft to bomb targets along the German front line. The defending Luftwaffe pilots, usually based close to the action, often flew as many as five or six sorties per day, knocking down the Russian aircraft almost unhindered. While the Soviets bore this inevitable attrition with stoicism, the Luftwaffe's 'Experten' reaped the rewards. ➤

> "MOST GERMAN PILOTS REMAINED ON OPERATIONS IN THE FRONT LINE WITHOUT RESPITE, UNTIL THEY WERE KILLED, CAPTURED, INCAPACITATED OR, PERHAPS, ELEVATED TO A STAFF POSITION"

Erich Hartmann's parents, Doctor Alfred Erich Hartmann and Elisabeth Wilhelmine Machtholf, one of the first German women glider pilots. **Editor's collection**

A young Erich Hartmann (seated) as a member of the Deutsches Jungvolk. By 14 he had his glider pilot's licence and was flying as a glider instructor, gaining his powered licence at 17. **Editor's collection**

"THE MOST SUCCESSFUL FIGHTER PILOTS THE WORLD HAS EVER SEEN."

While it is relatively easy to explain how high scores were obtained during the early period of fighting on the Eastern Front, many of the problems affecting the Soviet Air Force early in the war were gradually rectified as time wore on. By the time that Erich Hartmann entered the fray in October 1942, many of the early advantages for the Luftwaffe had been lost. By the close of 1943, with the Wehrmacht now in retreat, the air war in the east was very different from what it had been during the first year.

The opening days of the 'turkey shoot' had long gone, along with many of the Luftwaffe 'Experten' who had scored easily and massively at the expense of the Soviets in the early days, but who had now paid the price. The Russian pilots' training programmes were much improved and they had learned some tactical lessons. Although they normally operated at lower altitudes, they now tended to fly everywhere at maximum continuous power and high speed, making the surprise 'bounce' more difficult to achieve. The Soviets formed special Guards 'Red Banner' units with highly skilled and disciplined pilots who were much tougher adversaries.

The Soviet Air Force was also operating much better aircraft, in ever growing, and soon to be overwhelming numbers. New Soviet fighter aircraft such as the Lavochkin La-5 and the Yak-9 were sleek and powerful machines, comparable with the latest versions of the Bf 109 in speed and, in some cases with a better turn rate. The Bf 109 always retained an advantage in a zoom climb though, and most Luftwaffe Bf 109 veterans believed that they retained the 'edge' over the rank and file of Russian pilots even up to the end of the war, as long as they fought to the strengths of their own aircraft.

As the war went on, the Jagdwaffe was greatly reduced in strength on the Eastern Front by the transfer of units out of theatre to shore up other fronts. This meant that the German fighter pilots continued to operate in a target rich environment, but also meant that their chances of survival were reduced. Luck was needed to survive for long enough to accumulate high scores and while combat

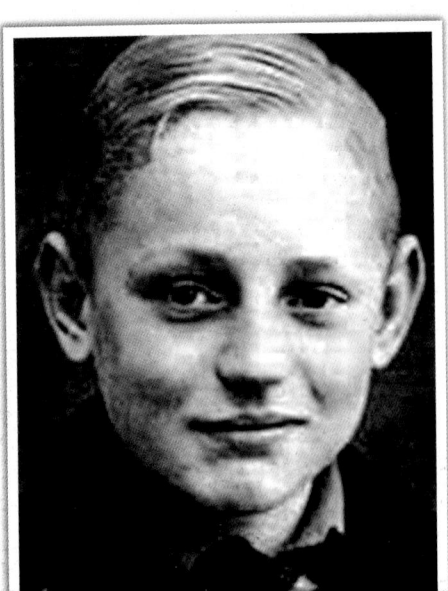

Erich Hartmann spent much of his childhood in China, where his father worked before the Chinese Civil War forced the family to return to Germany in 1928. **Editor's collection**

experience might have helped, it did not guarantee survival. Indeed, 75 of the 229 Luftwaffe Bf 109 'Experten' with scores of 50 victories or more were killed, went missing or were made prisoners of war on the Eastern front – a loss rate of about 33%. However, the Luftwaffe still had a large number of 'Experten' with plenty of experience on the Eastern Front, able to pass on the best tactical advice to their new, replacement pilots.

Against this background, it is much more difficult to explain why and how Erich Hartmann and his colleagues achieved their remarkable tally of aerial victories while operating against the Soviets from late 1942 to the end of the war, when the Luftwaffe's superiority was marginal. I am able to offer no other explanation for their amazing success rates than that these were just brilliant, aggressive and courageous fighter pilots and Hartmann was quite simply the best of all. They were, however, 'lions led by donkeys' at the top of the Third Reich's hierarchy.

Vastly outnumbered, with the war being lost on the ground and on all fronts against sheer numbers and the overwhelming industrial might of the Americans and Soviets, it was inevitable that the efforts of the German fighter pilots alone could not stave off defeat. As they were fighting on the wrong side and for a wrong cause, it is just as well that they were let down by their political masters as otherwise it might have been a different story.

This then was the broad and sombre canvas against which the most successful fighter pilots the world has ever seen – or is ever likely to see – achieved their record success rates. Erich Hartmann was to become the highest scoring of them all.

BLACK TULIP

While an Oberfeldwebel, Alfred Grislawski had been one of those formation leaders who taught Hartmann the tactics he would later use with great success. **Editor's collection**

Hartmann made a number of trips to the US to evaluate new equipment before he retired in 1970. Here he is seated in the cockpit of a Convair F-106 Delta Dart, an aircraft he particularly liked. **Editor's collection**

United States, where he was trained on USAF equipment. He had his JG 71 Sabre aircraft painted with the same spreading black tulip pattern used by him on the Eastern Front.

He served in the reformed Luftwaffe from 1956 and commanded JG 71. He retired from active duty in 1970.

On September 19, 1993, Erich Hartmann lost the ultimate battle for life, when an illness that originated back to his imprisonment by the Russians finally beat him and he died at Weil im Schönbuch, aged 71.

STYLE AND TECHNIQUE

On results alone, Erich Hartmann is indisputably the greatest fighter pilot the world has ever seen; if this honour was awarded not only on the basis of results but also for style and technique, I would still give him the place. What was it that made Hartmann such a great fighter pilot?

As we have seen, Hartmann did not favour dogfighting, which he believed was "a waste of time", but instead he was a master of stalk and ambush, hit and run tactics, saying that, "the element of surprise served me well". After a slow start, during which he learned the best way to employ the Bf 109 from other experienced 'Experte' pilots, he became a cool, calculating and cautious fighter pilot. He weighed up the risks and always sought the most advantageous position from which to attack. His careful approach was epitomised by his four-part formula for success in the air: "Locate, decide, attack, break away." By his own account, he was convinced that about 80% of the Soviet pilots he shot down never knew what hit them as he attacked unseen.

On many occasions he scored multiple victories, but he was also quite content to get just one and break off the engagement if that was the most sensible thing to do, repositioning for another attack or even disengaging completely. He made use of the Bf 109's powerful engine, its high speed in a dive and its excellent zoom climb performance to make fast diving attacks on formations of enemy aircraft, often taking advantage of the confusion that resulted when one of the Soviets was shot down, especially if it was the leader.

Hartmann had been taught – particularly by Alfred Grislawski and Walter Krupinski – not to open fire until he was extremely close to his target (often as close as 20m (66ft) or less). In common with many other top aces of the Second World War he had mastered this difficult skill and would then unleash a short and lethal burst from point-blank range. This technique compensated for the characteristics of the Bf 109 guns, it meant that he did not reveal his presence and position until the last moment; it conserved ammunition and also prevented the adversary from taking evasive action. However, firing at such close range carried the risk of flying through the debris of damaged or exploding victims and this was the principal cause of the many forced landings that Hartmann had to make during the war.

The remarkable thing is how his nerves stood the strain of continuous flying and fighting, especially as he had suffered a nervous breakdown in mid-1943 after his fifth crash landing. Somehow he was able to maintain his morale and spirits, and that of those around him, despite the circumstances in which he found himself and, stoically, he just got on with his job. Adolph Galland once described Erich Hartmann to *Aviation Classics* editor Tim Callaway as: "A knight, a man of principle, who rose above the conditions he was forced to operate under without making those around him feel lesser men; he led by

Walter 'Krupi' Krupinski chose Hartmann as his wingman, teaching him good tactics in the process. After the war, Krupinski joined the Bundesluftwaffe rising to the rank of Generalleutnant. **Editor's collection**

example." That is a fine tribute from another great fighter pilot, but considering all that Erich Hartmann went through and witnessed both during the war and during his years of captivity in Russia after the war, I think he should have the final words. In his last interview before his death he said of his experiences: "One thing I learned is this: never allow yourself to hate a people because of the actions of a few. Hatred and bigotry destroyed my nation, and millions died. I would hope that most people did not hate Germans because of the Nazis, or Americans because of slaves. Never hate, it only eats you alive. Keep an open mind and always look for the good in people. You may be surprised at what you find." ■
Words: Sqn Ldr Clive Rowley

The Canadair Sabres of JG 71 were painted in Hartmann's 'black tulip' scheme on the nose and fin. **Editor's collection**

being appointed as Staffelkapitän of 4./JG 52, based in Hungary, on October 1, 1944. In later life Erich Hartmann said: "Unit loyalty was important to me. I had many new pilots who needed guidance and instruction. They were getting younger all the time and had fewer and fewer hours of flight instruction before they were thrown into battle. I was needed and that was where I stayed."

By the end of 1944, Hartmann's victory tally was 331 and it continued to rise slowly through the remaining winter and spring months. From February 1 to 14, 1945, Hartmann briefly led I./JG 53 as the acting Gruppenkommandeur, a role he relinquished to Hauptmann Helmut Lipfert on February 15. In March 1945, Hartmann, his score now standing at 336 aerial victories, was asked a second time by General Adolf Galland to join the Me 262 units to fly the new jet fighter. Hartmann attended the jet conversion programme at Lechfeld, but declined to remain, instead returning to JG52 again.

In late April he was promoted to major and claimed his 350th aerial victory on April 17, in the vicinity of Chrudim. On May 8, 1945, he claimed his 352nd, and last, victory. During his wartime career he had flown 1404 combat sorties, resulting in 825 aerial combats, he had force-landed 14 times and had been forced to bail out once when he ran out of fuel after a combat. All his victories were achieved on the Eastern Front. His kill tally included some 200 various single-engine Soviet-built fighters, more than 80 US-built P-39s, 15 Il-2 ground attack aircraft, and 10 twin-engine medium bombers. He had been awarded the Iron Cross 1st and 2nd class, the German Cross in Gold and the Knight's Cross with Oak Leaves, Swords and Diamonds.

SURRENDER, PRISONER AND POSTWAR

At the end of the war Erich Hartmann disobeyed an order for the first and only time when General Seidemann ordered Hartmann and Hermann Graf to fly to the British Sector to avoid capture by the Soviet forces, leaving the rest of the wing to surrender to the Russians. Hartmann later explained: "I could not leave my men. That would have been bad leadership." As Gruppenkommandeur of I./JG52, Major Hartmann surrendered his unit to members of the US 90th Infantry Division on May 24.

In accordance with the terms of the Yalta Agreements, which stipulated that airmen and soldiers who had been fighting the Soviet forces had to surrender directly to them, the US Army handed Hartmann, his pilots and ground crew over to the Soviet Union. Subsequently, Hartmann was falsely accused on trumped up charges of war crimes and was sentenced to 25 years' hard labour by the Russians. He served 10 and a half years as a captive of the Soviets, suffering brutal treatment including long periods of solitary confinement in total darkness, before he was released and returned to Germany in October 1955, broken in body but not in spirit.

In 1956 Hartmann re-entered military service in the Bundeswehr and became an officer in the West German Air Force (Bundesluftwaffe), where he commanded West Germany's first all-jet unit, Jagdgeschwader 71 'Richthofen', which was equipped initially with Canadair Sabres and later with Lockheed F-104 Starfighters. He also made several trips to the

One of the JG 71 Sabres is now on display at the Luftwaffenmuseum at Gatow in Berlin. **Constance Redgrave**

The award of the Diamonds to the Knight's Cross earned Hartmann some leave, during which he married his long time sweetheart Ursula on September 10, 1944. **Editor's collection**

After his imprisonment by the Soviet authorities, Hartmann returned to West Germany in October 1955, rejoining the Bundesluftwaffe and taking command of West Germany's first all-jet unit, Jagdgeschwader 71 'Richthofen'. **Editor's collection**

fact that 40 of the 76 Soviet aircraft claimed by III./JG52 between January 8 and February 28 were shot down by him alone.

A Russian counteroffensive during May and June 1944 forced the Germans into a full retreat. On May 8, Hartmann flew his Bf 109 out of the Crimea with two of his groundcrew in the rear fuselage, a method that was used on several occasions to save the precious ground crew from capture and to ensure that operations could continue uninterrupted. During these two months Hartmann accounted for 60 Soviet aircraft, bringing his score to 267. He later described an incident that occurred in May 1944 when he and his wingman were jumped by Soviet fighters near Jassy. His wingman, Oberfeldwebel Freidrich Blessin, broke right and the enemy followed him down to the deck.

Hartmann called him on the radio to pull up and slip right in a shallow turn, which Blessin, with total faith in his leader, did without hesitation. Hartmann used the turn to cut the corner and close into firing range. He said: "I told Blessin to look back and see what happens when you do not watch your tail, and I fired. The Soviet fighter blew apart and fell like confetti." Despite the mounting difficulties facing the German pilots, Hartmann was able to achieve his 250th victory on June 4, a day when he shot down six LaGG fighters plus a P-39.

For a short period, Hartmann operated over Romania intercepting the American daylight bombing raids on the Romanian oil fields and installations, and on June 24 he tangled with USAAF P-51 Mustangs for the first time. In later life he told of destroying at least three of the P-51s, but he was credited with only one kill as his 265th victory. This is how he described the combat: "B-17s were attacking the railroad junction, and we were formed up. We did not see the Mustangs at first and prepared to attack the bombers. Suddenly four of them flew across us and below, so I gave the order to attack the fighters. I closed in on one and fired, his fighter came apart and some pieces hit my wings.

"I immediately found myself behind another and I fired, and he flipped in. My second flight shot down the other two fighters. But then we saw other P-51s and again attacked. I shot down another and saw that the leader still had his drop tanks, which limited his ability to turn. I was very relieved that this pilot was able to successfully bail out. I was out of ammunition after the fight."

Hartmann was awarded the 'Swords' to his Knight's Cross on July 4 for his 239th kill and, after another short stint of home leave, he returned to the fray and downed 35 Soviet aircraft during August, eight of them on the 23rd and no fewer than 11 in one day on 24th, bringing his total score to 302. By the end of the month 7./JG52 had shot down 1200 Soviet aircraft, more than any other Staffel in the Luftwaffe. Oberleutnant Hartmann was awarded the Brillianten – the Diamonds – to his Knight's Cross on August 25, 1944. He became one of only 27 German warriors to receive the Diamonds to the Knight's Cross during the Second World War; it earned him some more leave, during which he married his long time sweetheart Ursula on September 10. He was also immediately prohibited from further combat flying by Reichsmarschall Göring, who was fearful of the effect on German morale if such a hero should be lost.

> **"THEN HE PULLED UP AND ROLLED, AND WE APPROACHED EACH OTHER HEAD ON, FIRING, WITH NO HITS EITHER WAY"**

He was assigned to Erprobungskommando 262 to test fly the Me 262 jet fighter, but his heart and his friends were in JG52 and he felt that was where he belonged. His choice to return to the Eastern Front, with the eventual outcome of the war now obvious and the final defeat in sight, was courageous and principled to the point of being foolhardy and was subsequently to cost him dearly. His lobbying was successful and Hartmann was able to get the prohibition on his combat flying lifted, ➤

SQUADRON COMMANDER

On August 29, 1943, when the squadron commander of 9./JG52 – 113 victory 'Experte' Leutnant Berthold Korts – was reported missing in action, Hartmann was chosen to replace him. His year long leadership of 9./JG52 was to see Hartmann's personal score rise to an incredible 304 kills. His distinctively marked Bf 109, latterly with his personal black 'tulip' patterned nose, reportedly earned him the nickname of 'The Black Devil' among the Soviets, who placed a 10,000 ruble price on his head. His own pilots, inspired by their leader's simple but effective tactics, followed his example keenly and many achieved high scores. Soon the entire 'Karaya' Staffel (named after their radio call-sign – Hartmann was 'Karaya 1') was as famous as its youthful leader.

Hartmann generally avoided 'dogfighting', relying instead on the Bf 109's acceleration and speed in the dive and its excellent rate of climb to reposition, while taking advantage of the sky conditions to avoid being seen by the enemy pilots and crews. However, it was not always possible to dictate the fight conditions and sometimes a turning fight was unavoidable. On one occasion Hartmann became involved in an extended combat, what he described as "a duel", with a Red Banner Yak-9 flown by a pilot who he realised was both "good and absolutely insane".

The Yak-9 could turn inside a Bf 109 due to the Soviet fighter's smaller sustained turn radius at low speeds and lower levels, although the German fighter had a slightly superior turn rate. Hartmann later described his one on one, Yak-9 v Bf 109 combat thus: "He tried and tried to get in behind me, and every time he went to open fire I would jerk out of the way of his rounds. Then he pulled up and rolled, and we approached each other head on, firing, with no hits either way. This happened twice. Finally, I rolled into a negative G dive, out of his line of sight, and rolled out to chase him at full throttle. I came in from below in a shallow climb and flamed him. The pilot baled out and was later captured. I met and spoke with this man, a captain, who was a likeable guy."

Now an Oberleutnant, Hartmann was awarded the Diamonds to his Knight's Cross on August 25, 1944. **Editor's collection**

SPECTACULAR SUCCESS, FAME AND MEDALS

By September 18, 1943, Hartmann had completed 300 operational missions and had 95 victories to his credit. He claimed two more Soviet fighters the next day and on September 20 he shot down three Soviet LaGG fighters and a P-39 Airacobra to reach a total of 101 kills. There were now some 50 other German fighter pilots who had achieved 100 kills or more and this achievement was no longer sufficient to be awarded the Knight's Cross. By the end of the month Hartmann's score was 115 and during October he claimed another 33 kills, bringing his total to 148, at which point he was finally awarded the Knight's Cross. It was not that Hartmann particularly coveted such trinkets, although he appreciated the recognition of his efforts, but medals meant leave – time away from the front and a chance to see his beloved girlfriend 'Ushi'. He later said that if he had the choice of losing his 'Ushi' or returning the decorations, he would have sent all the medals back.

After this, Hartmann's scoring rate continued at an even greater pace. During the first two months of 1944 he claimed another 43 kills, including six LaGG fighters in one day on January 30, five more the next day and an amazing 10 P-39s shot down in three separate missions on February 26. The last three of these kills, claimed in 10 minutes between 2.40pm and 2.50pm, brought his score to over 200 (202 to be precise). His spectacular success rate raised eyebrows in the Luftwaffe High Command and his claims were double and triple checked.

For achieving more than 200 victories he was awarded the Oak Leaves to his Knight's Cross on March 2. Erich Hartmann's prominence at this time can be gauged by the

The Evergreen Aviation & Space Museum at McMinnville, Oregon, has a Bf 109G-10 painted in Hartmann's markings, including the 'black tulip' round the nose and Karaya markings. **Editor**

On August 29, 1943, Hartmann became the squadron commander of 9./JG52, taking the callsign Karaya One. **Editor's collection**

Between August 1 and August 20, Hartmann flew 54 combat sorties in the Kharkov area and, with a succession of multiple daily kills, shot down 48 Soviet aircraft, raising his total score to 90. This run ended on August 20, when his flight of eight Bf 109s encountered 40 LaGG and Yak fighters, escorting another 40 Il-2 Shturmoviks bombing German ground positions in support of the Soviet offensive. Hartmann shot down two of the Il-2s, but his Bf 109 was damaged by debris from the second and he was forced to crash-land behind enemy lines. He was quickly captured by Soviet soldiers, but managed to escape and made it back to the relative safety of the German lines, although as he approached he was challenged by a German sentry who fired a bullet at him that ripped open his trouser leg.

This incident also serves to highlight the strong bond of friendship that had developed between Hartmann and his crew chief, Heinz 'Bimmel' Mertens. Hartmann later said: "You rely on your wingman to cover you in the air, and your team mates in an aerial battle, but the man who keeps your machine flying and safe is the most important man you know. Mertens and I became best friends and none of my success would have been possible if not for him." When his pilot went missing behind enemy lines on August 20, the loyal Mertens took a rifle and went looking for him. Hartmann was very upset when he returned to find what his friend had done. Fortunately, Mertens also returned the next day and they had a 'birthday party', a party thrown in honour of a pilot who survived a situation that should have killed him.

The conditions that Erich Hartmann and his colleagues had to endure on the Eastern Front were dreadful. In common with many other combatants in other theatres of the war, they lived in daily fear of death and, in addition, they were particularly fearful of capture by the Soviets, with good reason. Many Luftwaffe pilots who came down behind Soviet lines were simply never heard of again.

The Soviet Union was not a signatory to the Geneva Convention; it did not follow its guidelines for the treatment of prisoners of war and the behaviour of some of its soldiers was barbaric. The weather on the Eastern Front provided extreme fluctuations, with severe cold during the winter months, waterlogged airstrips during the spring thaws and high temperatures during the summers on the steppes of the southern sector where JG52 operated. The Luftwaffe personnel seldom had hard shelter, living in tents even in the winter.

Hartmann later described the conditions thus: "The lice were the worst and there was little you could do but hold your clothes to a fire and listen to them pop. We had DDT and we bathed when we could. Illness, especially pneumonia and trench foot were a problem, especially among the ground crews. Food was always a concern, especially later in the war, when fuel restrictions made every mission count.

Hartmann also adopted a 'black tulip' colour scheme on the nose of his Bf 109G as commander of 9./JG52, as seen here over his shoulder as he checks the map for his next mission. **Editor's collection**

Hartmann in the cockpit of his personal Bf 109G, showing the 9./JG52 red heart and Karaya marking, but including his wife's name 'Ursel' in the heart. **Editor's collection**

"We always flew from grass airstrips and we were often bombed. These strips were easily repaired, but the terrain made every take-off and landing an adventure. Our Bf 109s would sometimes snap their landing gear, or just dig in and topple over. Maintenance was another nightmare, as supplies and parts were difficult to get, especially as we were moving all the time."

They learned from Russian prisoners how to start their engines in sub-zero temperatures by mixing petrol into the oil in the crankcase; the fuel thinned out the congealed oil and evaporated as the engine started. They also learned that dipping the guns into boiling water to remove the lubricants prevented them from freezing and kept them working. When these operating conditions are taken into account it is even more of a wonder that the German fighter pilots maintained their morale and were so successful. ➤

In March 1943, Hartmann was selected to be the wingman to his new squadron commander – Walter 'Krupi' Krupinski (sometimes known in jest as 'Count Punski') – who replaced von Bonnin as Gruppenkommandeur of III./JG52 and who had a reputation for being something of a 'wild man'. Hartmann's first introduction to Krupinski had been in October 1942 when, along with some other new arrivals to JG52, Hartmann was being addressed by Major 'Dieter' Hrabak, the Geschwaderkommodore. The novice fighter pilots were shocked when a Bf 109 approached the airfield smoking, flipped over on landing and exploded.

Hartmann later said: "We knew that the pilot must be dead. Someone said 'it's Krupinski', and then, out of the blinding smoke, this man walked out of the wreckage with a singed uniform, but with no other damage. He was smiling and complaining about the flak, but with no real surprise on his face." On his arrival with III Gruppe as the new Gruppenkommandeur, Krupinski introduced himself to the pilots, demanded an aircraft, went up, was shot down and was brought back by car. He then took another aircraft, scored two kills, returned and wanted dinner. Hartmann was in awe of Krupinski's coolness and later said that he seemed to treat the whole event as casually as a card game (Krupinski eventually scored a total of 197 kills, 177 of them on the Eastern Front).

Although the partnership was rather uneasy at first, Krupinski believed in Hartmann and took the promising youngster in hand with a relaxed approach, while constantly demanding that he got closer to his adversaries before opening fire. Krupinski never avoided combat, whatever the odds, and flying with him meant that Hartmann saw combat on almost every mission. Hartmann's victory tally began to rise but only slowly and both he and Krupinski were forced to crash land several times themselves.

By the end of March 1943, Hartmann had six confirmed kills and by the end of April – over 6 months since he first went into combat – his victory tally was still only 11. Speaking later about his partnership with Krupinski, Erich Hartmann said: "We worked well together. We both had strengths and weaknesses and managed to overcome these problems. It worked out well. Besides, I had to make sure that he came home to his many girlfriends always waiting for him. I won the Iron Cross Second Class while flying as wingman with 'Krupi'. One thing I learned from him was that the worst thing to do was to lose a wingman. Kills were less important than survival. I only ever lost one wingman – a former bomber pilot – but this was due to his inexperience with fighters (although he survived)." On May 23, Hartmann claimed his 17th victory – another Soviet LaGG fighter – but two days later he had to force-land for the fifth time after his Bf 109 was rammed by or collided with a LaGG-3. Following this incident, he suffered a nervous breakdown and was sent back to Germany to rest and recuperate.

LEADER

Erich Hartmann returned to the Eastern Front in late June 1943, determined to prove himself. It was from here that his meteoric rise to incredible success began. He had learned the lessons that he had been taught by Roßmann, Grislawski and Krupinski, and after 180 combat missions he had become a master of the Bf 109. This was proved on July 5, 1943, the first day of the German Panzer attacks on Kursk – part of Operation Zitadelle – when he flew four missions and returned from each with a kill. (It is estimated that the Soviets lost 432 aircraft in this single day of the war, mainly bombers and ground-attack aircraft, as they tried to halt the advancing German Panzers). Walter Krupinski shot down 11 aircraft himself on July 5, but was severely wounded claiming the last of these. Erich Hartmann was promoted to acting Staffelkapitän and led the Staffel for the next six weeks.

On July 7 Hartmann shot down seven enemy aircraft in four different engagements and by the last day of July his score had risen to 42. After only eight days, Hitler called off Operation Zitadelle; he withdrew many of his forces to other fronts and the die was cast for the closing chapters of the war in the east. From here on it was to be a retreat and, in the months that followed, the component Gruppen of JG52 would be constantly on the move, shuttling from one point of danger to the next with increasing frequency and desperation. To highlight this point, during the two years (from November 1942) that 'Dieter' Hrabak was Kommodore of JG52, the wing flew from 47 different airfields.

A strong bond developed between Hartmann and his Bf 109 crew chief, Heinz 'Bimmel' Mertens, to whom Hartmann attributed much of his success. **Editor's collection**

By September 20, 1943, Hartmann's score reached 100 victories. **Editor's collection**

Leutnant Erich Hartmann with Ursula Paetsch. Hartmann would paint the shortened version of her name, Ursel, on his Bf 109. **Editor's collection**

Oberleutnant Walter Krupinski became Gruppenkommandeur of III./JG52 and took the young Hartmann as his wingman. The pair became close friends as this picture clearly shows. **Editor's collection**

ERICH HARTMANN – EARLY DAYS AND TRAINING

Erich Hartmann was born near Stuttgart, Germany, on April 19, 1922, the son of a doctor. In the latter stages of his schooling, at Korntal, he met his sweetheart and wife to be Ursula 'Usch' or 'Ushi' Paetsch. Hartmann's flying career began early when he was taught to fly a glider by his mother, Elisabeth, who was one of the first female glider pilots in Germany. By the age of 14, Erich had earned his glider pilot's licence and had become a gliding instructor. In 1939 (aged 17) he gained his pilot's licence, allowing him to fly powered aircraft. His training as a Luftwaffe pilot began in October 1940 and the following year and a half saw him move through a series of flying training and fighter schools.

In March 1942, Hartmann arrived at Zerbst-Anhalt for training on the Bf 109. At the end of that month he was temporarily grounded and fined for performing unauthorised aerobatics over the airfield, an incident which taught him some discipline. When Leutnant Hartmann graduated in August 1942 he had built a reputation as a skilled marksman and he was qualified to fly 17 different types of aircraft including the Bf 109.

WINGMAN

In October 1942 Hartmann was assigned to JG52 on the Eastern Front to fly Bf 109Gs. For the fighter pilot who was eventually going to become the highest scoring of all time, it was a slow start. As we have seen, his combat debut was something of a debacle, but subsequently he knuckled under and concentrated on being a good wingman and learning from his experienced element leaders, Oberfeldwebels Paule Roßmann and Alfred Grislawski. It might seem odd that, as an officer, Hartmann was assigned to fly as a wingman to non-commissioned pilots, but rank mattered little over experience in the Jagdwaffe and these were seasoned combat veterans.

Grislawski thought that the novice Hartmann was a talented but highly individualistic pilot who had much to learn about tactics; it was he who invented the nickname for the youthful looking and eager fighter pilot – 'Bubi' ('Little Boy'). Having served on the Eastern Front for more than a year, Grislawski also thought that the contempt Hartmann initially displayed towards his Soviet adversaries was unhealthy; he told him that he would be a corpse in a matter of weeks if he did not change his attitude.

On November 5, 1942, Hartmann scored his first kill – an Il-2 Shturmovik of the 7th Guards Ground Attack Aviation Regiment – when his Schwarm of four Bf 109s attacked a force of 18 of the heavily armoured Russian tankbusters, escorted by 10 LaGG-3 fighters. Hartmann later said: "That was a day I will never forget… the Shturmovik was the toughest aircraft to bring down because of the heavy armour plate. You had to shoot out the oil cooler underneath otherwise it would not go down." He went on to say: "That was also the day of my second forced landing, since I had flown through the debris of my kill. I learned two things that day: get in close, but break away immediately after scoring the kill."

Leutnant Erich Hartmann was first posted to JG52 on the Eastern Front. **Editor's collection**

Grislawski repeatedly told 'Bubi' Hartmann to get closer to enemy aircraft before opening fire, but this was easier said than done; it was a tactic that took much nerve and had to be learned the hard way. It was almost another 12 weeks – January 27, 1943 – on his 41st combat sortie, that Erich Hartmann managed to down his second Soviet aircraft, reported as a 'MiG 1', but in reality, probably a misidentification of a Yak-1 or Yak-7. It was taking him some time to establish himself as a consistently scoring fighter pilot. ➤

Hartmann scored his first kill, an Il-2 Shturmovik ground attack aircraft, on November 5, 1942. **Editor's collection**

Major Erich Hartmann flies high over the Eastern Front in early 1945 in his Messerschmitt Bf 109G-14. At this time Hartmann was Staffelkapitan of 4./JG52 and was to end the war as the ace of aces with 352 confirmed victories, making him the most successful fighter pilot of all time.

'Toni' – Hitler's carrier fighter:
The Bf 109T: its ship, its unit, and its combat history

Arado's next attempt to fulfil the Luftwaffe's carrier-based multi-role aircraft requirement, the Ar 195, was an even greater disappointment. Three prototypes were constructed and were soon relegated to the Travemünde experimental station to test arresting equipment and other carrier operations systems. **Thijs Postma Collection**

In the frigid depths of the Baltic Sea, 34 miles (55km) off the Polish port of Wladyslawowo (near Gdynia), lies the 70-year-old wreck of the only aircraft carrier ever launched for the German Navy (Kriegsmarine). How it got there is a mystery only now being revealed as undersea expeditions explore the 861ft (265.5m) long hulk. But at one point it represented the dream of Hitler's navy to take the Luftwaffe's air power on to the high seas.

Arado attempted to develop its Ar 95 floatplane to meet the Luftwaffe's original specification for a shipboard reconnaissance/torpedo-bomber, but because of its poor performance, it was rejected. Of the dozen pre-production examples, half of them were sold to Chile while the others flew from Majorca during the Spanish Civil War. **Thijs Postma Collection**

It was during the halcyon days of 1940, when one Nazi conquest followed another, that KMS Graf Zeppelin was being fitted out at Kiel. Specific aircraft types were being developed to fly from her 787ft (240m) flight deck, and a Trägergeschwader or carrier air wing comprising one group each of fighters and dive bombers was being formed for that purpose.

Officially the ship began life as part of Grand Admiral Erich Raeder's 'Plan Z', an ambitious warship building programme designed to provide Hitler's Third Reich with a full-fledged battle fleet in 1942. With it the Kriegsmarine could challenge the Royal Navy's Home Fleet for superiority – if not supremacy – in the North Sea. Fortunately for Britain, der Führer chose to begin his European campaigns more than two years prematurely – resulting in the three components of the project never coming together on the carrier's flight deck. The history of these disparate components – especially that of the ship's intended fighter, the Messerschmitt Bf 109T – provide interesting stories in themselves and, in the end, an intriguing 'what if'.

THE SHIP: KMS GRAF ZEPPELIN

Named for Ferdinand Graf von Zeppelin, the famous producer of enormous rigid airships (many of them used by the Imperial German Navy to terrorize England during the First World War), Germany's first aircraft carrier was originally designed by the Kriegsmarine's K-Amt (construction bureau) under the direction of the naval chief architect, engineer Wilhelm Hadeler, during the winter of 1933/34. Created from the keel up to be a 20,000 ton through-deck fleet carrier, it was to hold 30-50 aircraft, make 33 knots, mount eight 8in (20.3cm) guns, and have the armour and interior protection of a light cruiser.

The designers had made a thorough study of the HMS Courageous – then considered the state of the art in carrier development – and toured HMS Furious during 'Navy week' at Portsmouth in 1935. However, mounting a flight deck atop a large hangar bay built upon a battlecruiser hull proved insufficient to guide the design of a ship from the keel up. A three man K-Amt team also visited the Imperial Japanese Navy carrier Akagi – another converted battlecruiser – that autumn, but this only confirmed the direction upon which the designers were embarking.

The design was well enough developed to be included in 'Plan Z' and the Reich's fiscal year 1936 budget (a second, unnamed, carrier was included in the 1938 budget). On November 16 that year Deutsche Werke Kiel AG shipyard was awarded the contract to build the ship and on December 28, 1936, within three weeks of the new battlecruiser Gneisenau being launched from Slipway 1, the keel of the Graf Zeppelin was laid. Almost exactly two years later – on December 8, 1938 – the shiny flat-topped hull of the Kriegsmarine's newest warship slid down the ways and into the water.

Finishing the ship proved difficult though, because the design was still evolving. The day Hitler invaded Poland and started the Second World War, the carrier was considered 85% complete. Its main antiship armament had been changed to 16 5.9in (15cm) guns paired in casement-mounted turrets, two forward and two aft on each side. Six dual 4.1in (10.5cm) flak gun turrets were to be mounted on the island side of the flight deck and numerous light flak automatic weapons were to be added.

The flight deck was fitted with three centreline elevators – forward, amidships, and aft – and two compressed air catapults, each 77ft (23.5m) long. The Germans' system used 'launching sleds' where an aircraft taxied on to the sled's cradle, then the catapult would sling the aircraft into the air, the sled coming to an abrupt halt at the end of the run, then was shunted sideways on to below deck return rails, to be raised into position for the next launch. K-Amt designers estimated it was possible to launch eight aircraft in three and a half minutes with this system. Aft, four cross-deck arresting cables were fitted to bring landing aircraft to a halt. ▶

SECOND WORLD WAR AIRCRAFT CARRIERS COMPARED GRAF ZEPPELIN VS HMS ARK ROYAL VS USS YORKTOWN SPRING 1940

Attribute	Graf Zeppelin	HMS Ark Royal	USS Yorktown
Date launched	December 8, 1938	April 13, 1937	April 4, 1936
Displacement	28,090 tons	27,700 tons	25,500 tons
Hull length	861 feet (262.5m)	800 feet (243.8m)	809 feet (246.7m)
Flight deck length	787 feet (240m)	780 feet (237.7m)	802 feet (244.5m)
Aircraft Complement			
Total Complement	43 aircraft	60 combat aircraft	91 combat aircraft
Fighters	12 Bf 109T	24 Skuas	18 F4F Wildcats
Dive Bombers	13 Ju 87C		37 SBD Dauntless
Torpedo Aircraft	18 Fi 167A	36 Swordfish	36 TBD Devastator
Armament			
	16 x 15cm (5.9in)		
	12 x 10.5cm (4.1in)	16 x 4.5-inch	8 x 5-inch
	22 x 3.7cm AA guns	48 x 2-pdr (40mm)	16 x 1.1-in AA guns
	28 x 2cm AA guns	32 x .5-in MGs	24 x .5-in MGs
Powerplants			
	16 La Mont boilers	Six Admiralty boilers	Nine Babcock & Wilcox boilers
	Four 50,000hp Brown, Boveri & Co. Steam Turbines	Three 34,000hp Parsons Geared Turbines	Four 30,000hp Parsons Geared Turbines
Performance			
Maximum Speed	33 knots	31 knots	34 knots
Steaming Range	8,000NM at 19kts	7,600NM at 20kts	12,000NM at 15kts
Crew Complement	1760 men	1600 men	1890 men

Construction of the German aircraft carrier Graf Zeppelin began on December 28, 1936, signalling the Kriegsmarine's intent of providing its battle fleet with an aerial strike and air defence capability. It was up to the Luftwaffe to develop the aircraft, train the crews, and form the units of the ship's Trägergruppe (Carrier (Air) Group). **Thijs Postma Collection**

Like HMS Ark Royal, the German carrier had two hangar decks. The upper hangar was designed to accommodate 13 Ju 87C Stuka dive bombers forward and 12 Bf 109T fighters aft, while the smaller lower hangar was to hold 18 Fi 167 torpedo biplanes.

The ship was due to be completed by October 1, 1940, and was scheduled for its sea trials in the winter of 1940/41. However, work slowed once Hitler initiated hostilities because his unprepared navy was forced to turn to U-boat production in an attempt to have a strategic impact in the conflict. While the incomplete carrier languished at Kiel, the Kriegsmarine launched the invasion of Norway and Denmark in April and the Wehrmacht rolled into France and the Low Countries. In the latter campaign, the Graf Zeppelin's two Trägergruppen **(1)** or 'carrier air groups', played substantial roles, even if their parts were not preformed from the flight deck of their carrier, or necessarily with aircraft designed for that purpose.

THE AIRCRAFT: THE FIRST ITERATION

Despite the bitterly acrimonious debates between Hermann Göring, the imperious leader of the Luftwaffe, and Grand Admiral Raeder – and by their minions beneath them – the Reichsluftfahrtministerium (RLM or Reich Air Ministry) did its part to stock the navy's carrier with defensive fighters and dual-role reconnaissance/torpedo bomber aircraft.

For the first, the RLM contracted with the Arado Handelsgesellschaft at Warnemünde (formerly the First World War Albatros concern) to develop its Ar 68 biplane into a more powerful navalised fighter under the designation Ar 197. Three prototypes were constructed in early 1937, the final (V3) example being powered by the 880hp BMW 132Dc nine-cylinder radial and mounting a pair of 20mm cannon and two 7.92mm machine guns. The result was a heavy biplane with a top speed of only 248mph (399kph).

Production and flight testing were agonisingly protracted, with the prototypes finally being evaluated in July and August 1938. Originally the RLM planned on ordering 10 pre-production examples and 18 definitive models, enough to equip one 12 fighter träger-staffel or carrier squadron with 50% reserves. However, the performance was so disappointing, only four pre-production aircraft were completed, three of them (plus the V2 prototype) being assigned to the Erprobungsstelle (See) Travemünde 'Research Station (Sea)', commonly abbreviated E-Stelle, in September 1939 for testing the carrier's developing cradle catapult and arresting cable technologies.

To fill the carrier-based reconnaissance/torpedo bomber requirement, Arado expected to adapt its two seat float biplane, designed in 1935 to replace the Heinkel He 60 aboard the Kriegsmarine's light cruisers, to carrier operations. First flown the next year, the Ar 95's performance was also disappointing; its maximum speed was only 171mph (275kph) at sea level. The Luftwaffe rejected it, and in 1937 the RLM issued a new specification: a shipborne multirole aircraft capable of reconnaissance, dive bombing, level bombing, launching torpedoes, and anti-submarine patrol/dropping depth charges.

The resulting Ar 195 was no improvement over Arado's previous offering, having the same engine, higher drag, and lower performance. The first of three prototypes flew in the summer of 1938, but by October all three had been relegated to E-Stelle Travemünde for use in arresting gear and other carrier-related trials.

The winning design was from Gerhard Fieseler Werke GmbH, (**[2]** an outstanding design exceeding the RLM's specification requirements in all respects. Powered by a 12-

The winning torpedo-bomber design was Fieseler's excellent Fi 167, but fighter priorities delayed early production. The dozen pre-production Fi 167As were assigned to Erprobungsstaffel (Evaluation Squadron) 167 and eventually flew coastal patrols from the Netherlands. **Thijs Postma Collection**

(1) There is considerable inconsistency and confusion, even in the Second World war Luftwaffe documentation, as to the exact command echelon and unit designation of the carrier air groups and their squadrons. For this article, the Kriegsmarine's simpler, numerals-only, designation (staffel or gruppe/186) will be used.

(2) Gerhard Fieseler was a 22-victory First World War ace and the 1934 world aerobatic champion. In 1930 he began acquiring various small sailplane and aviation manufacturers, using them to establish his own company three years later. In addition to his own sportsplane designs, in 1935 his GmbH produced under license Klemm Kl 35s, Focke Wulf FW 58s, Ar 68s, He 72s and Bf 109Bs.

The first fighter type designed to be embarked aboard the Graf Zeppelin was the Arado Ar 197, a navalized adaptation of the Luftwaffe's first real fighter, the Ar 68, using a BMW 132Dc radial engine and mounting two 20mm cannon and two 7.62mm machine guns. **Author's Collection**

cylinder 1100hp Daimler-Benz DB 601B liquid-cooled engine, this large, spindly-looking aircraft could lift twice the required load – a 1487lb (700kg) torpedo – at higher than the specified speed. Consequently Fieseler was contracted to provide a dozen pre-production Fi 167A-0s.

However, being one of Germany's smaller aeroplane manufacturers, Fieseler was soon directed to open an assembly line producing the new Bf 109E and by September 1939 the 'Emil' – along with Fieseler's own Fi 156A STOL liaison aircraft – was in mass production at Kassel/Waldau. The need for the outstanding Messerschmitt fighter, both for the air defence of the Reich and to clear the skies of the opposition in Hitler's upcoming offensive campaigns, far outstripped that for a carrier-based multipurpose biplane, so production priority was understandably low. Consequently, it took Fieseler two years to build the 12 pre-production shipboard torpedo bombers, by which time their careers as carrier-borne operations were moot.

Originally, in August 1938, the Luftwaffe had ordered the carrier's trägergruppe to form at Bug on the Baltic coast island of Rügen to undergo preliminary fighter training flying Ar 65s. But since the Ar 197 fighter had not proved acceptable and the Fi 167 was still in development, this order was cancelled 10 weeks later. In fact, in the crucible of combat of the Spanish Civil War, the Messerschmitt Bf 109B and Junkers Ju 87A had proven themselves outstanding aircraft, each within its own specialised role. Therefore, the Oberbefehlshaber der Luftwaffe or 'commander-in-chief of the Luftwaffe' staff postulated that the best mix for the Graf Zeppelin's air group was to have the Fi 167 as the reconnaissance/torpedo bomber, the Ju 87C as the carrier-based dive bomber, and a modified Bf 109E (this variant just beginning production) as the ship-board fighter. This decision was to result in the Bf 109T. ➤

THE LUFTWAFFE'S PROGRAMME TO PROVIDE TRÄGERGRUPPEN FOR KRIEGSMARINE'S AIRCRAFT CARRIERS

The German archives contain two documents which provide a fuller understanding of the Luftwaffe's plan to provide operational air groups to the Graf Zeppelin and the unnamed 'Flugzeugträger B' ('Aircraft Carrier B').* The first document, an ObdL report of April 4, 1939 confirms that one squadron each of Bf 109s and Ju 87s were available and were planned to grow to become two Messerschmitt and four Stuka squadrons by November 1 that year.

Report of the
Nr. 860/39g Kdos (II B)
M 1293/803288
04.04.1939

Inventory and Organisation of the Carrier battle groups

Available:
Trägergruppenstab I./186 (T)
[Carrier Group HQ] Kiel-Holtenau
4. (St)/186 (T) with Ju 87s Kiel-Holtenau
6. (J)/186 (T) with Me 109s Kiel-Holtenau

Under instruction (in training) until November 1, 1939:
Trägergeschwaderstab 186
[Carrier Wing HQ] Bremerhaven-Weddewarden
1. (St)/186 (T) with Ju 87s Bremerhaven-Weddewarden
2. (St)/186 (T) with Ju 87s Bremerhaven-Weddewarden
3. (St)/186 (T) with Ju 87s Bremerhaven-Weddewarden
5. (J)/186 (T) with Me 109s Bremerhaven-Weddewarden
A permanent onboard Fliegerkommando (flight command) on Aircraft Carrier A (Graf Zeppelin)

Ordered to relocate by October 1, 1939:
4. (St)/186 (T) with Ju 87s to Bremerhaven-Weddewarden
6. (J)/186 (T) with Me 109s to Bremerhaven-Weddewarden

Objective: To be established in Bremerhaven by the end of 1939:
1. -4. (St)/186 (T) with Ju 87s (4 carrier dive bomber squadrons)
5. -6. (J)/186 (T) with Me 109s (2 carrier fighter squadrons)
A permanent onboard flight command (equivalent to a Flughafenbetriebskompanie FBK [base repair company])
(the I.(Stuka)/186 and II.(fighter) /186 group HQs disbanded)

The second document, date unknown but apparently about one year later, added the CAG for 'Flugzeugträger B' (TrGr 286), which was to be operational by November 1941. It also adjusted the individual CAG's composition to include the acceptance of the Fi 167 torpedo biplane after November 1940. The final compliment for each carrier was to be 18 Fi 167As (three squadrons), 13 Ju 87Cs (two squadrons), and 12 Bf 109Ts (one squadron).

Conversions and/or Dispositions 1940/1941

Carrier Wing 186 – Bremerhaven:
1. /186   Ju 87   from 1 November 1940 convert to Fi 167
2. /186   Ju 87   from 1 November 1940 convert to Fi 167
3. /186   Ju 87   no change
4. /186   Ju 87   no change
5. /186   Me 109 from November 1, 1941 convert to Fi 167
6. /186   Me 109 no change

Carrier Wing 286 – Wilhelmshaven (Aircraft Carrier B):
1. /286   disposition as of November 1, 1941 Fi 167
2. /286   disposition as of November 1, 1941 Fi 167
3. /286   disposition as of November 1, 1941 Fi 167
4. /286   disposition as of November 1, 1941 Ju 87 Stuka
5. /286   disposition as of November 1, 1941 Ju 87 Stuka
6. /286   disposition as of November 1, 1941 Me 109 fighter

Those that were authorised on June 1, 1938 (to 1942):
2 Geschwaderstäbe (Wing HQs) (from 2 planned)
6 Mehrzweck-Staffeln Fi 167 (from 6 planned)
3 Stuka-Staffeln Ju 87 (from 4 planned)
2 Jagd-Staffeln Me 109 (from 2 planned) for Aircraft Carriers A and B

* Although repeatedly said to have been named the Peter Strasser, there is no documentary evidence of this. Although the keel was laid at Friedrich Krupp Germania Shipyard in the latter half of 1938, with a planned completion date of December 1941. Once Hitler began the Second World War, work was halted on September 19, 1939 and the material already built was broken up on February 28, the next year. Luftwaffe Lieferplan 15 (supply plan September 15, 1939) called for the construction of 155 Bf 109Ts in order to provide sufficient fighters to outfit 'Flugzeugträger B's' 6. Staffel/TrG 286.

'TONI' – THE TRÄGERJÄGER

Anticipating that the Ar 197 would be obsolete by the time the Graf Zeppelin became operational, the Luftwaffe's interest in the Bf 109 as a carrier-based aircraft began in October 1937 when the 10th 'Emil' prototype (Bf 109 V-17/actually a 'Caesar' model with a Jumo 210G motor) was reserved for development as a shipborne fighter. The first flight of this aeroplane (WkNr 1776/TK+HK) was from Messerschmitt's Augsburg airfield on February 28, 1938. Near the end of the year this aircraft was badly damaged during takeoff for its ferry flight to Travemünde, so a 'Berta' model (WkNr 301/TK+HM) was converted into the replacement, Bf 109 V-17a. It arrived at E-Stelle (See) in the first week of the new year and made the first use of the Messerschmitt-designed 70cm tailhook. This aircraft was used extensively to evaluate the landing gear modifications and arrestor hook design in numerous landing, taxi, and arrestor hook trials.

This aircraft was joined in July-September 1939 by the rebuilt TK+HK and two modified Bf 109Es (civilian registry D-(later WL+)IECY/TK+HL, WkNr 1781; and WkNr 1783/GH+NT) and a year later by a third 'Emil' (WkNr 1946/GH+NU). The type's arrested landings were problematic due to the pilot's very poor visibility over the nose on finals, it's propensity to bounce when 'dropped in' and the tailhook's tendency to skip over the wires if it hit the deck before engagement.

The fourth 'prototype' for Messerschmitt's carrier-borne variant was a Bf 109E-0 with DB 600G-2 engine. This aircraft was primarily used for arrested landing trials at E-Stelle (See) and testing the smaller (2.8m) diameter VDM propeller, in the hopes that the latter would reduce damage to the deck and propeller/engine during the all too frequent 'tip ups' experienced upon arrestor cable engagement. **Thijs Postma Collection**

The poor visibility resulted in some landings being as much as 20ft (6m) off centreline and the lack of rudder authority, even with the DB 601N at idle, always slewed the landing aircraft to the left on landing. However, when the 'traps' (arrested landings) were successful, the average stopping distance was reduced to only 85ft (26m).

These five, plus the definitive 'Toni' prototype (Bf 109E WkNr 6153/CK+NC) (3) and the seven pre-production aircraft, conducted almost 500 arrested landings using the production-standard 18mm thick DEMAG arrestor cables on Travemünde's 800-900m simulated carrier deck. Other E-Stelle (See) research aircraft – three He 50s, two Ar 195s, an Ar 197 and the prototypes of Fi 167s and Ju 87Cs – accomplished over 1000 more arrested landings at the Luftwaffe's naval aviation test facility.

Meanwhile, the plans for the Bf 109T were drawn up by Willy Messerschmitt's Bayerische Flugzeugwerke AG (Bavarian Aircraft Manufacturing) design office at Augsburg and sent to Fieseler for implementation. Rather than disrupt Messerschmitt's assembly line, the RLM initially decided that Fieseler should convert 60 Bf 109E-3s from its production run to T-1 models. This was changed, in Lieferpläne 11 (Supply Plan 11/August 1939), to 70 new-build Bf 109T-1s. Delays in producing 'Emils' – primarily caused by Messerschmitt's redesign of the wing spar and insufficient availability of DB 601 engines – during this period impacted the 'Toni' production as well. Consequently, the RLM's C-Amt (technical office) did not finalise the production plans until producing Lieferpläne 19 in October 1940.

The most obvious change from the basic 'Emil' was the increase in wingspan, the resulting larger wing area decreasing take off distance and the lengthened aileron span improving low speed handling (never a strong point with the Bf 109). Flap travel was also increased, a tail hook and four catapult cradle attach points were added, and a life raft was installed behind the pilot's headrest. Additionally, to reduce lift on demand and enable precision landings, small spoilers were

BF 109T PROTOTYPES AND RESEARCH VARIANTS

Type	WkNr	Engine Type	Civil Code	Luftwaffe Code	Known Present at E-Stelle (S)	Remarks
Bf 109C-1 V-17	1776	Jumo 210G	D-IYMS	TK+HK	March 10, 1939	Initial Modification Prototype; First Flight February 1938; Damaged at Augsburg December 1939; Repaired
Bf 109B-1 V-17a	301 (Erla)	Jumo 210D	D-IKAC	TK+HM	January 1939	Replacement for V-17 - First Arrestor and Catapult Tests
Bf 109E V-15	1773	DB 601A	D-IPHR	CE+BF	January 17, 1941	First to fly with T-1 Wings; Tested at Augsburg June 1939 - December 1940
Bf 109E-0	1781	DB 600G	D-IECY/ WL+IECY	TK+HL	September 1939	Arrestor Trials Aircraft; Tested Smaller VDM Propeller
Bf 109E-0	1783	DB 601A		GH+NT	July 18, 1939	Arrestor and Catapult Trials Aircraft
Bf 109E-3	1946	DB 601A	D-IGPY	GU+NU	October 1941	Trials Aircraft for New Arrestor Hook Design
Bf 109E-1	6153	DB 601A		CK+NC	June 21 1940	Full-up Prototype; All Mods; All Trials Performed
Bf 109T-1	7728	DB 601N		RB+OA	April 23 1941	First Pre-Production Example; First Flight at Waldau January 1941

(3) Called the 'Musterflugzeug' or 'master aircraft', this 'Emil' was the definitive Bf 109T-1 prototype, incorporating all Messerschmitt's design modifications, except it retained its DB 601A engine. Its first flight was at Augsburg on March 26, 1940, and was flown to Travemünde in July. It was used as the final check of the design's interface with and use of the production-standard catapult launch and cable arrestor systems, as well as evaluate its own components.

A pair of D.21s on patrol. Lt Herman Doppenberg is piloting aircraft #237. Aircraft #241 was flown by Jan Bosch on the morning of May 10 and was set on fire by strafing Bf 109Es as he landed; fortunately he escaped injury in the attack. **Thijs Postma Collection**

The first offensive mission of II.(J)/186 was to destroy the Dutch 1st Fighter Squadron. This unit was deployed to De Kooy airfield to provide fighter defence for the main Dutch naval base at nearby Den Helder. It was equipped with 11 Fokker D.21s, a nimble fighter, but slowed by its anachronistic fixed landing gear. **Thisj Postma's Collection**

In van Overvest's words: "Why I looked behind me I don't know, but it saved my skin, because I had four Messerschmitts on my tail. Flaps in, and climb and turn, full throttle. One of the Bf 109s came straight at me, and I for him. We fired simultaneously and missed. I went straight again into a turn. He made long runs and pulled twisting, climbing turns. Close to stalling speed, I made the tightest turn the D.21 could handle. After a few circles I was behind him and when he pulled up for another turn I took a full shot at his engine, taking one aeroplane length's lead; white smoke of glycol and fuel streamed and the Bf 109 slid away to make a belly landing on our airfield.'

Indeed, with his Daimler-Benz engine dead, Robitzsch made a wheels-up crash-landing into the middle of De Kooy airfield, where he was immediately taken prisoner.

Lt Focquin de Grave also latched on to a Messerschmitt, damaging it, and the whole swarm of fighters started a swirling, left turning fight at low altitude (1200ft/360m) directly over the airfield. Meanwhile, the six D.21s circling overhead came swooping down into the raging dogfight.

2nd Lt Doppenberg also quickly joined in and he shot down one Messerschmitt, sending it crashing to the east-southeast. This was Uffz Wilhelm Rudolf. With his Bf 109E badly damaged and being wounded in the back, Rudolf managed to glide his stricken fighter about five miles (8km) to the southeast and attempted a crash-landing in a polder field near Westerland. Unfortunately, the aeroplane flipped over on its back, mortally injuring the pilot.

As the raging fighters were wheeling overhead it only took an instant for an attacker to could become a target. The next thing van Overvest knew, "I then saw how one of our people was being followed by two Bf 109s, I attacked one which dived immediately down, and I flew just a moment too long in a straight line to take a shot at the second one. I should have looked around first! With a bang my instrument panel blew apart, fuel gushed through the cockpit and the engine started to smoke." The Fokker stalled and went into a spin. "With the windshield covered with oil, one eye smashed, and flaps shot off I put down the D.21 in a slip on the short landing strip of De Kooy. Our own soldiers hardly recognised me. My parachute appeared to be shot through twice, because big lumps of silk were hanging out: speaking of luck…!"

When the swirling 10 minute dogfight was over, the surprised Messerschmitt pilots had lost two of their number, but they claimed the destruction of seven Dutch fighters. Uffz Kaiser claimed two D.21s destroyed, the other five surviving members of the formation each claiming one 'kill' each. Indeed, one Fokker had been destroyed and six others were badly damaged.

As soon as possible the surviving two D.21s took off again to mount a standing patrol over the field. They were airborne when II.(J)/186's second wave (another pair of schwärme, probably from 6. Staffel, led by Lt Hans-Herbert Wulff) arrived, but this time the defenders were not well positioned to repel the attack. The 'Emils' strafed the grounded D.21s, destroying two of them. In this attack Lt Schopper and another member of 6. Staffel were credited with one victory each.

In the final attack of the day – this one at noon by Bf 110s (2./ZG 76) flying all the way from Aalborg, Denmark – another D.21 was destroyed and the remaining 1.JaVA aircraft abandoned De Kooy that evening, regrouping with the handful of other survivors at a secret, camouflaged 'campaign airfield' just north of Amsterdam.

THE CAMPAIGN CONTINUES

II.(J)/186 had achieved its initial objective – 1.JaVA was destroyed as a fighting unit – but the carrier fighters continued attacks against De Kooy and raided the MLD floatplane base at De Mok, on nearby Texel Island. During an attack on De Mok by the Aalborg-based Bf 110Cs, the Zerstörer aircrew spotted a number of Dutch aircraft at De Vlijt, the ML's advanced training base on Texel. Returning four hours later, accompanied by two staffeln

The strafing Bf 109Es of 6.(J)/186 set Lt Bosch's D.21 alight - destroying it. **Thijs Postma Collection**

Herbert Kaiser would become the highest scoring 'Experten' to have been a member of II.(J)/186. His first victory claimed was a Bristol Blenheim (235 Sqn) on May 5, 1940. Eventually he was credited with 68 aerial victories and was awarded the 'Knights Cross of the Iron Cross' as an Oberfeldwebel on March 14, 1943. Andre' Wilderdijk Collection

Relaxing on Alert: three Dutch pilots who would play important roles during the morning air attack on May 10, 1940. Left to right they are: Lts Jan Bosch, Herman Doppenberg, and Henk van Overvest. Doppenberg and van Overvest each shot down a Bf 109E during the dramatic dogfight over De Kooy. Thijs Postma Collection

Weddewarden made us one of the best units of the Luftwaffe at this manoeuvre.'

The Trägergruppe's first success was on April 1 when the local Freya coastal air defence radar **(4)** detected nine Blenheim IVs (82 Sqn) on an armed reconnaissance of the German Bight. 5.(J)/186 was scrambled and arrived as the RAF bombers were attacking a flotilla of patrol boats, Blenheim P8867 being shot down by Lt Otto Hintze. **(5)** This victory was followed on May 3 when the staffel attacked a pair of Coastal Command's new Lockheed Hudson maritime reconnaissance bombers (206 Sqn) reconnoitering the Elbe Estuary near Norderney island. The attackers concentrated their fire on aircraft N7319, killing the turret gunner and damaging the aircraft so badly that it crash-landed upon return to RAF Bircham Newton. **(6)** Two days later the staffel scrambled against a formation of Blenheim F MkIs (235 Sqn), damaging one (although two victories were claimed).

On May 7, six of the squadron's 'Emils' scrambled to intercept a like number of Bristol Beauforts (22 Sqn). Unteroffizier (Uffz or Corporal) Herbert Kaiser attacked and shot down aircraft OA-G (L4464), which crashed into the sea with the loss of all aboard, starting his run towards his eventual 68 aerial victories. Lt Hans-Wilhelm Schopper damaged the formation leader (Wg Cdr H M Mellor in L4518) so badly it crashed upon landing at North Coates; Schopper was credited with his first of 17 eventual victories.

THE DOGFIGHT OVER DE KOOY

In the pre-dawn darkness of Friday morning, May 10, 1940, the Luftwaffe launched massive formations to attack British, French, Belgian, and Dutch airfields, opening Fall Gelb ('Case Yellow'), Hitler's invasion of France and the Low Countries. While Dornier, Heinkel, and Junkers medium bombers struck at air bases deep in the enemies' rear, in the all-out attack the Luftwaffe's air defence units were also tasked to destroy elements of the Allies' and the neutrals' air power closer to the front. Even the carrier fighter pilots of II.(J)/186 headed west with a vengeance.

Their target was the Dutch fighter squadron defending the Koninklijke Marine (Royal Netherlands Navy) base at Den Helder, on the northernmost point of Holland west of the IJsselmeer (formerly called the Zuider Zee). The 1e Jacht Vliegtuig Afdeling (1.JaVA, literally the 1st Fighter Aircraft Unit) was one of three squadrons in the Dutch army air arm, known as the Militaire Luchtvaart (Military Aviation or ML), flying the Fokker D.21 single-engine fighter. An interim and obsolescent design, the D.21 featured an enclosed cockpit but still sported the old fashioned fixed undercarriage and mixed construction. Powered by a nine-cylinder 830hp Bristol Mercury VIII radial engine, the little fighter was not fast at 286mph (460kph) – in fact it was much slower than the Bf 109E (348mph/560kph) – but being very lightly built, it was exceedingly agile, able to out-turn the 'Emil' with ease.

The Trägerjagdgruppe's first mission was to destroy 1.JaVA's 11 D.21s based at De Kooy airfield. After flying down the chain of the Frisian Islands from Wangerooge, a small formation – probably the Stab Schwarm (a four-aeroplane fighter formation) led by Hptm Seeliger – spotted a single Dutch Naval Aviation Service (Marine Luchtvaart Dienst or MLD) Fokker C.14W float reconnaissance biplane on 'dawn patrol' along the coast. One rotte (two-ship element) split off to attack the seemingly hapless victim, but the biplane proved much more manoeuvrable than the Messerschmitts and the pilot and gunner were very skilful, fending off repeated attacks by their faster adversaries. Soon the 'Emils' had to withdraw, low on fuel, empty-handed.

The remaining pair of Bf 109Es arrived at De Kooy to discover that the D.21s had already departed, headed south as part of the LVD's response to Heinkels bombing Rotterdam's Waalhaven airfield. The two 'Emils' strafed the base, destroying a number of MLD training aeroplanes and riddling 1.JaVA's mobile command post/radio van, killing one radioman and causing the commander to issue a recall to his squadron.

Nine Fokkers **(7)** returned to De Kooy and, while the three-plane formation led by eerste luitenant (Lt) Francois 'Frans' L M Focquin de Grave, circled warily overhead, the other six went in to land and refuel. Within 15 minutes these six were airborne again and Focquin de Grave's formation came gliding in for a landing. Just as they touched down II.(J)/186's second wave – two schwärme from 5.(J)/186, led by their staffel commander, Oberleutnant (Lt) Dietrich Robitzsch — came roaring in, machine guns and cannon blazing. One D.21, piloted by tweede luitenant (2nd Lt) Jan Bosch, was hit and immediately burst into flames, but Lt Focquin de Grave and his remaining wingman, 2nd Lt Henk van Overvest, quickly took to the air again. ➤

---

(4) The Kriegsmarine had installed a chain of eight FuMG 39G (gB) Dete 1 Freya radars as part of its North Sea coastal defences. This system could detect aircraft at ranges of 50-60 miles (80-100km) and fed information directly to Jagdfliegerführer Deutsche Bucht (Fighter Commander German Bight) command centre.

(5) This was Hintze's only victory. He became a jagdbomber (Jabo) pilot flying the Bf 109E-4 on 'tip and run' raids during the Battle of Britain. On October 26, 1940, he was shot down over Kent by a 222 Sqn Spitfire flown by Sgt J H H Burgess, baled out and was a POW for the rest of the war.

(6) No victories were claimed by the German pilots on this occasion.

(7) Two D.21s became separated from the main formation, chasing after German bombers; one of them was shot down by the enemy's defensive fire.

After launch, the Graf Zeppelin was towed to a Kiel dockside where its outfitting – building the ship's island and adding its weapons, catapults, arrestor gear, and other machinery and equipment – was begun. Work proceeded well for the first eight months, but the initiation of the Second World War meant priorities immediately changed to producing U-boats.

For initial carrier-landing training, a mock flight deck was laid out at Bremerhaven's Weddewarden airfield, adjacent to the Kriegsmarine's warship dock basin, seen here in a post-Second World War overhead practice reconnaissance photograph. At this time the facility was a US Army Europe (USAEUR) port facility for unloading heavy equipment arriving for NATO units. **Ulrich Israel via Jorg Müchler**

As the unit trained, it also grew, spawning a sister staffel (5.(J)/186) which was formed on July 15, 1939. Equipped with 24 Bf 109Bs, the two fighter units were not yet combat-ready, so when Hitler issued the deployment orders for Fall Weiss – 'Case White', the invasion of Poland – 4.(St)/186 departed for Stolp-West being attached go II./Stukageschwader 2 to begin the Second World War. At this point the ObdL realised that the Graf Zeppelin's units could be very useful in the Wehrmacht's continental offensives and 10 days into the Polish campaign it established the Stab (staff) of I.(St)/186 and ordered the formation of two more squadrons (1. and 2. Staffeln, redesignating 4. Staffel as 3. Staffel).

Simultaneously Stab II.(J)/186 was established under Hauptmann (Hptm or Captain) Heinrich Seeliger, the two-squadron group moving to Hage where they transitioned to the much more powerful and effective Bf 109E-1 – the famous 'Emil'. Following rather hasty conversion training, the gruppe moved to Jever on September 21 to take up air defence duties as part of Jagdgeschwader (fighter wing) 1, expanding with the addition of its third staffel [4.(J)/186, formed from 2./JGr 101] on October 11.

During the battles of the Heligoland Bight - when RAF 3 Group's Wellingtons attempted to attack the Kriegsmarine's cruisers in harbour at Wilhelmshaven in December, II.(J)/186 was based inland, at Nordholz, and therefore never had sufficient advanced warning to enable them to engage the British bombers before they had completed their bomb runs and were heading home.

Leutnant (Lt) Wolf-Dietrich Huy, II.(J)/186's adjutant, later recalled: "In March 1940, our Trägergruppe 186 was moved to the island of Wangerooge, with the aim of protecting the German Bight against RAF attack. The tiny windswept island off the German North Sea coast made take offs and landings quite difficult… but the training we had received during the exercises on the artificial landing strip at Bremmerhaven-

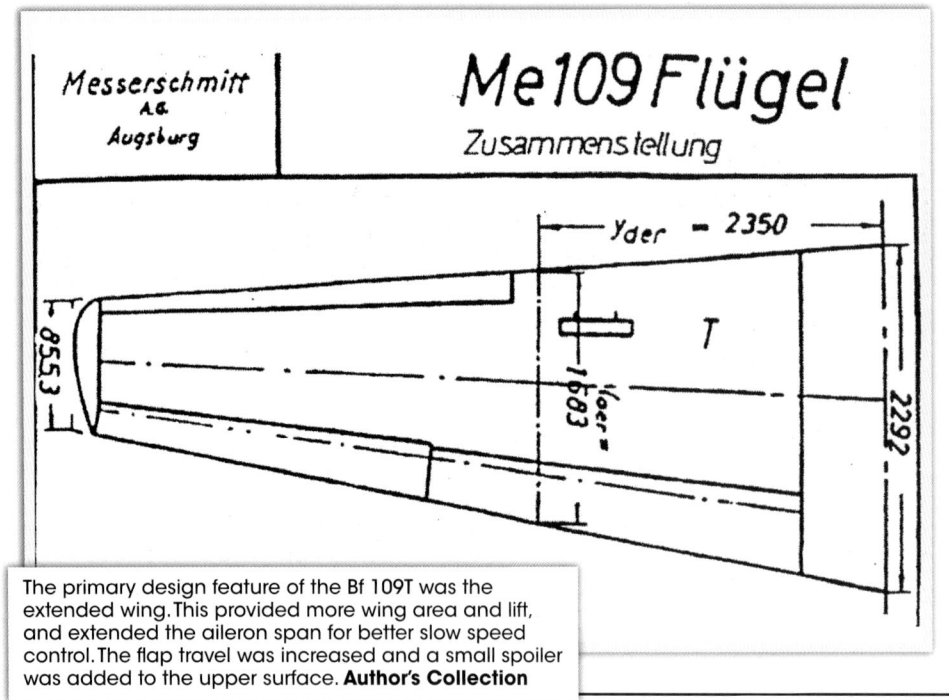

The primary design feature of the Bf 109T was the extended wing. This provided more wing area and lift, and extended the aileron span for better slow speed control. The flap travel was increased and a small spoiler was added to the upper surface. **Author's Collection**

Two of the 'Toni' modifications are seen here: a thicker padded headrest to help the pilot sustain the G-forces associated with the catapult acceleration and the inflatable one-man dinghy in case of a ditching at sea.
Thijs Postma Collection

added to the inboard section of the wing. The 'Toni' was to be fitted with the DB 601N engine which had a higher compression ratio and used 100 octane (C3) aviation fuel to produce 1175hp for better take off performance. To enable the pilot to better endure the sudden accelerations of catapult launches, a thicker headrest and seat arm rests were provided.

Finally, the longer range Telefunken FuG VII (2.5-3.75 MHz/45-50km/27-31 miles air-to-ground/ship) radio/telephone was provided, as well as a FuG 25 IFF transponder, and a large, more sensitive and stable Patin master compass. These features allowed the 'Toni' pilot to fly with confidence over the featureless sea and remain orientated to his carrier as well as permitted the carrier's radar operators to vector the fighter out for intercepts, and back to ship.

The first Bf 109T-1 (WkNr 7728/RB+OA) rolled out of the Fieseler factory in January 1940, followed by the remaining six pre-production examples over the next three months, all of which were sent to E-Stelle (See) for testing. One was lost when violent fluttering ripped off the left wing during a high speed dive. Once the trials were complete (and the wing design modified to eliminate the high speed flutter), five of these were placed into storage at Travemünde, minus their DB 601N engines which were desperately needed in operational units.

THE UNIT: II.(J)/TRG 186

While the engineers, pilots, and personnel at E-Stelle (See) were testing Messerschmitt's various prototypes, the workers at Gerhard Fieseler Werke GmbH were preparing the assembly line for producing the Bf 109T, and those at Deutsche Werke Kiel AG were preparing to launch the Kreigsmarineschiff (KMS) Graf Zeppelin, on November 1, 1938, the Luftwaffe formally established the ship's flying organisation. II. Gruppe/Tragergruppe 186 (II./186) was formed at Kiel-Holtenau, under the command of Major Walter Hagen, a Stuka pilot. The emphasis on its offensive capabilities also showed in the formation of its two squadrons: 4.(Stuka)/186 was established the same day, while the fighter unit – 6.(Jagd)/186 – followed two weeks later.

The Luftwaffe announced the formation of the Graf Zeppelin's CAG the same day that the ship was christened by Count Zeppelin's daughter, Hella Gräfin von Brandenstein-Zeppelin. Amid great fanfare and under the prideful gaze of Adolf Hitler, Hermann Göring, Erich Raeder, and 15,000 cheering onlookers, the nation's only real carrier was launched on December 18, 1938.

Meanwhile at Kiel-Holtenau, 6. Staffel inherited the Bf 109Bs from 4./JG 136, a recently established land-based squadron assigned to the traditionally float-plane fighter equipped I./JG 136. After learning to fly the fairly tricky and demanding (particularly in the take-off and landing phases of flight) Messerschmitt, in the spring of 1939 the pilots of the Luftwaffe's sole carrier-based fighter squadron began practicing 'coming aboard' a 2953ft (900m) mock flight deck laid out at Bremerhaven's Flugplatz Weddewarden, immediately adjacent to the warships' docking basin. The pilots also journeyed to Travemünde where they were instructed on cable-arrested landings using E-Stelle See's three hook-equipped He 50 biplanes. ➤

The Graf Zeppelin was launched on December 8, 1938, amid huge fanfare and some 15,000 spectators, including the highest ranking Nazi officials. That same day the Luftwaffe announced the formation of the ship's Trägergruppe 186, although at that time it consisted of only one Bf 109E and one Ju 87B squadrons. **Thijs Postma Collection**

Over Dunkirk II.(J)/186 encountered RAF Spitfires and lost one of their number – Lt Otto Hintze's 'White 5' – in the engagement. The next day the unit was transferred to Norway and Luftflotte 5. **Editor's Collection**

The two German battlecruisers were essential to the Kriegsmarine's strategy against Britain, and after safely returning to Germany – and having their battle damage repaired – they launched the most successful commerce raiding mission of the war, sinking 22 merchant ships before retiring to Brest, France. **Editor's Collection**

II.(J)/186 adjutant Oberleutnant Wolfdieter Huy was credited with shooting down a Spitfire Mk I over Dunkirk on May 31. He later went on to score 39 more victories on the Eastern Front and in North Africa before he being shot down by a 601 Squadron Spitfire Vc flown by P/O J.H. Nicholls on October 29, 1942 over the El Alamein area. Huy spent the rest of the war as a POW. **André Wilderdijk Collection**

from II.(J)/196, the overwhelming attack destroyed two FW 58Bs crew trainers, three FK.56 advanced trainers, an NA-27 Yale (precursor to the famous Harvard), and an ancient Fokker D.17 biplane fighter.

Dutch anti-aircraft (AA) fire proved particularly effective, especially the batteries defending Den Helder naval base, which shot down one strafing 'Emil' this day and two more the day after. During those two days two members of 6.(J)/186 were shot down, both surviving to become prisoners of war (POWs).

On May 12, II.(J)/186 was tasked to provide air cover for the Wehrmacht's only horse-mounted formation, the 1. Kavalerie Division. In two days, the German cavalrymen had crossed the breadth of Friesland and reached the east end of the long dyke connecting it to North Holland (called the Afsluitdijk) closing off the IJsselmeer from the sea. The cavalry dismounted and began determined assaults against the Dutch fortifications there. That afternoon the ML sent four equally ancient Fokker C.5d reconnaissance biplanes (IIIe Verkennings Groep or 3rd Reconnaissance Group) to attack the German cavalry. Flying combat air patrol (CAP) overhead the battle was a formation of 'Emils' from 5.(J)/186.

(8) Lt Emmerich later became the commander of 4./JG 51 during the opening months of 'Operation Barbarossa' and following his sixth victory (09/07/41) he was transferred to Jagdschule (fighter school) Gatow.

The Dutch pilots spotted the Messerschmitts and, decidedly outclassed, wisely turned and ran for home. The Germans sighted the Fokkers and gave chase. 1Lt Peter Emmerich claimed one Fokker shot down – his third victory of an eventual six. **(8)** The Dutch indeed lost one C.5d, but attributed the damage to their own overzealous AA batteries – it crash-landed and was abandoned near the IIIe Verk Grp base at Middelmeer, the crew surviving the encounter unhurt.

Meanwhile, II.(J)/186 was also still 'sitting alert' guarding the Deutsche Bight. That morning, 5. Staffel intercepted an RAF Hudson (N7353/206 Sqn) patrol bomber reconnoitring the German coastline and 1Lt Lorenz Weber shot it down into the sea just north of Borkum Island.

Two days later, on May 14, the Dutch capitulated and the battlefront moved beyond II.(J)/186's ability to participate. Guarding the approaches to the Kriegsmarine's naval bases was still the unit's highest priority. The next day, the local Freya radar detected a formation of three Hudsons (206 Sqn) approaching Heligoland and scrambled 5. Staffel to intercept. The staffel commander, 1Lt Wulff, led the intercept and shot one of the Hudsons down; it fell into the sea some 55 miles (88km) northwest of the island.

As can be expected, operations diminished considerably as Guderian's panzers broke through at Sedan (also during the same) and drove pell-mell across Picardy, focusing everyone's attention on them as they approached the Channel Coast. As the panzers came within range of England-based RAF units, the Luftwaffe's previous, almost hermetical, air supremacy became more diluted the further Guderian drove far ahead of his fighter coverage. Among the many units called forward to extend the Luftwaffe's fighter umbrella, II.(J)/186 transferred to Antwerp's airport on May 24.

The unit was rewarded with a victory being scored that day over an RAF Blenheim bomber, credited to 1Lt Emmerich. A week later, while the RN's 'Operation Dynamo' was evacuating the British Expeditionary Force (BEF) from Dunkirk, the II.(J)/186 group adjutant, 1Lt Wolfdieter Huy, was credited with a Spitfire shot down over the beleaguered port. However, no RAF losses correlate to these claims.

Early the following morning II.(J)/186 joined I./JG 26 to patrol above the embattled beaches of Dunkirk. They soon spotted a dozen Bf 110Cs (I./ZG 1) being attacked by about twice that number of Supermarine Spitfires (19 and 222 Sqns) two miles northeast of the port city, at 4500 feet (1370m). Immediately the 'Emils' dived to the rescue. In the expansive engagement, six Spitfires were shot down (none were claimed by II.(J)/186 pilots) while three Bf 110Cs and four Bf 109Es were lost to the Supermarine fighters. One of the latter was 1st Lt Otto Hintze (4. Staffel) who managed to nurse his stricken fighter to Furnes, just outside the BEF perimeter, where he crash-landed at 0540hrs. While 'White 5' was destroyed, Hintze escaped with superficial injuries. ➤

THE NORWEGIAN ADVENTURE BEGINS

This was the final major air battle for II.(J)/186. Even while 'Operation Dynamo' was continued, in Norway the RN and RAF mounted regular attacks on Kriegsmarine fleet units, particularly against the two battlecruisers Scharnhorst and Gneisenau which were ensconced in Trondheimfjord, having just sunk the aircraft carrier HMS Glorious. Consequently, Luftflotte 5's sole single-engine fighter gruppe, II./JG 77, **(9)** which was based at Stavanger-Sola airfield, required urgent reinforcement further north.

Fittingly, II.(J)/186 was selected and on June 2, Hptm Seeliger's unit was ordered northeast to Scandanavia. They flew via Jever and Aalborg to Trondheim, leaving 4. Staffel at Oslo's Gardermöen and Fornebu airfields. The two battlecruisers, with an escort of four destroyers and three torpedo boats, departed for Kiel on June 20. RAF Coastal Command coordinated a number of strikes the next day and provided a pair of Short Sunderland flying boats (204 Sqn) to shadow the German warships.

II.(J)/186 provided an overhead CAP, flying in relays as the two staffeln shuttled southward to their new base at Stavanger-Sola. Midday, a 6. Staffel schwarm led by Lt Wilhelm Schopper spotted one of the Sunderlands (N9028) and engaged it in a 15 minute running firefight. The large four-engine 'Flying Porcupine' defended itself well - claiming one 'Emil' shot down (no losses occurred) - but returned to Sullom Voe in the Shetland Islands seriously damaged. So much so that Schopper was credited with a victory, his third. The subsequent raids by Swordfish (821/823 Sqns), Hudsons (233 Sqn), and Beauforts (42 Sqn) failed to obtain any hits, attacking at significant loss to shipboard flak and Bf 109Es from II./JG 77.

Another important Kriegsmarine warship covered by II.(J)/186 was the 'pocket battleship' Lützow, which attempted a breakout into the North Atlantic in mid-June. The 'Tonis' shot down two Blenheims and a Beaufort torpedo bomber attempting to locate and attack the warship, but could not prevent another one from achieving a telling hit, sending it back to Germany for repairs. **Bundesarchiv**

The most successful 'Toni' pilot was Lt Franz Wienhusen, who was credited with four victories RAF aircraft during his tour of duty. In November 1944 Weinhusen, who had flown over 300 combat sorties, became the commander of the newly-formed IV./JG 4 at Frankfurt-Rhein Main. He was killed flying a Bf 109G-10 while attacking US Army forces approaching Aachen on December 3. **André Wilderdijk Collection**

The Norwegian campaign cost the German navy one heavy cruiser, two light cruisers, 10 destroyers and six U-boats. Furthermore, both battlecruisers, an armoured cruiser ('pocket battleship') and a light cruiser were all seriously damaged by torpedoes. Obviously, the Kriegsmarine needed shipyards and workers dedicated to repairing these warships much more than it needed to finish an aircraft carrier. Consequently, three weeks into the campaign, on April 29, GAdm. Raeder suggested to Hitler that the work on the Graf Zeppelin be halted temporarily, and resumed once the 'quick war' was over.

At this stage the Nazi carrier was considered more than 90% complete: all primary machinery was installed and the 15cm casement guns were mounted. The auxiliary machinery, main battery weapons controls, and flak battery fire control system were still lacking. Hitler agreed to defer completing the vessel and subsequently Raeder ordered its 15cm guns dismounted and sent to Norway to strengthen the Kriegsmarine coastal batteries there. The ship's flak guns were also removed and redistributed.

The stripping of the carrier's guns was completed by July 6 and six days later the ship was towed from Kiel to Gotenhafen (now Gdynia, Poland), to moor it beyond the reach of RAF bombers. With no carrier to fly from, the Luftwaffe reorganised the CAGs: on July 5 II.(J)/186 was redesignated III./JG 77. **(10)** By this time, the gruppe's 4. Staffel had already been split off, transferred to Cologne's Ostheim airfield to become the third squadron of the newly-created Erprobungsgruppe 210, established to evaluate the Bf 109E as a fighter-bomber delivering 250kg (550lb) bombs in 'tip and run' harassment raids during the Battle of Britain.

THE NORWEGIAN ADVENTURE CONTINUES: BF 109T IN COMBAT

It would have been a poetic end to this story had the Bf 109Ts – when they finally came off Fieseler's assembly line – been issued to III./JG 77, the progeny of the unit originally intended to fly the 'Toni' from the flight deck of the Graf Zeppelin. But it was not to be. In April 1942, Jagdgeschwader 77's Stab, II. and III. Gruppen departed Scandanavia for the Balkans where they participated in the Nazi conquest of Greece and Yugoslavia, and eventually campaigned in North Africa and against the Soviet Union.

This left the daytime air defence of Norway to the newly formed I./JG 77, established that February specifically to fly the newly-built Bf 109Ts. Fieseler's completion of the 63 production 'Tonis' began in April and was finished within three months. Since this was well after Hitler's fateful decision to defer completion of the Graf Zeppelin, the now unnecessary carrier specific equipment was removed, and the designation was changed to Bf 109T-2s. With 'Toni's' increased wingspan and more powerful DB 601N engine, it was perfect for the short, mountain-encircled Norwegian airfields.

> "MIDDAY, A 6. STAFFEL SCHWARM LED BY LT WILHELM SCHOPPER SPOTTED ONE OF THE SUNDERLANDS (N9028) AND ENGAGED IT IN A 15 MINUTE RUNNING FIREFIGHT."

A Bf 109T undergoing maintenance at a Norwegian airfield, very possibly Lister. The Bf 109T's returned to Lister in November 1943 when the type's last operational unit – Jagdstaffel Helgoland – was withdrawn there and redesignated 11./JG 11 and lived out its existence providing convoy escort. The extra-long wingspan of the 'Toni' is readily apparent when viewed from this angle. **Glory Archive**

I./JG 77 was formed at Stavanger-Sola in February 1941 under Hptm Walter Grommes and became operational on Bf 109Es in April, just as the geschwader's other two gruppen departed for the Balkans. Initially, it consisted of the normal 1., 2., and 3. Staffeln, but in May the first of these was transferred to Kirkenes in the far north of Norway to become the basis for Jagdgruppe zbV (zur besonder Verwendung – for special purposes) to participate in 'Operation Barbarossa' operations against Soviet forces defending the Arkhangel'sk area. **(11)**

While the Wehrmacht turned against the USSR, the Kriegsmarine increased its attempts to strangle the UK's maritime lifeline. For 1941, GAdm. Raeder had planned a series of forays by his most powerful fleet units to drive into the North Atlantic to destroy the convoys crossing from North America. The first of these was 'Operation Berlin': the Gneisenau and Scharnhosrt sallied via the North Sea and the Denmark Strait (between Greenland and Iceland) in January and sank 22 merchant ships (115,600 tons total) before retiring to Brest, France. The next was 'Operation Rheinübung' (Rhine Exercise), originally scheduled for late April, using the navy's newest battleship – the dreaded Bismark – and heavy cruiser, Prinz Eugen. After a sortie to attack convoys in the North Atlantic, these two were to join the battlecruisers at Brest for a subsequent – and potentially decisive – foray.

It was the mission of I./JG 77 to provide defensive fighter cover over these warships while they were in Norwegian waters. Their adversaries were the RAF Coastal Command's No. 18 Group based in Scotland, flying Hudsons and Blenheims on maritime reconnaissance missions, and Bomber Command's No. 2 Group flying anti-ship strikes with Blenheims and Beauforts, the latter armed with Mark XII aerial torpedoes.

On May 21, the KMS Bismark, Prinz Eugen, and three destroyers arrived at Grimstadtfjord near Bergen and JG 77's 3. Staffel, flying from nearby Herdla airfield, flew CAP fending off one snooping Blenheim (254 Sqn). The Nazi task force was eventually located by a reconnaissance Spitfire Mk I Type D (1 PRU) and a large strike was laid on for the next day, but by then the two heavy warships had slipped out into the North Sea unobserved. ➤

Even after launching the Graf Zeppelin's design continued to evolve. Here the 'Atlantic prow' is added to the ship while being outfitted at Kiel. **Bundesarchiv**

(9) JG 77's I. Gruppe was attached to JG 51 for the Battle of Britain and, afterwards, on November 21, 1940, it was absorbed into the jagdgeschwader as IV./JG 51.

(10) I.(St)/186 was redesignated III./StG 1 on the same date.

(11) On the I./JG 77's order of battle the departed squadron was replaced by 1.(Z)/JG 77 with eight Bf 110Cs. Its presence, when the Bf 109Ts arrived, resulted in the group re-establishing its third single-engine fighter squadron as the 13. Staffel (4.-through-9. Staffeln were with II. and III. Gruppen and 10.-through-12. Staffeln designations were reserved for IV. Gruppe, normally the operational training establishment of a jagdgeschwader).

By the time Hitler became interested in completing the carrier, the Fi 167 was completely obsolete as a carrier torpedo plane, so the RLM directed Junkers to update their ship-borne 'Stuka' design using the newer Ju 87D 'Dora' as a basis. Prototype Ju 87 V25 'BK+EF' demonstrated the design's ability to carry aerial torpedoes. **Thijs Postma Collection**

In June Luftflotte 5 received all 63 production Bf 109Ts, issuing 42 to I./JG 77, which established a fourth squadron (13./JG 77) at Sola. The 21 additional 'Tonis' were sent to Trondheim where they were issued to Jagdgruppe Drontheim's 1. (Einsatz) Staffel. **(12)** Each of the I./JG 77 squadrons were given nine fighters as their frontline strength and the Trondheim unit had a dozen, the rest being held in reserve or undergoing maintenance.

The first major effort for the 'Tonis' was associated with Raeder's 'Operation Somerreisen' ('summer journey') the commerce raiding foray by the armoured cruiser Lützow that began June 11. Two days later, as the 'pocket battleship' was making its way towards Trondheim accompanied by five destroyers, it was spotted by a Blenheim (114 Sqn) and two waves of Beauforts – nine from 42 Squadron (Leuchars) and five from 22 Squadron (Wick) – were launched to attack it. Due to thick cloud, only one from each wave located the target and the 42 Squadron machine evaded both the Bf 109Ts and Bf 110Cs to score a torpedo hit on the ship's port side. Its armoured belt was not penetrated but the concussion caused sufficient damage to the ship's machinery for Kapitän zur See Leo Kriesch to abort his mission and return to Kiel for repairs.

The RAF lost two Blenheims and a Beaufort to the newly-arrived Bf 109Ts during these missions. The Beaufort (OA-R/W6521 of 42 Sqn) was one of several intercepted by a rotte of 'Tonis' flying CAP over the Lützow, and was shot down by Lt Franz Wienhusen, who was awarded the Eisernes Kreuz II ('Iron Cross 2nd Class') for this achievement. **(13)** Two days later the same pair scrambled from Sola to intercept a 114 Sqn Blenheim (RT-Q/V5887) bombing the Norwegian steamship Tromösund 18 miles (30km) south of Stavanger, this time Lt Rudolf Glöckner getting the victory - two

The remaining 'Tonis' were split between Jagdstaffel Heligoland and Nachtjagdgeschwader 101. The latter used them, such as this example displaying its NJG 1 badge on the cowling, as night-fighter trainers from Manning airfield near Ingolstadt. Also prominent on the cowling is the white 'N' indicating the aircraft has a high-compression DB 601N engine, thus requiring the 100-octane C3 fuel being pumped into the tank aft of the cockpit. **Glory Archive**

While the Kriegsmarine was successful in gathering its major warships in Norwegian/North Sea waters - such as the Lützow, seen here in a Norwegian fjord in 1942 - it failed to employ them effectively against Murmansk-bound convoys resupplying the Soviet army. Subsequently Hitler lost all faith in his navy and ordered the warships 'paid off', a decision that resulted directly in the immediate, final and complete cancellation of the dream of German carrier-based aviation. **Editor's Collection**

survivors (the observer was KIA) being rescued/captured.

In September, Raeder wanted to have the armoured cruiser Admiral Scheer breakout into the Atlantic, raid the convoys to Britain, and join his three fleet units at Brest. However, Hitler disapproved, having become disillusioned with the Grand Admiral's 'Atlantic Strategy' because of the national humiliation associated with the loss of the Bismark and the fact that all three of the Kriegsmarine's warships at Brest had been heavily damaged and immobilised by RAF bombing during the intervening months. Instead der Führer allowed the Scheer only to go as far as Oslofjord, and thus remain available for operations against the Soviet Baltic Fleet if needed.

Found in Oslofjord, the German 'pocket battleship' immediately became a high priority target for the RAF, Bomber Command electing to use its new four-engined, long-range Boeing Fortress Mk Is (90 Sqn) to try and destroy the raider. The RAF had accepted 20 B-17Cs and despite a host of problems was anxious to attempt, and assess, the American version of high altitude precision bombing – in broad daylight. On September 8 four Boeings were launched from Kinloss, Scotland, crossing the North Sea in a loose 'gaggle' at 24-28,000ft (7315m-8535m) altitude. Due to their high altitude German radars detected them 150 miles (240km) from their target and since they were drawing white contrails across the clear blue skies, the 'Toni' pilots of 13. Staffel had no difficulty in spotting and intercepting them.

Lt Alfred Jacobi led the first attack, later reporting "I observed two condensation trails stretching from west to east. I climbed up towards the trails… (and) after about 12 minutes, I came up to within 400 metres (1312ft) of a four-engined Boeing. There were two defence positions (on the empennage sides) shooting at me; in addition two guns were firing at me from a turret just behind the cockpit. I opened fire with both MG 17s at a range of 400 metres, then used my cannon as well. I obtained hits on the right side of the rear fuselage, while the Boeing jinked from side to side apparently in order to give the rear gunners a chance at a good shot. Meanwhile because of my speed I came up alongside the enemy aircraft and saw a large hole in the rear third of the fuselage and flames coming from the upper part of the tail. I did not notice while firing but the left outer motor was alight and beginning to smoke.

"During my second attack in which both rear guns fired at me, I saw hits in the left wing of the Boeing, which tore out a large piece of wing structures. Between the engines was a fire and from the whole aircraft equipment and skinning were falling off, with smoke coming from the cockpit. The aircraft went spiralling down into a gradually steepening angle (then) went into a vertical dive and exploded about 2000 metres (6560ft) beneath me."

A second Fortress was shot down by Uffz Karl-Heinz Woite 31 miles (50km) southwest of Stavanger and a third was so badly damaged it made a wheels-up crash-landing at Kinloss, and was subsequently written off. The leader of this raid aborted the mission 80 miles (130km) short of the target. The disastrous performance resulted in the remaining Fortresses being transferred to Coastal Command's 220 Squadron for long-range maritime patrols over the North Atlantic and the RAF declined the opportunity to follow the American's into daylight precision bombing. ➤

(12) This was a training organisation containing four squadrons, equipped with 26 Avia B534 Czech biplane fighters, 37 Ar 96s two-seat monoplanes, 60 Bücker Bü 131 aerobatic biplane trainers, and 63 Bf 109Es and Ts. The last mentioned was also charged with the air defense of the Trondheim area anchorages, as well as training replacement fighter pilots for the other Luftflotte 5 units.

(13) In February 1944, Weinhusen was transferred to 4./Jagdgruppe Süd in Marignane airfield near Marseille, France, to train fighter pilots, then was posted to command the newly-formed IV./JG 4 at Frankfurt-Rhein Main. After over 300 combat sorties and with four victories to his credit, he was killed flying a Bf 109G-10 while attacking US Army forces approaching Aachen on December 3.

Nevertheless, the costly raid (and its weather-aborted predecessor two days prior) had one positive effect: on September 8, the Admiral Scheer departed Oslo and retired to Swinemünde.

While RAF's autumn operations settled down to routine armed reconnaissance missions along the Norwegian shoreline, I./JG 77's sorties were mostly 'küstensperrflug' ('coastal protection flights') protecting the many ships plying the coastal routes. From June through December, the 'Tonis' are known to have shot down a total of four Beauforts (22 and 42 Sqns), five Blenheims (114, 235, and 248 Sqns), seven Hudsons (220 and 608 Sqns and 320 (Dutch) Sqn), one Spitfire PR I and a Mosquito PR I (both 1 PRU). These encounters were not entirely one sided, however: in July one Bf 109T (2./JG 77) was lost to a Beaufort's (42 Sqn) defensive fire, killing Lt Werner Minz, his 'Black 8' immediately crashing into the sea. **(14)**

By the end of November I./JG 77 had 31 Bf 109Ts on strength, 26 of which were operational, while Jagdgruppe Drontheim had another 16 available. At this time the decision was made to 'withdraw (the type) from service', but this was not because its usefulness had expired. On the contrary, it was because of a suddenly renewed interest in finally completing the type's intended carrier, the Graf Zeppelin.

THE END OF THE DREAM
When Hitler's over-ambitious campaign to crush the Soviet Union in 1941 ('Operation Barbarossa') stalled at the gates of Moscow, Leningrad, and Rostov-on-Don the Eastern Front became an overriding obsession for der Führer. Believing that the Kriegsmarine surface combatants would be better utilised attacking Stalin's maritime resupply convoys passing through the Norwegian Sea and around the North Cape he ordered Raeder's Brest-based units returned to German ports. This resulted in the daring – and surprisingly successful – 'Operation Cerberus' aka the 'Channel Dash'.

The idea of gathering the Kriegsmarine's fleet units along the North Sea coast **(15)** represented a return (albeit for different reasons) to the navy's original strategy. Furthermore, the fact that the mighty Bismark had been crippled by an ancient Swordfish biplane torpedo bomber – thus allowing the Royal Navy's heavy warships to close on and destroy it – and that the Lützow's 'summer journey' was aborted by damage from a single aerial torpedo highlighted the Kriegsmarine's renewed need for carrier-based air cover. Consequently, in August 1941 Hitler directed Raeder to complete the Graf Zeppelin after all, and have her in service by October the following year.

Anticipating the necessity to re-establish the trägergruppen, on September 28 the Oberkommando der Marine (the High Command of the Navy, Raeder's HQ) requested the Luftwaffe withdraw the remaining 'Tonis' (and Fi 167As) from combat operations and store them awaiting completion of their ship. During December the 47 Norwegian-based Bf 109T-2s were ferried back to Fieseler for overhaul and reconfiguration back to the 'T-1' standard, then they would be flown to Pillau-Neutief airfield on the coast near Königberg, East Prussia, for storage. **(16)**

Since Fieseler was now producing the badly-needed FW 190, the overhaul and modification of the 'Tonis' was a secondary priority, taking almost all of 1942 to accomplish. The five original pre-production Bf 109T-1s, stored at Luftzeugamt Erding, were also overhauled by Fieseler and joined the 47 combat veterans at Pillau. **(17)**

Meanwhile a reappraisal of the air group's composition – based largely on IJN's experience in combat operations during 1942 (Midway and the Guadacanal sea battles) – led to the decision that the Fi 167A was totally obsolete as the ship's torpedo plane. Consequently, Junkers was directed to examine the feasibility of converting the updated Ju 87D to a multi-role carrier borne attack aircraft. The resulting design, the Ju

The Graf Zeppelin was moved to Stettin and moored there in a river, becoming a derelict. Even though it was scuttled in 1945, it proved relatively easy for the conquering Soviets to refloat two years later. **Thijs Postma Collection**

A side view of Messerschmitt Bf109E-4, Black 1, 'Der Alte', flown by Staffel Kapitän Oblt Dietrich Robitzsch and shot down during the De Kooy airfield attack. **Tom Cooper**

87E, could carry and launch a standard navy torpedo as well as performing dive bombing and reconnaissance tasks. The Marineleitung ('Supreme Navy Staff') stated to the RLM a requirement for 54 examples, 28 of them to be embarked as the ship's strike force. (Ma: 141)

The 'Toni' had also been surpassed by the Allies' carrier fighter technology, so the RLM directed Messerschmitt design a new ship-borne fighter. Since long wingspans were needed for high altitude interceptions as well as carrier operations, Messerschmitt initially paired the navy's new fighter requirement with the RLM's specification for a new high-altitude interceptor (to combat the USAAF B-29 then in development), initially designated the Me 155. Messerschmitt was fully engaged in developing the improved versions of the Me 109G so the design work was passed to Blohm & Voss as the BV 155. In any event, the 'Toni' was to be relegated to training pilots for the new design.

With the German fleet now concentrated in Norwegian waters (those not being repaired in German shipyards, anyway), on March 16, 1942 the OKM ordered the completion of the Graf Zeppelin to resume. Some redesign was necessary: larger, more powerful catapults to launch the newer, heavier aircraft; an 'Atlantic bow'; increased flak batteries; and other changes in light of the RN, USN, and IJN experience in carrier combat operations. All of these resulted in the renewed design displacing almost 36,000 tons. ➤

(14) In addition to the solitary combat loss, one 'Toni' was destroyed by RAF bombing, seven had been lost in operational and training accidents with an equal number being damaged beyond repair (DBR) in similar mishaps.

(15) By the time of 'Operation Cerberus' the Nazi's newest battleship, Tirpitz, was already deployed to Trondheim, and as soon as the 'Channel Dash' was concluded, the Prinz Eugen and Admiral Scheer joined her there.

(16)] The 'Tonis' were stored with the 10 surviving Fi 167As and one Ju 87C. The Fieselers would eventually be sold to Croatia, where their short-field and high load-carrying abilities made them ideal for transporting ammunition and other supplies to besieged Croatian army garrisons between their arrival in September 1944 and the end of the Second World War.

(17) The replacement of the 'Tonis' by new Bf 109Fs (and some older 'Emils') resulted in I./JG 77 becoming the basis of JG 5, controlling all the fighters in Luftflotte 5. Later, in southern Russia the veteran I.(Jagd)/Lehrgeschwader 2 became the new I./JG 77 since it was operating with JG 77.

As proud and elegant a warship as was never commissioned: The last known photograph of the Graf Zeppelin, reportedly after it was towed to Swinemünde in preparation for her last trip, ostensibly to Leningrad in June 1947 to be 'inducted' into the Soviet navy. The carrier's protective anti-torpedo 'bulge' amidships is very evident in this poignant photo. **Author's Collection**

A Fokker DXXI, 219, of the Royal Netherlands Air Force 1st Fighter Squadron. **Tom Cooper**

> "FOUR DAYS BEFORE RAEDER LEFT THE OKM, COMPLETION OF THE GRAF ZEPPELIN WAS FINALLY AND IRREVOCABLY CANCELLED. IN APRIL IT WAS TOWED TO STETTIN WHERE IT WOULD BE SCUTTLED TWO YEARS LATER TO (UNSUCCESSFULLY) KEEP IT OUT OF THE HANDS OF THE SOVIETS."

The ship was not towed to Kiel until December 1942, and work began immediately, but like so many other aspects of this story, it was not to be. Already reeling and enraged from the encirclement and decimation of the Wehrmacht's Sixth Army at Stalingrad (besieged beginning November 23), Hitler finally lost all confidence in Raeder and his Kriegsmarine surface warships when the Admiral Hipper, Lützow, and six destroyers failed utterly against Russia-bound convoy JW51B in December. In a typically apoplectic decision, in January 1943 he ordered all major fleet units 'paid off' and their big guns mounted in the 'Atlantic Wall' and other coastal defences. He now placed his faith in unrestricted submarine warfare, turning the Kriegsmarine over to the U-boat admiral Karl Dönitz on January 30, 1943.

Four days before Raeder left the OKM, completion of the Graf Zeppelin was finally and irrevocably cancelled. In April it was towed to Stettin where it would be scuttled two years later to (unsuccessfully) keep it out of the hands of the Soviets.

That same month, the 'Tonis' at Pillau began to be issued as night fighter trainers to I./Nachtjagdgeschwader (NJG) 101 at Manching, near Ingolstadt in southern Germany, and the newly-established Jagdstaffel Helgoland ('fighter squadron Heligoland', administratively attached to II./JG 11). The latter was established with 16 Bf 109Ts on a brand-new airfield on nearby Düne Island – thus returning the erstwhile carrier fighter to the mission pioneered by its originally intended trägerjagdgruppe: the defence of the Deutsche Bight.

From this exposed, windswept rock, with its runways of less than 800 metres (2624ft) length, the 'Toni' was well-suited. Since the Deutsche Bight was the preferred bomber ingress route to targets in northern Germany, the 'Toni' would again meet one of its former opponents: the Boeing B-17 Flying Fortress, this time flown by the US Army Air Forces in immensely larger formations, and with far greater defensive fire-power, than the paltry numbers of underarmed Fortress Is employed by the RAF 18 months earlier. Additionally, they were escorted by large numbers of USAAF's excellent P-51 Mustang fighters, in every way superior to the Bf 109E-derivative 'Toni'.

Consequently, victories were few and losses were high and by November Jagdstaffel Helgoland was withdrawn to Lister airfield in southern Norway, one of the 'Toni's' bases two years prior. There it was redesignated 11./JG 11 and lived out its existence providing convoy escort in what had become – with the demise of the Kriegsmarine – a quiet backwater combat zone.

Though the Bf 109T never flew from the flight deck of the Graf Zeppelin – and the pilots trained to do so were eventually transferred to other fronts and duties – with its 1941 successes against the RAF's maritime patrol/strike forces (and assuming a far more cogent naval strategy for its employment with the German fleet units) the knowledgeable reader can now thoughtfully ponder, weigh and argue the rather poignant 'what if' in the event it had. All three components – the ship, the aircraft, and the pilots/unit – of the Kreigsmarine's intended carrier operations were developed in parallel, and to near fruition. Fortunately, perhaps, for the Royal Navy they never came together to form the threat that they could have been. ■ *Words: Colonel Douglas C Dildy*

The *Graf Zeppelin* was moved to Stettin and became derelict. The Soviets refloated the vessel and towed it to Leningrad. **Thijs Postma Collection**

Inside 'Red 7's' cockpit, the only modern avionics being the radios, GPS and transponder. **Constance Redgrave**

Mike Schwarz and Olaf Rohrer turn the mighty DB 605B over by hand. **Constance Redgrave**

When the EADS Heritage Flight visited the ILA, the Berlin Air Show, *Aviation Classics* was lucky enough to be allowed to photograph the aircraft inside and out while the flight's aircraft were at the show. Among them was a Bf 109. Test pilot Klaus Plaza describes flying it and photographer Constance Redgrave gives a visual perspective.

Main image: In flight on the way back to the Flight's home base of Manching, the shark-like lines of the Bf 109 are evident. **Joe Rimensberger**

Opposite left: Along with his crew chiefs, Klaus makes his pre-flight inspection, a pilot tradition that goes back to the earliest days of flight. **Constance Redgrave**

Opposite right: The man and the machine. Klaus ready to display. **Constance Redgrave**

The EADS Bf 109 was originally built as an HA-1112-M1L number 139, as attested by the manufacturer's plate on the rear bulkhead of the cockpit, but has since been re-engined with a Daimler-Benz DB 605B and returned to 109G-4 standard. It is registered D-FWME and painted as 'Red 7'. *Aviation Classics* was given a rare opportunity to see it at close quarters and EADS Heritage Flight engineers kindly opened the aircraft up for our cameras. Two other examples examined at the superb RAF Museum at Hendon also yielded some fascinating additional detail, including as it does both an original Bf 109E-3 and a G-2.

Based at Manching, home of the Messerschmitt Stifftung and Museum, 'Red 7' was one of the stars of the film The Battle of Britain, where it appeared as 'Yellow 11' and 'Red 14'. Its first flight after undergoing an extensive rebuild, which saw its new engine installed, was in the hands of Walter Eichorn in 2004. Flying historic aircraft is never straightforward however, as Klaus Plaza, from Cassidian, an EADS company, knows only too well. He describes it here.

"..so, Klaus, how DOES she fly after all?"

I've heard this question so many times, and yet I don't really know a good, probably cool sounding answer.

Maybe: "Oh, nothing much to it, she handles just like any other, really."

A blunt lie.

Okay then: "Man! It is pure luck to bring her up and then back again in one piece."

Another lie.

But somewhere between both answers may be the truth. So come on and join me on a typical mission and see for yourself. First things first: get your flight order, fill out your flight card (remember, test pilots never depart without a task) and get the weather.

If you plan to perform vertical manoeuvres, the ceiling should be at least about 4000ft AGL (above ground level) because a loop takes between 3500 and 3700ft in diameter.

And the wind, please, gently from head on. If not: you can handle a steady 10 knot crosswind assuming that your drum brakes put out sufficient power, which is anything less than certain. I long for the day we refit Dave Kumlers' disc brakes.

Crosswinds must not be gusty: it happened to me just recently on the first display day at the 2012 ILA at Berlin. 'Tower' gave me a final wind reading of 260° (Runway 25) and three knots. ➤

The reality was about 300° with 15, gusts 25 knots and… Christ! Just after touchdown a gust grabbed my right wing and threw the airplane on its left wing tip, scraping the runway while coming off track to the left at the same time. Not much time to think. I kicked left rudder despite its left going tendency to let inertia bring her back on to both feet. It worked. I cut the power while she crossed the sideline at about 30 or so knots and soon came to a standstill. Phew!

Needless to say, I had to restart both the engine and my heart to taxi uneventfully back to parking (the boys did a splendid paint repair job during the night, so the show was on again the next morning).

Both wind and clouds being okay today, let's walk out and meet the 'boys'. Olaf Rohrer and Mike Schwarz, my trusted crew chiefs, both wait for me at the aeroplane. We discuss briefly what has been done since the last flight and I tell them what we are about to do: a 15 minute local flight doing a display practice. Without them I couldn't do it. Whatever wishes I have, they do the utmost in trying to achieve them and they also give me valuable hints about this and that. It is all about teamwork and boils down purely to flight safety. And I love it.

After my walk around, which is a fixed part of my flight operation, it is time to put the seatback parachute on and strap in. Many say "wow, this is a tiny office" but I don't really think so. Well, it is not the dancing room of a Corsair or Mustang, but certainly not a Fw 190 either. Even with my height of 185cm, I feel very comfortable in it. My right arm rests on my thigh with the hand naturally reaching the unique, slightly canted control stick. My left hand 'falls' on the power lever. Trim and flap wheels are on the left side at the bottom. I admit they are a bit hard to work, especially the flap wheel with its high air load even if you crank them down well below the maximum flap operation speed, which is 280kph.

A last pass in front of the audience, undercarriage down… **Constance Redgrave**

The instruments are grouped in the typical, somewhat scattered way they did it in those days.

Flight instruments to the left and middle, engine monitoring instruments more to the right.

Two radios and a mode S transponder are grouped together on the lower centre console.

Not original, I know, but a tribute to small modern avionics and the needs of today's airspace. Ah, and on top of everything, that's not the rounds counter, but a Garmin 495 GPS. I want to go to places like the Air Tattoo at Fairford, without causing London ATC too much trouble.

Make sure you sit high enough in the three position bucket seat to feel okay. At least it gives you the subtle feeling to see, ahem, maybe not much, but a little less 'nothing'. That settled, I close the heavy canopy. No Ray-Ban wearing, arm-hanging P-51 taxiing along the crowd line. They can't even see me grinning at them because I wear a full mask. Mark Hannah once told me: "If you want to ever have a chance that someone can hear you on the radio you've got to wear a mask. Too noisy, these cockpits." Hence, I wear them. I also think it adds to the 'bad guy' look.

Before I start the mighty DB 605 engine I radio to tower for start-up clearance. They would tell me any expected delay: I have no more than 10 or 11 minutes from cranking to take off to avoid coolant overheating, or I would have to shut down again. Start up granted, I signal the ground crew, turn mags to 'M1+2' and energise the flywheel starter while giving her some four pressure strokes with the heavy duty primer pump located under my left knee.

Now, engage and cautiously feed in some throttle. Being a direct injected engine it 'always' starts well, but you've got to be aware of the excessive oil pressure (more than 10bar) when turning it above 800 to 900rpm. Even a 1943 service bulletin warned crews about possible damage if this was not adhered to.

…before turning in for the difficult bit, the landing!
Constance Redgrave

The forward left side of the cockpit, including the throttle and mixture levers, tailwheel lock and canopy release. **Constance Redgrave**

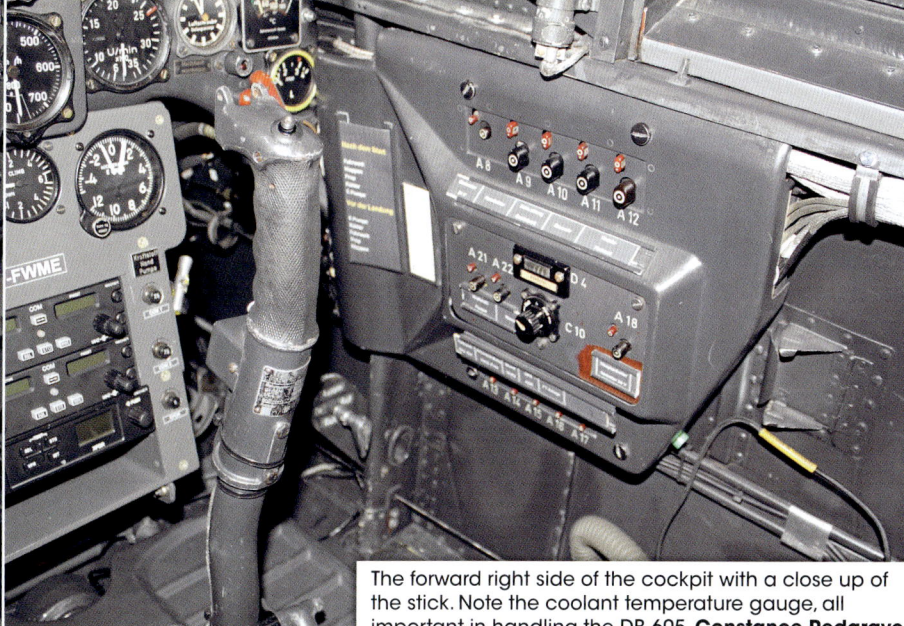
The forward right side of the cockpit with a close up of the stick. Note the coolant temperature gauge, all important in handling the DB 605. **Constance Redgrave**

The remarkably original cockpit of the RAF Museum's Bf 109E-3. Note the offset Revi reflector gunsight. **Editor**

The canopy of the RAF Museum's Bf 109G-2, note the position of the gunsight. **Constance Redgrave**

Chocks off, I S-turn toward runway 07 at Manching, the turns enabling me to see over the long nose. 40°C oil temperature is okay for a quick run up, coolant temp at that time is already at 80°C, soon to cross the 100°C mark. If you hit 110°C you get white smoke! The brakes won't hold much more than 2000rpm. With the take off checks complete and clearance received, I taxi into position, straighten the tail wheel and lock it. Don't you forget that! If you do, you'll be very busy during landing roll out, I can tell you.

Take off roll: feed in 1ata and gain speed, holding her straight as well as you can by getting sideways looking clues, feeling for effectiveness with the rudder, then come forward with the stick and apply 1.15ata manifold pressure. This equals maximum continuous power and I rarely use any more than this at all, saving wear and tear on the engine. Of course there are all sorts of adverse effects tearing on my little aeroplane, enough to make me look like I am waving at you with the rudder! But be sure you are ready in case she does 'something' towards a direction not aligned with the runway. I believe this is due to the canted angle of the main wheels, being far forward of the centre of gravity anyway, which apparently love to develop a sense of direction of their own. ▶

> MARK HANNAH ONCE TOLD ME: "IF YOU WANT TO EVER HAVE A CHANCE THAT SOMEONE CAN HEAR YOU ON THE RADIO YOU'VE GOT TO WEAR A MASK. TOO NOISY, THESE COCKPITS." HENCE, I WEAR THEM. I ALSO THINK IT ADDS TO THE 'BAD GUY' LOOK.

The canopy of the RAF Museum's Bf 109E-3, including the early lower front glazed panels. **Constance Redgrave**

A close up of the starboard leg housing including the undercarriage lock. **Constance Redgrave**

Looking up into the port main wheel bay with the undercarriage locks in the leg housing. **Constance Redgrave**

Looking down on the main undercarriage wheel with the brake lead and oleo calliper. **Constance Redgrave**

'Red 7's' spinner and forward cowling detail. **Constance Redgrave**

Once airborne, I bring up the undercarriage and flick the 'Propellerautomatik' on, then roll up the flaps, crosscheck 280kph and commence climbing. The initial climb rate is near 2500ft per minute. Check the coolant temperature and adjust if necessary. Fuel boost pump off. Airplane: happy. Pilot: commence breathing again (happy too). Before we play a bit I have to close the split flap coolant air exit door all the way and then crack it open again. Two indicators: left eye, right eye.

Now let's play: I trade some altitude (I checked the ceiling above 4500ft AGL – above ground level) for speed. As the operator we limited the Vne (velocity never exceed) to 550kph indicated air speed (IAS) instead of the original 750kph. Fast enough to make you look all right but still saving the aeroplane. After all, we want to pass it along to the generations to come. I have to use both hands if you load her up. She stiffens a lot while at speed. Torque factors are a big player when going vertical. I still have to work on a way to make her go straight up every time I try.

Rolls are quite a charm, but especially to the right again I have to use both hands. Too much air load, or not enough workout from my side. The part I like the best is the inverted flyby, which she performs with ease despite losing some power while doing so. Her non fuel-injected Allied opponents would have coughed and spit a long time ago if they tried. Sometimes it is good to be the bad guy. A normal display routine uses −1 to +4.6G. Again we limited ourselves to use a maximum 5G instead of the original 7G.

Let's return to land. Power back, she puffs and barks protesting against it like a dog after a walk having to enter the yard again. Use the coolant doors as an airbrake to slow down and at the same time bring down the coolant temperature as much as you can to allow for some taxi time after landing. Below 280kph, I select the undercarriage down and watch two little pointers unevenly 'walk' down and wait for the two clunks, telling me it has locked down and that I can believe my two green lights.

Flaps need to come down now, an act of intense workout, taking as long as the full downwind plus some of the base leg. Propeller to 'manual' and then set with the thumb switch on the throttle lever to 11:45, read by a clock-like indicator, which is the setting for a possible go-around. Air speed 220kph IAS on the base leg. Then 200 on turning finals, 180-ish on final with some power on to control the descent rate. Stop breathing.

No runway in sight any more on final. If you have, better go around, because you won't land on it.

Don't flare too high, an intuitive thing to do if you can't see where you are going. Power further back to idle and then touchdown or sometimes to touchdown and then idle. She feels (and is) awfully nervous, dancing from one foot on the other just after touchdown, which should always, always be attempted in a three point attitude. Because you need the assistance of the locked tail wheel to keep her going straight while rapidly losing rudder effectiveness. Roll out using rudder and sometimes differential brakes. Once down to cyclists' speed, snap the tail lock open and taxi to parking. The mask is limiting the wide grin on my face, still being the bad guy, but a happy one.

And now start breathing again. The aircraft: no matter how well, or not so well my display may have gone, the applause is always hers.

Cut the engine by the mixture lever, cut the mags, cut the electrics and open the canopy shouting the words "magnete aus" to the crew.

"So, what do you think, how is she handling?" I am asked.

Certainly a handful of an aeroplane, that's for sure. Probably the most demanding of my career.

It's also a great honour for me to be selected and allowed to fly and display this rare classic under the roof of Cassidian and be part of the team.

Let's hope it will grace the sky and fill it with its unique sound for many years to come. ➤

Top left: The starboard exhausts and forward cowling of the RAF Museum's Bf 109G-2, with its large tropical air intake cover and filter. The forward clamshell doors of the intake could be closed to prevent sand ingress and force the air through the cylindrical filter. **Constance Redgrave**

Top right: A close up of the external tank, its mounting brackets and fuel feeds on the RAF Museum's Bf 109G-2. **Constance Redgrave**

Above right: The port exhaust and cowling of the RAF Museum's Bf 109G-2. **Constance Redgrave**

Right: The starboard exhausts and forward cowling of the RAF Museum's Bf 109E-3, note the small engine air intake cover and grill. **Constance Redgrave**

Far left: The rear of the port side of the engine bay showing the supercharger air intake and the impeller behind its mesh screen. **Constance Redgrave**

Left: Looking aft in the bottom of the engine bay showing hose, connector and cooling pipe details. **Constance Redgrave**

Below left: The port side of the engine bay with all the cowlings open. **Constance Redgrave**

As well as the sheer joy of Klaus' description of flying the Bf 109, *Aviation Classics*' photographer Constance Redgrave was also moved by the experience of working with the EADS Heritage Flight to put pen to paper. She writes:

Serendipitous: the joy of finding something you weren't looking for. *Aviation Classics* has been full of these surprising moments over the past two years; the Hurricane, the Mosquito and the Harrier being my particular favourites.

I recently had my fourth trip to ILA Berlin with the added remit of photographing the Bf 109. Needless to say, my experience with this aircraft has been extremely limited. After all, weren't they the bad guys?

Anyway, on the first day when I first crossed what I was reliably told was the 'Messerschmitt Line', I was immediately caught by the incredible buzz around me of excited Germans trying to photograph these four amazing machines. I did manage a few shots of the 108 with John's help, but the 109

'Red 7' in the hanger after the display with everything open, for which we gratefully thank the EADS Historic Flight ground crew. **Constance Redgrave**

was really not an option in that crush. A lovely man named Olaf Rohrer suggested that I come down to the hanger at the end of the day where it would be much quieter.

Later, the 109's graceful shark-like display convinced me to take him up on his offer. When I arrived, they were in the process of doing the end of the day once-over inspection. Olaf and his magic screwdriver proceeded to open every compartment, door and even the funny little cubby hole on the underside for me. He then dragged a ladder over and allowed me to climb up, put my foot on the wing and photograph the cockpit at my leisure. By the end, I was covered in concrete dust, oil smudges and a huge smile. I never expected to fall in love with another aircraft after the Hurricane. If this keeps up, people are definitely going to talk… ■ *Words: Tim Callaway, Klaus Plaza and Constance Redgrave*

Top: The starboard side of the immaculate DB 605B engine in the nose of 'Red 7'. **Constance Redgrave**

Top right: The under nose oil cooler housing with its rear adjustable flap to control the oil temperature. **Constance Redgrave**

Middle right: The exit from the coolant radiators on 'Red 7' passes between an upper and lower flap, the bottom half of which is also part of the wing flaps. **Constance Redgrave**

Above: Under 'Red 7's' starboard wing tip, showing the leading edge slat, inspection panel and that the G retained the aerodynamic aileron mass balance from the earlier E model. **Constance Redgrave**

Left: A rear view of the RAF Museum's Bf 109E-3, showing a major difference between this and later models, the external bracing struts to the tailplane. **Constance Redgrave**

Messerschmitt Bf 109 105

Czech Mules and Spanish Pigeons

Postwar Bf 109 variants and their surprising roles in war and peace

The cessation of hostilities in 1945 saw the retirement of many fine but redundant piston engined aircraft; naturally the fighting aircraft of the defeated Axis powers disappeared almost instantaneously, with one notable exception – the Bf 109.

In 1939, the Bf 109Es of the Condor Legion were donated to the Spanish Air Force. **Editor's collection**

Spain was the first nation to see combat involving the Messerschmitt Bf 109 and yet was also the last nation to abandon the Bf 109 airframe, having built variants of the German fighter from the mid-1940s through to the late 1950s. The final version, with Rolls-Royce Merlin power, remained an operational fighter into the 1960s.

The first version of the fighter supplied to the Condor Legion was the Bf 109B. **Editor's collection**

For 30 years, Spanish aviation history was directly tied to the Messerschmitt fighter which had flown its first combat missions with the Condor Legion in support of General Franco during the Spanish Civil War.

But the story begins even earlier, during the First World War. Wolfram Freiherr von Richthofen (cousin of Manfred 'The Red Baron' and Lothar) had survived three years of fighting in the cavalry before he took the advice of his cousins and joined the German Air Force. By the end of the war, he had become an ace flying with Jasta 11, part of JG 1, Manfred Richthofen's Flying Circus. No doubt the fame of his family name combined with his service record played a part in his

A single Bf 109E was modified to test the installation of the V12 Hispano-Suiza 12Z-89 of 1300hp. Note the large under fuselage radiator which caused unacceptable drag. **Editor's collection**

The Hispano Ha-1112-K1L was later fitted with wing racks for eight unguided 80mm rockets and a pair of 20mm Hispano HS-404 cannon. Wing fences were fitted just outboard of the cannon. **Editors collection**

The Hispano Ha-1112-K1L featured a far more elegant Hispano-Suiza 12Z-17 engine installation and was initially unarmed. **Editor's collection**

career and Wolfram served with the Weimar Republic's armed forces in the pre-Nazi era. He was involved from the earliest days of the Luftwaffe, no doubt also helped by his connections at the top since following the 1918 deaths of first his cousin Manfred and then JG 1's subsequent commander Wilhelm Reinhard in a testing crash, his final commanding officer there had been Hermann Goering.

In the Spanish Civil War, von Richthofen was chief of staff to Hugo Sperrle, the head of the Luftwaffe's Condor Legion, which operated under the direction of General Franco's command. The concept of terror bombing, which had been introduced by the Zeppelin raids on England during the First World War, was raised to a far higher level of accuracy with the Condor Legion's utter destruction of the Spanish city of Guernica on April 27, 1937. Although Basque troops had been retreating through the area, the bombing of Guernica raised deliberate airborne destruction to previously unseen levels, and set a sad example for the carnage that was be wrought upon all sides throughout Europe during the Second World War. Wolfram von Richthofen became the commander of the Condor Legion in October 1937, and later served as a part of Army Group South fighting in Russia, before being given command of the Luftwaffe operations in Italy. He died soon after Germany's surrender in 1945, while a POW in an Austrian prison camp. But it was von Richthofen's years with the Condor Legion in Spain that had a direct effect upon the long service life of the Messerschmitt Bf 109 and its variants.

BUILDING THE BUCHON

The Condor Legion Bf 109Es gifted to General Franco in 1939 gave sterling service. Indeed the last example, werknummer 790, was not retired until 1954. During the war the Ejercito del Aires also received 15 ex Luftwaffe Bf 109F-4s to familiarise pilots destined for Escuadron Azul, the Spanish contingent of JG 51 fighting on the Russian front. However planned licence production of the Bf 109G-2 was made impossible by the rapidly deteriorating fortunes of Nazi Germany. Only 25 airframes, lacking engines, propellers and tail assemblies, were delivered to the Hispano Aviacion company which also lacked essential assembly jigs and technical drawings. Forced to seek an alternative power plant to make use of these airframes, the Spanish turned to the locally produced V12 Hispano-Suiza 12Z-89 of 1300hp.

Unlike the DB 605 motor the new engine was designed to be installed in the more orthodox upright position. Even more problematic was the fact that it rotated in the opposite direction, badly affecting the aircraft's flight characteristics. A single prototype adapted from a Civil War veteran Bf 109E made its maiden flight on March 2, 1945. While the German fighter's wing mounted coolant radiators were amenable to the new engine, the under slung oil cooler and carburettor were a cumbersome, ugly affair causing excessive drag. The disappointing performance was further blunted by an unsuitable VDM three bladed propeller, which limited the maximum engine rpm. Despite these limitations, the decision was made to assemble the 25 stored G-2 airframes as the HA-1109-J1L. Production progressed at a leisurely pace, the first flight not taking place until mid-July 1947, but the type proved to be so unsuitable that it was never issued to the air force and was placed directly into storage after only limited flying time.

Another attempt to utilise the German airframes was made using a French built Hispano-Suiza 12Z-17 engine installed in the 10th HA-1109-J1L coupled with a de Havilland Hydromatic propeller permitting the full use of the 1300hp available. The nose was considerably cleaned up, with the oil ➤

A rare Hispano Ha-1112-K1L with the Hispano-Suiza 12Z-17 engine, on display at the Museo del Aire, Madrid, Spain, in 2010. **Diego Dabrio**

Like the earlier Ha-1112-K1L, the HA-1112-M1L Buchon was armed with a pair of 20mm cannon and underwing 80mm unguided rockets. **Editor's collection**

coolers placed on either side of the lower forward fuselage in long half round fairings and the carburettor air intake was moved rearwards between the main undercarriage legs. The first flight was made in May 1951 and production of the HA-1109-K1L commenced in the following year. An equivalent of the two seat Bf 109G-12 trainer was designated as the HA-1110-K1 but only a pair were built, the first being a conversion of the prototype HA-1109-K1L. An elegant blown canopy covered the crew and the 93 gallon (423 litre) fuel capacity was re-arranged into three small tanks in the wings and lower fuselage removing the need for external tanks as seen on both the German and Czech versions of the trainer.

Most early examples were completed without armament but later versions were cleared to carry eight unguided 80mm rockets under the wings. Eventually a pair of 20mm Hispano HS-404 cannon were installed in the wings creating the HA-1112-K1L. The cannon were very neatly packaged within the wing and did not require blisters to accommodate the breeches and ammunition feeds as had been the case in the earlier MG FF installation of the Bf 109E. Lastly, wing fences appeared between the guns and the automatic leading edge slots to maintain lift. The HA-1112-K1L possessed a maximum speed of 382mph (615kph) at 13,780ft (4200m) and had a maximum loaded weight of 6834lb (3100kg); at 29ft 6in (8.99m) it was slightly longer than the Bf 109G but had an identical wing span.

Production of the Hispano-Suiza 12Z-17 was terminated in 1953, forcing the search for yet another power plant. The ubiquitous Rolls-Royce Merlin 500/45 was still available in large numbers and when the HA-1109-M1L so equipped made its maiden flight it marked just over 19 years since the Bf 109 V1 took to the air under the power of a Kestrel from the famous British company. The new 1635hp engine proved far more successful than all previous substitutes. Its two speed supercharger gave it a maximum speed of 419mph (674kph) and its installation produced by far the best performing and most handsome member of the re-engined Messerschmitt family. Long eyebrow shaped bulges in the upper engine cover similar in style to the Griffon powered Spitfire were necessary to cover the Merlin's cylinder heads and it was also the only production version of the Bf 109 to be fitted with a four bladed propeller.

Many earlier Hispano-Suiza examples were converted, alongside 170 new build aircraft, but Willy Messerschmitt's delicate little fighter was still instantly recognizable as aft of the fire wall very little else was altered. Production was later standardised on the HA-1112-M1L version, the two trainers were also converted, but unlike the fighters they were fitted with

The two elegant Hispano HA-1110-K1 two seat trainers were retrofitted with the Merlin engine, having originally been equipped with the Hispano-Suiza 12Z-17. **Editor's collection**

The production HA-1112-M1L Buchon featured a four bladed propeller and the characteristic deep nose that earned the type its nickname. **Editor's collection**

The Tillamook Air Museum, in Oregon, is home to HA-1112-M1L Buchon serial number 193, later G-AWHN. It was used in the film The Battle of Britain. **Norm DeWitt**

Lenart with his S-199 in 1948, a painting by Boris Yaro. **Boris Yaro via Norm DeWitt**

Lenart in the cockpit of the Avia S-199 in 1948. **via Norm DeWitt**

Boris Yaro's painting 'Lenart attacks, the mission that saved Tel Aviv'. **Boris Yaro via Norm DeWitt**

formerly occupied by the Ottoman Empire. The day of the expiration for the Mandate, the State of Israel declared its independence on May 14, 1948. On the following day, the armies of Egypt, Transjordan, Syria, Saudi Arabia, and Iraq invaded.

Egypt had acquired a large number of war surplus Spitfire Mk.IXs from England, however the Israelis had nothing to deploy in response. Lou Lenart said: "Let me tell you the status of the situation in May of 1948. There was a total embargo against Israel; we had no air force whatsoever. The Arab countries had established armies and air forces… some good and some not so good. They had everything that they needed, and we had almost nothing. We couldn't buy a pistol, we couldn't land anywhere for refuelling. It was a very desperate status with the Mediterranean at our side, surrounded by Arab countries."

How was a handful of Jewish pilots able to obtain and transport these Czech fighters to the theatre of war? Lou said: "It was the genius of Al Schwimmer. He was a visionary, an ex-flight engineer at TWA. He started this whole thing in a hangar in Burbank, California, with four mechanics and a plan to buy C-46s that were in the desert as surplus. As pilots, each of us had a right to buy one if we showed them our certificate. I bought one for five thousand dollars that a Jewish agency gave me. Of course the FBI was after us all the time, and they would park their car in front of our C-46 so that we couldn't take off. There was also a desperate search for pilots. David Ben-Gurion (first prime minister of Israel) said it best: 'In the final analysis, Israel can only depend upon our own strength and sacrifices'. Perhaps another of Ben-Gurion's quotes applies to this mission as well: 'If an expert says it can't be done, get another expert'."

In the end, Schwimmer fled to Canada as he was being pursued on charges of violating a US embargo on weapon sales. Lou said: "We set up a fictitious airline in Panama to try and get around the embargo. We didn't have any fighter planes at all, so we took the C-46s from Panama to the Azores and then over to Czechoslovakia. It was a newly communist state that had armaments and was desperate for dollars so they were a big help to us. The original Messerschmitt was a very fine fighter plane but these used the original planes with a different engine and propeller… with two guns firing through the prop… when it didn't shoot the prop off or jam. It was a monster; in Czechoslovakia they called it the Mule."

HANDLING THE MULE

They could just as well have called it the Death Trap. Lou said: "We went to an air base outside of Prague. They were pretty challenging and I almost got killed on my first flight. The runway was just a big grass field with no boundaries to provide a point of perspective, as there is a tail wheel and you can't see anything. There were no two seaters, so you did your ground study and then you got in. What I used to do with the Corsair was to hold on to the brakes and bring up as much power as I could until I felt the vibration from the wings telling me that it wants to fly… I'm very spiritual about those things… and then I slam full throttle immediately because if something is going to happen I want it to happen in the first third of the runway, not the last.

"It was very important to bring the tail up as soon as possible, so I picked a cloud in the sky for a reference point, there was nothing else. I pulled the power on and started fairings over the fuselage mounted guns which were unnecessary due to the installation of smaller rifle calibre machine guns. When issued to the Czech National Air Guard the S-99 sported red undersides and engine cowlings with light grey upper surfaces. The national insignia was applied to the upper wings and tail only.

Despite a promising start the programme was dealt a massive blow when the entire stock of DB 605 engines was destroyed by fire alongside other military material stored in warehouses. The Czechs were forced to turn to the Junkers Jumo 211 intended for the Heinkel 111 medium bomber. Although it was an inverted V12 of almost comparable power, its greater weight and higher torque made it less than ideal for a fighter. Mating the Jumo to the narrow confines of the 109's forward fuselage could only be achieved by installing wider and stronger engine bearers necessitating long horizontal channels which blended into the 13mm MG 131 heavy machine gun bulged fairings which were reintroduced as the new engine could not accept the installation of a motorkanone. A smaller diameter spinner and a massive wooden paddle bladed propeller were also installed and if the 109's appearance was marred by this unhappy marriage its handling was utterly ruined.

The first flight was made on March 25, 1947, exposing the type's unpleasant characteristics which included a vicious swing on take-off and sluggish throttle responses, but worse was to come when attempting to land. This delicate procedure frequently ended in a ground loop. Despite these serious limitations, production orders were placed and to distinguish the new variant the designations S-199 and CS-199 were applied. The aircraft was universally unpopular and many accidents occurred due to the unsuitable engine/propeller installation combined with the 109s dangerously narrow and angled undercarriage. Nicknamed the Mezek or Mule for its obstinate behaviour, the S-199 possessed a theoretical maximum speed of 367mph (590kph) at 19,600ft (6000m), however in reality the performance was markedly inferior to the Bf 109E of 1940 vintage.

Additional design work was undertaken during the production run that surprisingly for such an unloved machine lasted until mid-1950; the heavy framed sideways opening canopies of both the fighter and trainer were replaced with aft siding blown sections of taller profile and the main wheel geometry was slightly altered. In Czech Air Force service the S-199 was frequently finished in an overall dark green scheme with a red spinner, the National Air Guard also operated the type

Lou Lenart with downed Egyptian Spitfire. **via Norm DeWitt**

in the red and grey scheme previously described. A second production line was established at the Letov factory at Letnany which eventually went on to build 129 of the 551 examples produced.

Despite its obvious failings the S-199 did provide the Czechs with a cheap home grown fighter until the adoption of more modern aircraft of Soviet origin. Amazingly, it even achieved export orders, albeit clandestinely. In 1948 the emerging state of Israel was in serious need of combat aircraft; surrounded by hostile Arab governments and prevented from purchasing military equipment by a United Nations arms embargo it was forced to acquire weapons by unorthodox means. Discrete approaches were made to the Czechoslovakian government and a deal to supply 25 complete S-199s with spares in two batches was agreed in exchange for US dollars cash in April 1948. Disassembled and crated, the aircraft were secretly delivered individually to Israel's Chel Ha'avir which was able to form 101 Squadron, its first fighter unit at Ekron in central Israel, as Norm De Witt takes up the story.

LOU LENART AND THE S-199

American Major Lou Lenart was one of the original four volunteer pilots in the Israeli Air Force, having previously been a Marine pilot flying Corsairs in the battle for Okinawa. The Middle East was undergoing massive change in 1948 with the expiration of the League of Nations Mandate for Palestine which had been created after the First World War to institute British rule in the southern areas ➤

Lou Lenart was a major in the US Marine Corps during the Second World War, seen here with his Vought F4U Corsair. **via Norm DeWitt**

A side view of Israeli Air Force S-199 120-D, now in the Israeli Air Force Museum. **Keith Draycott**

Messerschmitt Bf 109 111

the Tillamook Air Museum in Oregon, which has one of the Buchons used in the movies. He said: "Regarding the museum's Buchon (an HA-1112-M1L, serial number 193, carrying the British registration of G-AWHN), the aircraft is one of 28 Buchons that were purchased by executives from United Artists in 1968 for the film The Battle of Britain. After the film, most of the aircraft were sold to private individuals.

"Among those purchasing them was well known pilot Connie Edwards (who also flew in the film) who purchased nine of the Buchons and exported them to the United States in 1969 where they were sold to owner Jack Erickson in 1989."

Today at least 13 remain either on display or in storage in the United States including the sole surviving HA-1112-M4L two-seater. In Europe several have been reverse engineered to accept original Daimler Benz engines creating realistic G versions, while in the UK the Aircraft Restoration Company has recently returned Buchon C.4K 102 to her 1968 film identity Yellow 10 complete with replica wing cannon and fuselage machine guns. Bearing the civil registration G-AWHE this aircraft is currently based at Duxford where it is a highly popular addition to the UK air show circuit.

A Czech Bf 109G-14, known as the S-99, built at the Avia factory in Cakovice near Prague. A lack of Daimler Benz engines forced the development of the postwar S-199. **Editor's collection**

As for where the Buchon saw action as a combat fighter, nothing remains resolved. Although Spain returned Ifni to Morocco in 1969, to this day Spanish Sahara is considered an occupied state, with numerous claims to sovereignty from Morocco, Mauritania, as well as from independence advocates. As for the post colonial legacy, it goes without saying that Northern Africa and the Middle East are seemingly a never ending hotbed of conflicting territorial claims and counter claims between various ethnic and religious groups, where further armed conflict is possible at any time. One of those post colonial hotspots was to be the scene of another Bf 109 variant's introduction to war.

THE MULE IS BORN.

After the Second World War, the Bf 109 was briefly retained in service with several European air forces, but with Germany's industrial base in ruins the ageing Messerschmitt rapidly succumbed to a chronic lack of spares. However the situation in Czechoslovakia was somewhat different as production of the Bf 109G-14 had been established at the Avia factory in Cakovice near Prague as part of the plan to minimise the debilitating effect of Allied bombing on German fighter production. These assembly lines were abandoned almost completely intact when the Germans were forced to make a hasty withdrawal ahead of the irrepressible Red Army. With at least 20 fighters and a pair of G-12 trainers near completion the Czechs set about gathering components from the chain of local subcontractors with the intention of recommencing production. Prior to using the parts, careful inspection was necessary to detect possible sabotage by either those forced to build them or by Nazi sympathisers. Once production commenced, the Avia built machines were designated the S-99 fighter and CS-99 trainer. Both were identical to their German built equivalents with the exception of the prominent bulged

The production Avia S-199 with the sliding canopy and Jumo 211 engine. **Editor's collection**

The Avia S-199 now in the Israeli Air Force Museum, seen here while still in service. **Editor's collection**

Hispano HA-1112-M1Ls in Luftwaffe markings for the Battle of Britain movie in 1969. **via Norm DeWitt**

the taller tail and rudder seen on the S-199 and the last German 109 variants. The deep nose housing the oil cooler and air intake led to the adoption of the nickname Buchon after the common high breasted local pigeon. In service the type was most commonly operated in a smart overall dark blue scheme or silver over pale blue undersides. Production of the Spanish Messerschmitt finally ceased in 1958 after 239 of all versions had been built, used mainly as ground attack and training aircraft. They remained in service until 1967 in a country still ruled at that time by a fascist government. With a postwar embargo on providing weapons to Spain, they made do with what they had.

THE BUCHON IN WAR AND THE MOVIES

Into the 1950s, for the European powers, typical postwar usage for obsolete piston engine fighters and bombers was in attempting to retain control over their colonies. Spain's colonial battleground was the Western Sahara, or Spanish West Africa, from 1957-58. The Ifni war was a battle to maintain Spain's presence in the region, which was being challenged by the newly independent neighbour to the north, Morocco. In response to widespread rioting and attacks against the Spanish population, General Franco sent in the Spanish Legion to defend the city of Sidi Ifni, which was coming under siege from the Moroccans.

It wasn't just the 109 variants being used in these desert battles along the Atlantic coast, as given General Franco's relationships with Nazi Germany, the Spanish Air Force also had Spanish built versions of the Heinkel He 111, called the CASA (Construcciones Aeronauticas SA) 2.111. The Heinkel had been operational within Franco's Spanish Air Force during the Spanish Civil War, and during the Second World War was being built under similar licensing agreements as Hispano had done with the 109. Well before the Ifni war, the embargo against weapon sales was

The 1969 movie poster for the Battle of Britain. **via Norm DeWitt**

The 1957 movie poster for Der Stern von Afrika. **via Norm DeWitt**

Hispano HA-1112-K1L with Hispano-Suiza engines were used in filming of Der Stern von Afrika. **via Norm DeWitt**

removed and Spain was to build the 'Buchon' or final version of the HA-1112. Both the mid-50s versions of the Hispano Aviation HA-1112 and Heinkel aircraft were now to be powered by Rolls-Royce Merlin engines. Twenty years after the 109s and He 111s had wrought annihilation upon Guernica, Franco's forces again called upon the latest versions of these same German aircraft to rain destruction upon a different foe. With help from France, the Moroccan Liberation Army was stopped and a treaty was signed in April 1958. In Spain, the Ifni war is often known as the Forgotten War, as General Franco ordered it stricken from the history books.

Today, the HA-1112 Buchon is perhaps best known from the silver screen, as it was used in a number of Second World War movies, masquerading as the original Messerschmitt Bf 109, given the relative scarcity of the originals and the similar profile. Christian Gurling is the curator of ➤

pushing right rudder. I'm at full throttle and when the tail comes up, I look in horror that this thing had taken me 45° around the hangar towards a fence down the side. Even now it's terrifying just to think of it. I just went on instinct, pulled back on the stick and the airplane had just enough speed to go over the fence and landed on the other side. It scared the s**t out of me. It was a lesson to everybody else that even with full right rudder you had to put in gradual power, you couldn't fly it like the Corsair. They had told me that they had a lot of torque… we knew what the airplane was, but we had nothing else. Desperation is a good motivator.

"None of us had flown fighters since the Second World War, and the four of us were the foundation of the future air force. The other three guys had gotten their wings with either the British Air Force or South African Air Force, but not one of them had pulled a trigger in war. So obviously I was the leader being the most experienced, having seven years in the Marine Corps, and had flown the Corsair there. The Corsair… you either mastered it or it mastered you, and I just loved it. If I'd had four Corsairs instead of the junk I had, I could have changed the map of the Middle East.

"I told the Czech commander, 'look, we can't stay here'; we'd just heard Ben-Gurion announce the declaration of the State of Israel, and of course all the Arab armies had come in from the north, the east and the south. In one hangar we had the four Mules, with a Czech mechanic and a couple of Israeli mechanics taking the planes apart as the range on those planes was only about 50 minutes of flight. We brought them back in the C-46s, with fuselage in one, wings in the other… and then we put them back together.

"When you put a plane back together, there is always a test flight, but we didn't have time as the Egyptian army had crushed the settlements on the road from the Egyptian border to Tel Aviv. We didn't test the guns, we'd never flown them, and we had no radios. I didn't even know if the things would turn on. My mechanic who had helped put it together told me 'anybody who sits in this thing deserves a medal'. Meanwhile the Egyptian air force was flying over, bombing the s**t out of everything, and strafing the streets. What do you do when you have four airplanes and the other side has 40? You try to get them on the ground at first light."

THE MAN WHO SAVED TEL AVIV

"There was a bridge 22 miles from Tel Aviv that the boys had bombed, and it was damaged enough that there were about 500 Egyptian vehicles there… trucks, fuel tankers, artillery and tanks along with about 12,000 soldiers. They were about six miles south of where our airfield was. My plan was to take off the next day, the 30th, and attack the Egyptian air base headquarters right at the tip of Gaza. But the Israeli forces commander Shimon Avidan heard we had airplanes and drove to our airfield and told us they had knocked out the bridge at Ashdod and that the whole Egyptian army was bumper to bumper as far as the eye could see. He told me that if we 'don't stop them tonight, they will be in Tel Aviv in the morning and Israel is finished'. That was the critical moment, there was no alternative.

"It was about 6pm, but it was May and there was good light. But the airplanes were nose to tail in the hangar where they were built. We only had one tender to pull the planes out to where they could take off from. If we had done that, they would have been wiped out, one by one. So, I had them open the hangar doors all the way and started the engines in the hangar. One spark would have blown up the whole place. We never tested it, there was no time. I looked at the other three pilots and they were just white with fear, but as the leader if you show fear your mission is doomed to failure. It worked, and we did our takeoff towards the sea. My number two was Modi Alon, my number three was Ezir Weizman who became head of the air force later, and then president. Number four was a South African kid named Eddie Cohan. I had told them that I wanted them flying abreast of me, to the right. Not below me and not behind me because they were going to be shooting at the leader and hit whoever was dragging behind. The steeper the dive, the more accurate your aim, and I learned from flying the SBDs (Dauntless dive bombers) that if you wanted to do a steep dive, you've got to do an upside split S down. That's how it got started and my number four got hit right away, which was rough because we were like brothers. When I was in the Pacific when somebody got hit, there were 50 planes to take his place, and 50 pilots." There was no Plan B, these four pilots were all there was.

Lou said: "I must have lucked out because I hit a tanker and I only had one bomb… it was pure luck. It was the maximum effort at the minimum place, and a big fire started. Then I did cloverleafs back and forth strafing the column and then got out of there. That night our intelligence people intercepted a communication from the Egyptian commander to his headquarters in Cairo. It said 'we are heavily attacked by enemy aircraft and we are scattering'. They never moved one inch forward from that point. They moved to the southeast and joined up with the Jordanians.

"The Arabs were talking about how it was going to be a war of total annihilation, the likes of which hadn't been seen since Genghis Khan. I'd like to think I was born to be there for that precise moment in history when the entire Egyptian army was just 22 miles from Tel Aviv. It was luck… it's not that I'm better, smarter, or braver. It was my destiny." Today, Lou Lenart is known as 'the man who saved Tel Aviv'. That bridge where the Egyptian advance was halted is now called 'Ad Halom', which translates to 'up to here (and no further)'. ➤

> "… WITH TWO GUNS FIRING THROUGH THE PROP… WHEN IT DIDN'T SHOOT THE PROP OFF OR JAM, IT WAS A MONSTER; IN CZECHOSLOVAKIA THEY CALLED IT THE MULE."

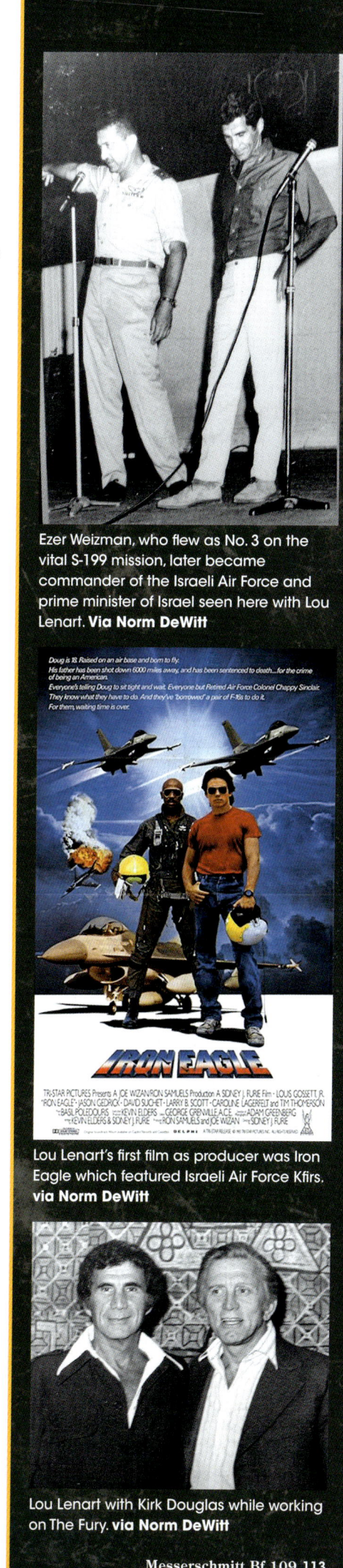

Ezer Weizman, who flew as No. 3 on the vital S-199 mission, later became commander of the Israeli Air Force and prime minister of Israel seen here with Lou Lenart. **Via Norm DeWitt**

Lou Lenart's first film as producer was Iron Eagle which featured Israeli Air Force Kfirs. **via Norm DeWitt**

Lou Lenart with Kirk Douglas while working on The Fury. **via Norm DeWitt**

RETIREMENT AND AFTERMATH

As the fighting progressed further, losses, to both accident and enemy action, were compounded by poor availability due to technical issues as there was little or no time for flight testing following the hasty assembly of each aircraft. On June 3, Lou's number two on the fateful raid, Modi Alon, a former RAF pilot, gained the type's first air-to-air kill. He intercepted a pair of Egyptian Douglas C-47 transport aircraft converted into makeshift bombers over Tel Aviv; the enemy had already made several raids on the town causing several civilian casualties and wide scale fear among the civilian population. Alon skilfully evaded a pair of enemy Spitfires and intercepted the bombers, destroying them both and causing much rejoicing on the ground; he added a Spitfire to his tally on June 18 but was killed when his aircraft crash landed following mechanical problems on October 16, 1948. The S-199's career in the Middle East lasted less than two years. Blighted by technical difficulties and an alarmingly high accident rate, the type's operational effectiveness was vastly overshadowed by its propaganda value. A single Israeli survivor is displayed at the Haterzim Air Force Museum while at the Prague Aviation museum visitors may view both an S-199 and its trainer variant.

Al Schwimmer, who had envisioned the entire Israeli operation, recently passed away in 2011 at age 94. Israeli president and pilot Ezer Weizman passed away in 2005. The last surviving pilot from those first missions is the founder of the Israeli Air Force, Lou Lenart, age 92. He went on to be a pilot for El Al, but quickly became bored… "like driving a bus". Lou became part of a Mossad operation to fly Jews from Baghdad in 1952, before moving into making films, eventually becoming the associate producer of the movie Iron Eagle. Later he was involved with the movies Iron Eagle II, Operation Thunderbolt, about the Entebbe rescue, and The Fury with Kirk Douglas. In March 2013, Lou begins filming a movie about how the Israeli air force destroyed the Iraqi nuclear facility in 1981. Number eight on that Iraq mission was Ilan Ramon, later killed when the Space Shuttle Columbia broke up on re-entry. Lou said: "He was a very close friend of mine. He called me a week before the launch and wanted me to be his guest there. I told him I'd watch him on television and I'd see him when he got back…

"The young pilots in the Israeli Air Force now are very interested, because they want to know how this mighty air force started. Man for man, they are now the best in the world because they've been fighting wars continually since 1948, and they can't afford to have anything less than the best… otherwise we're wiped out."

Today, the situation seems no closer to resolution than it was in 1948 when those four desperate Jewish pilots used a junkyard version of what had once been Nazi Germany's most successful fighter in a mission that saved the State of Israel. There could be no greater irony than that.

Aviation Classics would like to express our thanks to Lou Lenart for opening his archive to Norm DeWitt, and to Boris Yaro for allowing us to reproduce his paintings of the S-199 and its vital mission. ■ *Words: Norm DeWitt and Julian Humphries*

Above: Ilan Ramon's STS-107 mission patch. **via Norm DeWitt**

Colonel Ilan Ramon became an astronaut, sadly he died when the space shuttle Columbia broke up on re-entry on February 1, 2003. **via Norm DeWitt**

Left: Lou Lenart and his daughter with the Israeli Air Force Museum's S-199, D-120. **via Norm DeWitt**

Right: Lenart recently giving a talk in Israel about the 1948 air operations. **via Norm DeWitt**

Cut down on your excess baggage...

Aviation Classics is now available to read on your favourite device, including the iPad, iPhone, iPod touch, Samsung Galaxy Tab and Kindle Fire*. Buy the latest issue anywhere in the world on the day it is published, or catch up on back issues at a fraction of the cost of the paper edition.

Simply search for 'Aviation Classics' in the Apple App store or Android Market. The Aviation Classics app is priced at £2.49 (US$3.99) which includes one free issue, further issues are priced at £3.99 (US$5.99). A one year (four issue) subscription is available for £10.49 (US$14.99).

Direct download links - Apple: http://bit.ly/aviationipad
Android: http://bit.ly/aviationandroid
*Kindle Fire only available in the US

www.aviationclassics.co.uk

EMILS OVER THE ALPS

The Swiss Air Force had purchased 80 Messerschmitt Bf 109E-1s and E-3s in 1939 and was to keep these fighters in frontline service until December 1949. These aircraft patrolled and defended Swiss airspace throughout the Second World War, being painted in bright red and white identification stripes in the latter stages of the conflict.

A pair of Messerschmitt Bf 109G-2s of the Finnish Air Force. **Editor's collection**

The 109 abroad

Messerschmitt's fighter in service with other countries

As already covered in this magazine, the Messerschmitt Bf 109 was produced by both Spain and Czechoslovakia under licence and saw postwar service with both those air forces and that of Israel. However, there were 10 other nations that operated the type, including the short lived air force of the Slovakian Republic.

A Messerschmitt Bf 109G-2 of the Bulgarian Air Force. **Editor's collection**

BULGARIA

At the beginning of the Second World War in 1939, the Bulgarian Air Force placed a number of orders for more modern combat aircraft to supplement its fleet of largely ex-Czechoslovak Air Force aircraft it had purchased after Czechoslovakia had been occupied by the Third Reich. Among these were 12 Bf 109E-3s which formed the only really modern Bulgarian fighter unit up to the time the country entered the war as a German ally in 1941. From this small start, up until mid-1944, a total of 145 Bf 109E-3, G-2s, G-6s and G-10s were purchased, equipping the third and fourth regiments of the 6th Fighter Regiment. Throughout 1942 to 1944, these fighters defended Sofia and other important targets against Allied bombing raids and also intercepted attacks aimed at the Ploesti oilfields in Romania. On September 9, 1944, a pro-Allied coup in Bulgaria meant its remaining Bf 109Gs were used against the Luftwaffe in Serbia, Macedonia and Greece in co-operation with the Soviet 17th Air Army. By the end of 1944, the last Bulgarian Bf 109Gs were unserviceable due to lack of spares.

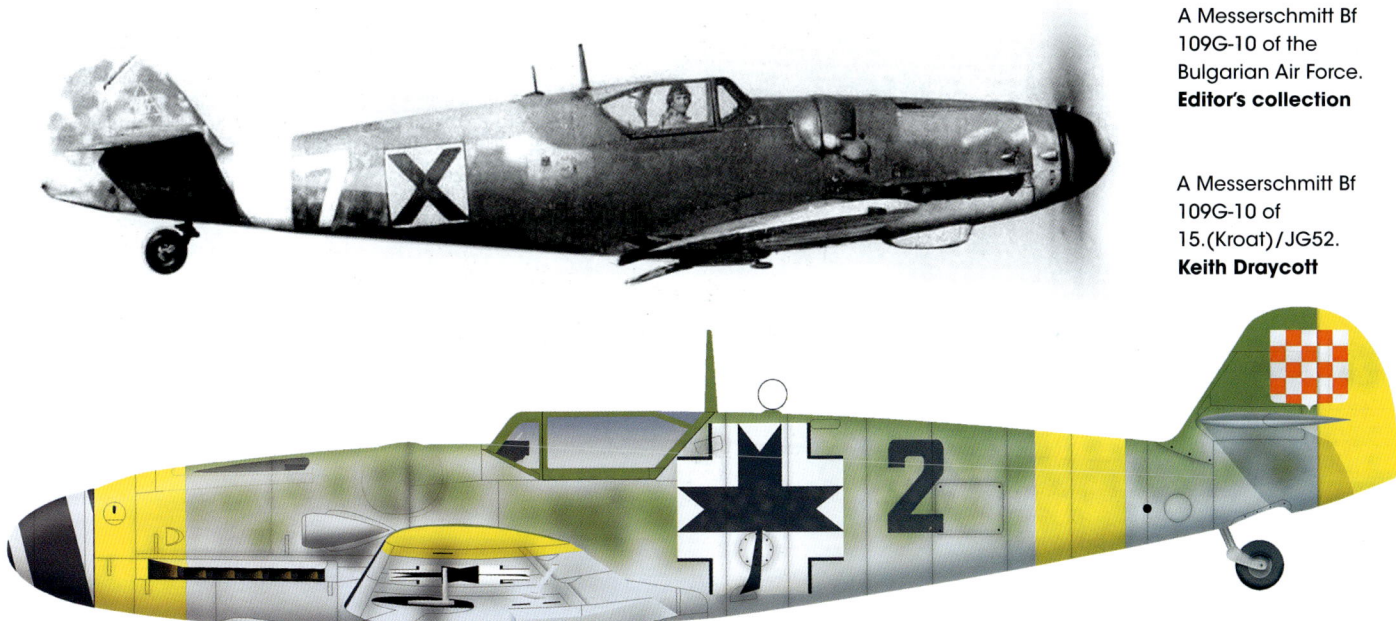

A Messerschmitt Bf 109G-10 of the Bulgarian Air Force. **Editor's collection**

A Messerschmitt Bf 109G-10 of 15.(Kroat)/JG52. **Keith Draycott**

CROATIA

The air force of the Independent State of Croatia, Zrakoplovstvo Nezavisne Države Hrvatske, or ZNDH, was founded with the support of Germany in April 1941 and was to be equipped with a variety of types, including the Bf 109E-4 and F-2, many of which served on the Eastern Front as the Kroatische Luftwaffen Legion of the Luftwaffe. The Croatian Bf 109 pilots were formed into a Staffel of the hightly successful Jagdgeschwader 52, known as 15.(Kroat)/JG52. Following the Allied invasion of southern Italy in September 1943, most of the ZNDH units returned to Croatia to defend against the growing Allied air threat in the region. The older fighter types operated by the ZNDH units were replaced with 21 new Bf 109Gs by the end of 1944, equipping the First Fighter Squadron.

Deliveries continued into 1945 including some of the latest Bf 109K models which allowed the Croatian pilots to meet the Allied fighters on near equal terms for the first time. Aside from attacking USAF and RAF raiders in its area, the ZNDH was also active against the Yugoslav Partisan Forces of Marshal Tito. The last Bf 109Ks were delivered on April 25, 1945, which was also the day the last victories by Croatian Bf 109s were claimed when two RAF P-51 Mustangs were shot down by Captain Bencetic and Lieutenant Jelak. Despite not receiving modern fighters until relatively late in the war, there were a number of Croatian aces who scored highly due to their extensive service on the Eastern Front with the Luftwaffe, including Lieutenant Major Mato Dukovac who was credited with 44 victories and Lieutenant Cvitan Galic with 38.

FINLAND

Four squadrons of the Finnish Air Force were to operate the Bf 109 during the Continuation War against the Soviet Union, Nos 24, 28, 30 and 34. These units were tremendously effective in combat, claiming 667 confirmed victories for the loss of only 34 Bf 109s and 23 pilots in combat and 16 further aircraft in accidents. The Continuation War was to last from June 25, 1941, to September 19, 1944, with the Finns pushing the Soviet Army back to their prewar borders by September 1941. For the next two and half years, the Finns were content to hold their original territory until the Soviet Union began a counterattack on June 9, 1944, which was fought to a standstill by the Finnish Army along the line occupied at the end of the first Winter War by early July 1944.

A ceasefire ended the war on September 5, followed by an Armistice on September 19. The war was not officially ended until the Paris peace treaty was signed in 1947. With the realisation that the Soviet Union was building up for its counterattack, in 1943 the Finnish Air Force ordered 162 Bf 109s, including 48 G-2s, 111 G-6s and three G-8s. Three of these, two G-6s and a G-8, were destroyed during delivery but the remaining 159 began to arrive on March 13, 1943. Known as the Mersu in Finnish service, the same nickname as Mercedes-Benz cars, the last were delivered on August 20, 1944, just prior to the Armistice. The last of the 102 Finnish Bf 109s that survived the war did not leave service until early 1954, when they were replaced with the first jet aircraft. Major Erkki Heinilä made the last operational flight in MT-507 on March 13, 1954. The Finnish Air Force had a number of high scoring aces among its Bf 109 pilots, including Ilmari Juutilainen, who, with a score of 94 confirmed victories, is the highest scoring non-German fighter pilot of the Second World War.

HUNGARY

The Royal Hungarian Air Force (Magyar Királyi Honvéd Légiero or MKHL) had received three Bf 109D-1s and 50 E-3s and E-4s between 1938 to the early days of the Second World War. Deliveries were clandestine initially, as the country was forbidden from having an air force by the Treaty of Trianon, signed between Hungary and the Allies in 1920 after the First World War. From October 1942, the first Hungarian Bf 109F-4 fighter unit was established, like that of the Croat Air Force, as part of the Luftwaffe's JG52 on the Eastern Front. Known as the 1./1. vadászszázad (fighter squadron), the Hungarian Bf 109Fs began combat operations on October 15, 1942. More units followed throughout 1943, equipping with the Bf 109F and G, again, fighting on the Eastern Front as part of the Luftwaffe. At the time, Hungarian home defence was conducted by licence built Reggiane Re.2000 Héja fighters, which began to be replaced by Bf 109G-6s from late 1943 onwards. The majority of these new fighters were built in the Hungarian Messerschmitt factory at Gyor and equipped the 101. Honi Légvédelmi Vadászrepülo ➤

MT-201, a Messerschmitt Bf 109G-2 of the Finnish Air Force. **Editor's collection**

A Messerschmitt Bf 109F-4 of the Hungarian Air Force. **Editor's collection**

Six Regia Aeronautica Messerschmitt Bf 109G-6s of the 150th Gruppo, 365 Squadriglia, on Sciacca airfield in Sicily. **Luigino Caliaro**

Osztály (101st Home Air Defence Fighter Wing). The G-6 was replaced in service by the G-10 and G-14 from November 1944, with the 101st Wing, or 'Red Pumas' as they were known, being forced to retreat into Germany in the face of the advancing Soviet Army during March 1945. The last combat victory for the Royal Hungarian Air Force occurred on April 17, 1945, when Senior Lieutenant Kiss shot down a Yak-9. On May 4, 1945, the Wing burned its remaining aircraft on Raffelding airfield in Austria to prevent them being captured by the advancing US Army. Altogether, the Royal Hungarian Air Force was supplied with 66 Bf 109Fs and more than 490 Bf 109Gs. The highest scoring Hungarian Bf 109 pilot was Szentgyörgyi Dezso, with 30 victories.

ITALY

The great Italian aviation photographer Luigino Caliaro has written this history of the Bf 109 in Italian service, and supplied the excellent historic photographs that accompany this piece.

Despite the fact that during the prewar period, the Regia Aeronautica had been considered one of the most modern and prepared air forces, an impression garnered by the series of impressive long distance tours and individual records which added lustre to Italian prestige, on the outbreak of the Second World War it found itself totally unprepared, with a limited number of aircraft available, few of which were effectively up to date.

Evidence of this is clear from the first few months of the war, when the Regia Aeronautica fighter fleet comprised three different types of fighter, characterised among other factors as having open cockpits and radial engines, the Fiat G 50, Macchi MC 200, and the Fiat CR42 biplane, aircraft inferior in terms of both performance and armament to the Spitfires and Hurricanes of the RAF. This technical inferiority was in part mitigated by the undoubted courage and capacities of the Italian pilots and the arrival in service of the Macchi MC 202, an aircraft of excellent flying performance but produced in small numbers that cannot be compared with British and German output.

However, in the early months of 1943, faced with a critical combat situation, the Italians turned to their German ally for assistance in the shape of aircraft of various types, among them the Bf 109 fighter. In reality, the Regia Aeronautica had already had an opportunity to try out the German fighter, when just before the beginning of the conflict four Bf 109Es were sent to Guidonia to be subjected to a extensive cycle of flight testing and comparisons, resulting in effusive and enthusiastic comments from the Italian pilots.

There was even a proposal submitted by the aeronautical section of the Alfa Romeo company to licence produce both the German airframe and its engine, but it was never followed up. It was therefore necessary to wait until the spring of 1943 to see the first Bf 109 in the colours of the Regia Aeronautica when the Germans supplied 122 aircraft. More specifically, these were 15 Bf 109F-4s previously utilised by the Luftwaffe in the Aegean sector, six Bf 109G-2s, 10 Bf 109G-3s and 91 Bf 106G-6s, almost all of the latter of new construction. The first unit of the Regia Aeronautica to receive the German fighter was the 150° Gruppo, composed of the 363a, 364a and 365a Squadriglia, and based at Sciacca in Sicily, followed shortly after by the 70a Squadriglia of the 23° Gruppo and by three Squadriglie of the 3° Gruppo, the 153a, 154a, and 155a.

It is also of note that in mid-May the 4° Stormo was also equipped with a few Bf 109Gs, but after only a month these aircraft were passed on to the 23° Gruppo of the 3° Stormo, based at Ciampino, being substituted by the first Macchi MC 205s. The Bf 109G of the 3° and 150° Gruppo were intensively utilised on the Sicilian front, and the first aerial victories obtained by the Italian fighters were recorded on May 31, 1943, by Tenente Ugo Drago and Tenente Giovanni Chiale, serving with the 363a Squadriglia. On June 9, Tenente Drago, flying Bf 109G-6 '363-7', obtained a second victory, downing the Spitfire V of Lt McMann of the USAAF 308th FS/ 31st FG. In a subsequent air combat during the afternoon, Tenente Drago was shot down by Allied aircraft, although he managed, after bailing out, to return to his base. The only confirmed victory recorded by the 3° Gruppo, however, was achieved by Sergente Maggiore Cavagliano, who shot down Spitfire V ER811 piloted by Sergeant Sheehan of 249 Squadron on June 13.

In July, despite intense activity as the Allies prepared to make landings in Sicily, problems caused by spare parts shortages reduced the overall availability levels of the aircraft, resulting in the complete cessation of activities in August. The only unit with serviceable machines in August was the 70a Squadriglia, based at Cerveteri and protecting the capital, Roma, but even this, at the time of the Armistice on September 8, could muster only a single aircraft in flying condition out of a little over 10 that were serviceable.

After the Armistice, a second phase of the history of the Messerschmitt in Italy commenced, as the Germans, from the middle of 1944, provided the ANR with around 200 Bf 109G-6, G-10, G-12, G-14, G-14AS and K-4 aircraft, which equipped, for various periods, the two fighter Gruppi and a third that was under formation. The first unit of the ANR to fly with the Bf 109G was the II Gruppo, based at Villafranca in late May 1944, which operated the aircraft in defence of the principal cities of Northern Italy from attack

A pair of Regia Aeronautica Messerschmitt Bf 109G-6s of the 150th Gruppo, 365 Squadriglia, on Sciacca airfield in Sicily. **Luigino Caliaro**

A Regia Aeronautica Messerschmitt Bf 109G-6 of the 150th Gruppo, 365 Squadriglia, on Sciacca airfield in Sicily. **Luigino Caliaro**

A close up of the squadron markings on a Messerschmitt Bf 109G-6 of the Regia Aeronautica's 150th Gruppo, 364 Squadriglia. **Luigino Caliaro**

An ANR Messerschmitt Bf 109G-10 of 3 Squadriglia of I Gruppo Caccia has its undercarriage tested at Lonate Pozzolo in March 1945. **Luigino Caliaro**

A close up of the nose markings on the Bf 109G-6 of Tenente Ermete Ferrero of 3 Squadriglia of 2 Gruppo of the ANR, Villafranca, November 1944. **Luigino Caliaro**

A Bf 109G-6 of 2 Gruppo of the ANR, Aviano, November 1944. **Luigino Caliaro**

Below: One of the unarmed Messerschmitt Bf 109E-7s purchased for evaluation by the Japanese Army Air Force. **Editor's collection**

by Allied bombers, deploying detachments of aircraft to various airfields.

After a period of grounding caused by a series of problems with the Germans, who attempted to take complete control of the activities of the aircraft and the personnel by incorporating them into the Luftwaffe, operations were resumed in the month of October, with the first combat victory being recorded on the 19th of the same month; the aircraft were continuously moved around the airfields in Northern Italy to escape the attacks of Allied aircraft. The Gruppo of the ANR equipped with the Bf 109G was the I Gruppo, formed in December 1943 under the command of Capitano Visconti, which replaced its Macchi MC 205s and Fiat G 55s with the first Bf 109Gs and Ks in February 1945 after its personnel had returned from Germany, where they had been sent to undergo training on the Me 163 Komet.

The activities of the I Gruppo were, however, extremely limited due to the deterioration of the operational situation for the ANR, and there was a complete cessation of operations at the end of April. The critical wartime situation of mid-1944 resulted in the decision to cease the formation of the III Gruppo, which, although reorganised in early 1945, never ever became operational, as its allocation of aircraft never arrived, with the exception of a few Bf 109Gs delivered just a few days before the cessation of hostilities. In the postwar period 11 Bf 109Gs were recovered by Italian manufacturer Agusta, which offered to return at least half of them to operational condition in order to provide an initial nucleus of aircraft for the new Aeronautica Militare. Nevertheless, the conditions of the Armistice, coupled with a lack of spares, resulted in the decision to scrap the remaining machines.

The importance of this aircraft to the Italians is illustrated by the fact that fewer than 400 fighters of the 'Series 5' were constructed (the Macchi MC 205, Fiat G 55 and Reggiane RE 2005) while the Germans, in the period 43-45, provided Italy with some 300 examples of the Bf 109 in its various versions.

JAPAN

Five unarmed Bf 109E-7s were purchased by the Japanese Army Air Force for evaluation against the fighters then in service, the Nakajima Ki-43 Hayabusa, Nakajima Ki-44 Shoki and the Kawasaki Ki-61 Hien. The Daimler-Benz DB 601 engine was built under licence and fitted to the Ki-61, but no interest was evinced in acquiring the Bf 109 itself.

ROMANIA

The Royal Romanian Air Force (Fortele Aeriene Regale ale României or FARR) received Bf 109s from German factories, but like the Hungarians, also flew licence built examples, produced by IAR at Brasov. A total of 75 Bf 109G-6s were produced locally, along with over 235 German built Bf 109G-2s, G-4s, G-6s and G-8s. Prior to the G models, some 69 Bf 109E-4s and seven Bf 109Fs had been supplied to the country. Most of these operated on the Eastern Front and over the Black Sea in their own units, under Luftwaffe command, between June 22, 1941, and August 22, 1944. The FARR fighter force also cooperated with the Bulgarian Air Force in patrolling the Black Sea and protecting the Ploesti oilfields and Bucharest against Allied air attacks. On August 23, 1944, King Michael I launched a royal coup, moving Romania on to the Allied side and assisting the invading Soviet Forces.

The FARR fought against the Luftwaffe and Hungarian Air Force in both Slovakia and Transylvania, but a number of Romanian pilots remained in Luftwaffe volunteer units until the end of the war. Several Romanian pilots became famous aces, the most successful being Captain Prince Constantin Cantacuzino with 68 confirmed victories and Captains Horia Agarici and Alexandru Serbanescu, both of whom shot down 60 enemy aircraft. ➤

SLOVAK REPUBLIC

Interestingly, the Bf 109 served with two air forces in Slovakia, one allied with Germany, and one fighting it. The Slovak Air Force (Slovenské vzdušné zbrane or SVZ), was, like the Croatian Air Force, the air arm of an artificial state created by Germany after its annexation of the country. The SVZ received 30 Bf 109Es which were later replaced by the same number of G-6s. Their first combat operations were against the Hungarian Air Force during the reoccupation of Carpatho-Ruthenia, territory taken from Hungary by the Treaty of Trianon, in March 1939. Between 1939 and 1945, the SVZ supported the Luftwaffe in the invasion of Poland and then in operations on the Eastern Front. It was also responsible for the air defence of Bratislava and strategic targets inside the Slovak Republic. On August 29, 1944, the Slovak military resistance organised an uprising to fight against Germany. Three Bf 109G-6s were captured by the resistance and used against the Luftwaffe, before the resistance forces were overrun by the German Army in October 1944. The remaining insurgent air units withdrew to Soviet held airfields in Poland, joining the 1st Czechoslovak Combined Air Division which assisted in the liberation of Poland and Czechoslovakia in 1945.

SWITZERLAND

Ten BF 109Ds were purchased in 1938 to form a fighter force to defend the neutral country's airspace. A further 80 Bf 109E-3s were purchased to bolster this force in April 1939, when it seemed a war in Europe was inevitable. Eight more fighters were licence built by Doflug, largely constructed from the spare parts supplied with the original order. Four more Bf 109s, two Fs and two Gs, were acquired during the war after they landed in Swiss territory, and 12 more G-6s were supplied by Germany in April 1944, in return for the destruction of a Bf 110G night fighter and its radar which had made an emergency landing in Switzerland. These 12 aircraft proved to have numerous defects, and were withdrawn from service in 1948; however, the earlier Bf 109Es proved reliable and remained as front line fighters until December 1949. The Swiss Bf 109s intercepted a number of Luftwaffe raids that entered Swiss airspace during the war, shooting down 12 German aircraft in the process. With the increase in Allied air presence in the area, the Bf 109s were painted with large red and white stripes in 1944 to prevent them being mistaken for Luftwaffe aircraft.

YUGOSLAVIA

Between 1939 and 1941, 83 Bf 109E-3s were delivered to the Royal Yugoslav Air Force, but kept short of spare parts, a deliberate tactic on the part of Germany. In April 1941, Germany invaded Yugoslavia, the Yugoslav Bf 109Es meeting their Luftwaffe counterparts in combat. After 12 days of intense combat, only a few of the Yugoslav aircraft survived, many being lost in combat as well as those destroyed by their crews to prevent their capture. The remaining aircraft and few spares were distributed between the air forces of Bulgaria, Romania and the newly formed state of Croatia. Near the end of the war in early 1945, the Yugoslav Partisan forces under Marshal Tito included air units trained and equipped in Britain, known as the Balkan Air Force under RAF control; others were trained and equipped by the Soviet Union, and a number using captured Luftwaffe and Croatian aircraft. Some 17 captured Bf 109Gs were supplemented by additional aircraft purchased from Bulgaria and operated by the newly formed Yugoslav Air Force (Jugoslovensko Ratno Vazduhoplovstvo or JRV) as the equipment of the 172nd Fighter Regiment until 1952.

ALLIED USE

A number of different version of the Bf 109 were captured by the Allies during the war and flown for evaluation purposes against British, Russian and US fighters. ■

Words: Tim Callaway

A Messerschmitt Bf 109E-3 of the Swiss Air Force. **Editor's collection**

A Messerschmitt Bf 109E-3 of the Swiss Air Force. **Keith Draycott**

A Messerschmitt Bf 109G-2 of the Yugoslav Air Force, now on display in the Belgrade Aeronautical Museum. **Keith Draycott**

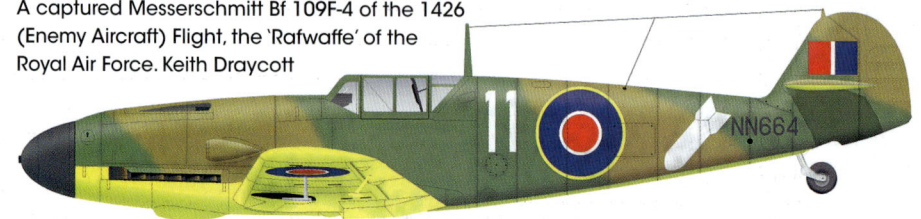

A captured Messerschmitt Bf 109F-4 of the 1426 (Enemy Aircraft) Flight, the 'Rafwaffe' of the Royal Air Force. **Keith Draycott**

 # Back Issues

From £6.99 PER BACK ISSUE!

MISSING A BACK ISSUE? Fear not, we've got a few left for you to complete your collection of the Aviation Classics series, but remember, when they're gone, they're gone, so get your order in soon! Order today: www.classicmagazines.co.uk or call 01507 529529.

www.classicmagazines.co.uk

ISSUE 9 – F-86 SABRE

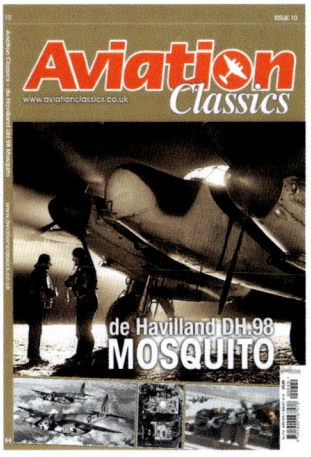
ISSUE 10 – MOSQUITO

ISSUE 11 – HARRIER

ISSUE 12 – F4U CORSAIR

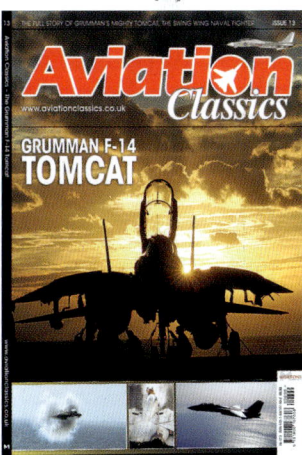
ISSUE 13 – GRUMMAN F-14 TOMCAT

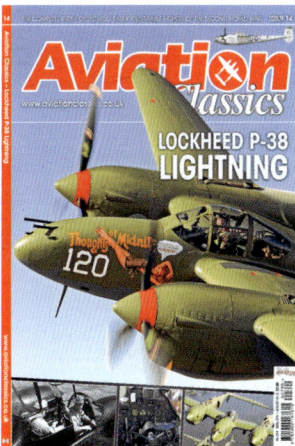
ISSUE 14 – LOCKHEED P-38 LIGHTNING

ISSUE 15 – THE HAWKER HURRICANE

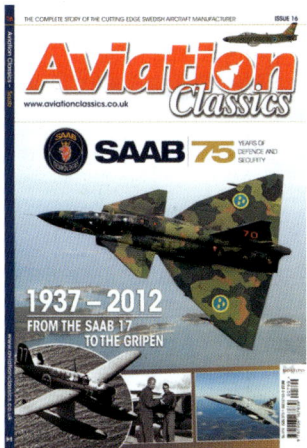
ISSUE 16 – SAAB

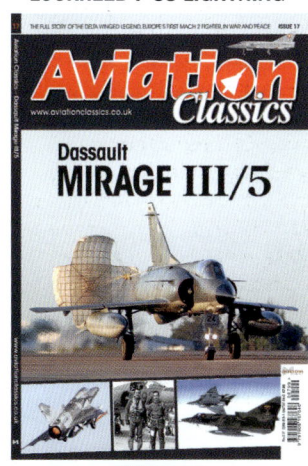
ISSUE 17 – MIRAGE III/5

www.classicmagazines.co.uk

BACK ISSUES

Title............. Forename.............
Surname.............
Address.............
.... Postcode.............
Email.............
Telephone.............
Are you a subscriber? ☐ YES ☐ NO

Mortons Media Group may wish to send you details of other special offers and promotions in the future that we think may be of interest to you. We will NOT pass your details on to any other third party. If, however, you do NOT wish to be contacted, please tick here ☐

I wish to order the following back issues:.............
Free P&P for UK. For EU and ROW visit www.classicmagazines.co.uk
☐ I WISH TO PAY BY CHEQUE
I enclose my cheque for £............. (payable to Mortons Media Group Ltd)
☐ I WISH TO PAY BY DEBIT/CREDIT CARD
☐ EUROCARD ☐ VISA ☐ AMERICAN EXPRESS ☐ DELTA ☐ MAESTRO
Card number:
Valid from:............. Expires:.............
Security code:............. Issue number (MAESTRO ONLY):.............
Card holder:
Signature:

FINEST HOUR ART

'60TH FIS AEROBATIC TEAM'

Aviation artist Adam Tooby has produced some beautiful limited edition A2 fine art prints from his work especially for *Aviation Classics*. These stunning images are perfect for framing or the perfect gift for the aerophile in your life. To order your limited edition *Aviation Classics* prints, complete the form on the opposite page, or a photocopy of it, and send it along with your cheque to Finest Hour Art. Alternatively, you can order your prints online at
www.finesthourart.com/aviationclassics

'JAIL BREAKERS'

'TO THE RESCUE'

'HIDE & SEEK'

'IRAQI FREEDOM'

'FLEEING HAWKS'

'THE CHECKERBOARDERS'

'DEATH RATTLERS'

'THE POLKA-DOTS'

'MARGE'

'YIPPEE!'

'FLYING CAN OPENERS'

'DESERT DELTAS'

'FIRST MIG DOWN'

MESSERSCHMITT Bf 109

CHECK SIX

DESERT DUEL

BLACK TULIP

EMILS OVER THE ALPS

FINEST HOUR ART LIMITED EDITION FINE ART PRINTS
WWW.FINESTHOURART.COM

Title .... Forename ....

Surname ....

Address ....

....

.... Postcode ....

Email ....

Telephone ....

Are you a subscriber? ❏ YES   ❏ NO

❏ I WISH TO PAY BY CHEQUE

I enclose my cheque for £............................ (payable to Finest Hour Art)

Mortons Media Group may wish to send you details of other special offers and promotions in the future that we think may be of interest to you. We will NOT pass your details on to any other third party. If, however, you do NOT wish to be contacted, please tick here ❏

Send to: Finest Hour Art, PO Box 265, Winsford, Cheshire, CW7 3FL
www.finesthourart.com/aviationclassics

Please send me:	Price	Qty	Total
60th FIS AEROBATIC TEAM	£39.95		£
TO THE RESCUE	£39.95		£
JAIL BREAKERS	£39.95		£
HIDE & SEEK	£39.95		£
IRAQI FREEDOM	£39.95		£
FLEEING HAWKS	£39.95		£
THE CHECKERBOARDERS	£39.95		£
DEATH RATTLERS	£39.95		£
THE POLKA-DOTS	£39.95		£
YIPPEE	£39.95		£
MARGE	£39.95		£
HURRICANE FORCE	£39.95		£
FLYING CAN OPENERS	£39.95		£
DESERT DELTAS	£39.95		£
FIRST MiG DOWN	£39.95		£
CHECK SIX	£39.95		£
DESERT DUEL	£39.95		£
BLACK TULIP	£39.95		£
EMILS OVER THE ALPS	£39.95		£
P&P	£5.95	1	£5.95
Grand Total			£

Survivors
The Bf 109 and its derivatives in the air and on display.

Altogether 33,984 Messerschmitt Bf 109s of all types were built, an astounding number which makes it the most produced fighter aircraft in aviation history. Despite this record, only a few remain in existence today.

The disparity between the number of 109s produced and the number surviving can be explained because of high losses caused by three distinct factors. First of these was the tricky handling of the type, mostly caused by its narrow track undercarriage and the increasingly powerful engines fitted to it. It is estimated by some historians that perhaps as many as a third of all 109s built were lost in landing accidents. Secondly, the difficult conditions the aircraft were operated under, such as in the desert and on the Russian front, caused their own hazards from the likes of sand ingestion and frozen or waterlogged airfields. Lastly, this was a combat aircraft, designed to go in harm's way. Operational losses were the inevitable consequence of this, reducing their numbers still further.

Bf 109E-3 1190 is on display in this diorama setting at the Imperial War Museum Duxford. **Constance Redgrave**

AUSTRALIA
Bf 109G-6/U4 163824 (G-SMIT, ex-NF+FY), Australian War Memorial, Canberra.
Bf 109G-2 14798 (VH-EIN), ex-GJ+QP, ex 8./JG 5 Black 10, Christopher Kelly, Seaforth.

AUSTRIA
Bf 109G-14 784993 ex-IV./JG 53 White 13, Aviaticum Wiener Neustadt.

BELGIUM
AIRWORTHY
HA-1112-M1L c/n 201 C.4K-131 (OO-MAF), movie: Battle of Britain, ex-Victory Air Museum, White 1 Sabine, Eric Vormezeele Collection, Brasschaat.

STORED OR UNDER RESTORATION
Bf 109F-4 w/rn unknown, ex-JG 5 White 4.

BRAZIL
Bf 109G-2, 14256, Yellow 14, Wings of a Dream Museum, São Carlos.

CANADA
AIRWORTHY
Bf 109E-3 3579 (CF-EML), ex-JG 2 White 14, ex-Bf 109E-7 4/JG 5 White 7 – crashed August 2, 1942, The Russell Group, Ontario.

ON DISPLAY
Bf 109F-4 10132, Canada Aviation and Space Museum, Rockcliffe, Ontario.
HA-1112-M1L c/n 164 C.4K-114, ex-471 Squadron 471-28, ex-7 Squadron 7-82, movie: Battle of Britain, on temporary display at the Western Canada Aviation Museum.

CZECH REPUBLIC
S-199 199178, UC-25, Aviation Museum – Kbely, Prague.
CS-199 199565, UC-26, Aviation Museum – Kbely, Prague.

FINLAND
ON DISPLAY
Bf 109F-4 7108, ex-NE+ML, ex-9./JG 5, Central Finland Aviation Museum, Tikkakoski.
Bf 109G-6 14743, ex-RJ+SM, ex-Finnish AF MT-208, Finnish Aviation Museum.
Bf 109G-6/U2 165227, ex-BV+UE, ex-Finnish AF MT-452 Yellow 4, Suomen Ilmailumuseo, Utti.
Bf 109G-6/Y 167271, ex-VO+GI, ex-Finnish AF MT-507, Yellow 0, Central Finland Aviation Museum (FAM), Tikkakoski.

STORED OR UNDER RESTORATION
Bf 109E-3 3285, ex-Bf 109E-7, ex-4./JG 5 Black 12, White 4, now Yellow 2, Finnish AF Museum, Tikkakoski.

FRANCE
STORED OR UNDER RESTORATION
Bf 109G-6 26129 ex-RV+IS, ex-II./JG 54 Black 3, Aéronautique Provençale.

GERMANY
AIRWORTHY
Bf 109G-10 w/n unknown (D-FDME), Black 2, EADS/Messerschmitt Foundation.
HA-1112-M1L c/n 139 C4K-75 (D-FWME), movie: Battle of Britain Yellow 11, now Red 7, Messerschmitt Air Company, re-engined with DB 605.
HA-1112-M1L c/n 156 C.4K-87 (D-FMBB), FM+BB, EADS/Messerschmitt Foundation, rebuilt with DB 605.

ON DISPLAY
Bf 109E-1 790, ex-J/88/2 (Condor Legion) 6-106, ex-Bf 109E-3, ex-Spanish AF C4E-106, Deutsches Museum, Munich.
Bf 109E-3 1407, ex-2./JG 77 Black 2, ex-Bf 109E-4, ex-14/JG 77, Red 5, Deutsches Technikmuseum, Berlin.
Bf 109G-2 trop 14753, ex-1./JG 27, White 3, Luftfahrtmuseum, Hannover-Laatzen.
Bf 109G-4 19310, ex-BH+XN, ex-4./JG 52 White 3 Nesthäkchen – crashed March 20, 1943, Technikmuseum Speyer.
HA-1109-K1L C.4J, Yellow 4 Luftwaffen Museum, Gatow, rebuilt as Bf 109G-2 with DB 605.
HA-1109-K1L c/n 54 C.4J, Messerschmitt Museum, Manching.
HA-1112-M1L c/n 194 C.4K-134, movie: Battle of Britain, ex-Victory Air Museum, on limited display at Wittmundhafen AB, marked as Black 12, rebuilt with DB 605 engine.
HA-1112-M1L c/n 228 C.4K-170 (N170BG), movie: Battle of Britain, movie: Patton (as P-51B) 743652, Yellow 4, Auto und Technik Museum, Sinsheim, rebuilt with DB 605 engine as a G-6.
HA-1112-M1L c/n 213 C.4K-1 (D-FEHD), Black 15, Messerschmitt Foundation.

STORED OR UNDER RESTORATION
Bf 109B/V10a 1010 (D-IAKO), Oberschleißheim, Munich.
Bf 109F-2 8993, ex GC + KQ, ex-2./JG 3, ex-Bf 109F-4, ex-JG 54 White 2, ex-9/III JG 5 Yellow 3 (pilot Obgfr. Eugen Britz) - crashed April 3, 1943.
Bf 109G-2 13605, Yellow 12.
Bf 109G-6 410077 (VH-BFG), ex-RK+FY, ex-IV./JG 54.

ISRAEL
S-199 782358, ex-Israel AF, D 112 Israeli Air Force Museum, Hatzerim Air Force Base.

Bf 109E-3 4101 on display in the Battle of Britain Hall at the RAF Museum Hendon. **Constance Redgrave**.

That there are as many surviving airframes as there are is a result of the postwar use of the type by the Spanish and other air forces. Many of the Merlin-engined Hispano built HA-1112s have been preserved in flying condition, several have been re-engined with the original Daimler-Benz inverted V-12s such as those of the EADS Heritage Flight. These re-engined aircraft are also to be found on static display in museums around the world, the basic airframe behind the engine changing surprisingly little between the production lines.

A flying display by a DB engined 109 is a tremendously powerful thing to witness. The speed, grace and sheer performance of the shark-like fighter is breathtaking, showing why it was still successful as a fighter against much later, more advanced designs. There is a powerful presence about this aircraft, perhaps a shadow cast by the dark political elements of its history, or perhaps simply because it was such a dangerous opponent, its reputation seems embodied in its sleek lines.

Other fighters from the period are as aesthetically pleasing in shape, or can outperform the 109 in some aspects of its performance envelope, but there are none that match its implacable sense of deadly purpose. As Cassidian test pilot Klaus Plaza so eloquently puts it, with the biggest smile on his face: "This is the bad guy!" Aside from its superb performance, there is another unique element to the 109 in flight, the sound of the DB 600 series engine. Many have described the sound of a Rolls-Royce Merlin to be music to the ears, an evocative and emotional sound, which it certainly is. The DB engine has a completely different tone, there is a deep, snarling growl quite unlike the Merlin which seems to suit the dangerous presence of the aircraft extremely well. The combination of the two elements produces a flying display of incomparable power. ➤

NETHERLANDS
Bf 109G-5 15343, ex-5./JG 53, Black 11, Aviation Museum at Seppe, Breda.
Bf 109G-6 15678 ex-9./JG 54 Brown 7 – crashed July 1943, fuselage only at the Atlantic Wall Museum.

NORWAY
STORED OR UNDER RESTORATION
Bf 109G-2/R1 13470, ex-CI+KS, ex-8./JG 5 White 4, Norsk Luftfartsmuseum, Bodo.
Bf 109G-1/R2 14141, ex-DG+UF, ex-2./JG 5 Black 6, Sola.

POLAND
Bf 109G-6 163306, ex-RQ+DR, ex-JGr. West Red 3 – crashed May 28, 1944, Fundacja Polskie Orły, Warszawa.

STORED OR UNDER RESTORATION
Bf 109E-3 1185, ex-Bf 109E-6, Lotnictwa Astronautyki Museum, Krakow.

RUSSIA
Bf 109G-2 14658, ex-KG-WF, ex-6./JG 5 Yellow 2, Museum of the Air Forces of the Northern Fleet, Severomorsk.
Bf 109G-6 411768 ex-FN+RX, ex-RW+ZI, ex-II./JG 5 Black 1, Vadim Zadorozny Technical Museum, Moscow.

STORED OR UNDER RESTORATION
Bf 109F-4/Z 7504, ex-7./JG 3 White 10 (pilot Fw. Rudolf Berg) – crashed March 28, 1943.
Bf 109G-2 13427, ex-9./JG 5 Yellow 2.

SERBIA
Bf 109G-2 14792, ex-GJ+QJ, ex-Yugoslavian AF 9663 63, Yugoslavian Aviation Museum, Belgrade.

SOUTH AFRICA
Bf 109E-3 1289, ex-SH+FA, ex-2./JG 26 (Schlageter) Red 2, South African National Museum of Military History, Johannesburg.
Bf 109F-2 trop, unknown Werknr, ex-I./JG 27 White 6, South African National Museum of Military History, Johannesburg.

SPAIN
HA-1109-K1L c/n 56 C.4J-10, ex-94 Squadron, 94-28, Museo del Aire, Madrid.
HA-1112-M1L c/n 211 C.4K-148, ex-471 Squadron, 471-23, Museo del Aire, Madrid.

SWITZERLAND
Bf 109E-3 2242, ex-Swiss AF J-355, Swiss Air Force Museum, Dubendorf.

UNITED KINGDOM
AIRWORTHY
HA-1112-M1L c/n 67 C.4K-31 (G-AWHE), movie: Battle of Britain Red 8, Yellow 14, Spitfire Ltd, Humberside Airport, maintained and operated by the Historic Aircraft Company, Duxford.
HA-1112-M1L c/n 172 C.4K-102 (G-BWUE), movie: Battle of Britain Red 7, now Yellow 10, Historic Flying Ltd.

ON DISPLAY
Bf 109E-3 1190, ex-Bf109E-4/N, ex-4./JG 26 White 4, Imperial War Museum Duxford.
Bf 109E-3 4101, ex-GH+DX, ex-6./JG 52 Yellow 8, ex-2/JG51 Black 12, ex-RAF DG200, ex-No. 1426 Flight, RAF, used in Battle of Britain film, Black 12, RAF Museum Hendon.
Bf 109G-2 trop 10639 (G-USTV), ex-PG+QJ, ex-III./JG 77 Black 6, ex-3 Squadron RAAF CV-V, ex-RAF RN228 No.1426 Flight, Black 6, RAF Museum Hendon.
Bf 109E-4 4853, ex-2./JG 51, wreck on display at the Kent Battle of Britain Museum, Hawkinge.

STORED OR UNDER RESTORATION
Bf 109E-1 Wknr unknown, ex-Spanish AF C4E-88, Robs Lamplough, Hungerford.
Bf 109E-1 854, Charleston Aviation Services.
Bf 109E-3 1983, ex-5./JG 5 Red ?, Charleston Aviation Services, Colchester.
Bf 109E-3 3523, ex-CS+AJ, ex-Bf 109E-7, ex-5/JG 5 Red 6, Jim Pearce, Sussex.
Bf 109E-3 4034 (G-CDTI), ex-1/JG 77, ex-8./JG 53 Black 5, Black 6 – crashed 11 February 1940, Rare Aero Ltd, Jersey.
Bf 109F-4 7485, ex-9./JG 5 Black 1, Charleston Aviation Services.
Bf 109F-4 8347, ex-6./JG 54 Yellow 10, Charleston Aviation Services.
Bf 109G-2 15458, Charleston Aviation Services.
Bf 109G-6 15458, ex-8./JG 1 Black 10, ex-III./JG 1, CW Tomkins Ltd.

UNITED STATES
AIRWORTHY
Bf 109E-3 1342 (N342FH), ex-6./JG 51 Yellow 8 (Pilot: Eduard Hemmerling) – crashed: July 29, 1940, Yellow 8, Flying Heritage Collection, Everett, Washington.
Bf 109G-14 610937 (N109EV), ex-Bf 109G-10/U-4, ex-Bulgarian AF, Ex-Yugoslavian AF 9664, 172 Group / 83rd SQ 44, Evergreen Aviation Museum, McMinnville, Oregon.
HA-1112-M1L c/n 234 C.4K-169 (N109W), movie: Battle of Britain Red 5, Harold Kindsvater, Castle Air Force Base, California.
HA-1112-M1L c/n 235 C.4K-172 (N109GU), movie: Battle of Britain, ex-Victory Air Museum, Cavanaugh Flight Museum, Addison, Texas. ➤

ON DISPLAY

Bf 109E-7 5975, ex-6./JG 5 Yellow 4 – shot down May 10, 1942, Mighty Eighth Air Force Museum, Savannah, Georgia.

Bf 109G-6 trop 160163, ex-KT+LL, ex-3./JG 4 Yellow 4, ex-USAAF FE-496, White 2, National Air & Space Museum, Washington DC.

Bf 109G-6 610824 (N109MS), ex-II./JG 52 Black 2, ex-USAAF FE-124, T2-124, Blue 4, National Museum of the United States Air Force, Wright-Patterson AFB, Ohio.

Bf 109G-10/U4 611943, ex-II./JG 52 Yellow 13, ex-USAAF FE-122, T2-122 Yellow 13, Planes of Fame, Valle, Arizona.

Bf 109G-14, ex-II./JG300 Red 3, restored by Sandy Air Corp, National WWII Museum, New Orleans, Louisiana.

HA-1112-M1L c/n 120 C.4K-77 (N700E), Yellow 3, Planes of Fame, Chino, California.

HA-1112-M1L c/n 171 C.4K-100 (N76GE), ex-71 Squadron, 71-9, movie: Battle of Britain Red 13, C.4K-19 71-9 Kalamazoo Aviation History Museum, Portage, Michigan.

HA-1112-M1L c/n 186 C.4K-122 (N109J), movie: Battle of Britain Yellow 7, Museum of Flight, Seattle, Washington, rebuilt as a Bf 109E with DB 601 engine.

HA-1112-M1L c/n 193 C.4K-130 (N90602), movie: Battle of Britain, Tillamook Air Museum, Tillamook, Oregon.

HA-1112-M1L c/n 199 C.4K-127 (N109BF), movie: Battle of Britain – Hurricane Ml-S, ex-Edwards Collection, Yellow 1, EAA Aviation Museum, Oshkosh Wisconsin.

STORED OR UNDER RESTORATION

Bf 109E-3 2023, ex-Bf 109E-7, ex-8./JG 5 Black 9 (pilot Ofw. Walter Sommer) – crashed May 27, 1943, Military Aviation Museum, Virginia Beach, Virginia.

Bf 109F-4 8461, ex-5./JG 27, Malcolm Laing.

Bf 109F-4 10144, ex-6./JG 5 Yellow 7 (pilot Fw. Albert Brunner) – crashed September 5, 1942, Air Assets International, Colorado.

Bf 109G-2 10394, ex-6./JG 5 Yellow 2 (pilot Fw. Erwin Fahldieck) – crashed April 29, 1943, Malcolm Laing, Texas.

Bf 109G-2 13500, ex-II./JG 54 Red 4.

I witnessed this as Klaus ran in to begin his display in Berlin. Everybody on the airfield stopped what they were doing to watch and listen. Even now, the 109 causes a stir, an emotional reaction, partly through its political history, partly by its sheer presence. I would prefer to think that after so many years, the latter is beginning to outweigh the former; that a display today is a fitting memorial to those who flew and maintained such a remarkable piece of aviation history.

As ever, the list of aircraft here is as complete as we can make it, but we realise there may be aircraft we have missed or which have moved to new owners. As already mentioned, there are a surprisingly large number of preserved examples of the 109 design, so if you know of any that are not listed here, please do let us know and we will publish the details on the Aviation Classics website. ■

Words: Tim Callaway

Rebuilt with a DB 605 engine, this HA-1112-M1L, c/n 156 (D-FMBB), FM+BB, is part of the EADS Heritage Flight. **Julian Humphries**

HA-1112-M1L c/n 172 C.4K-102 (G-BWUE) as it appears today as Yellow 10, owned by Historic Flying Ltd. **Editor**

Originally an HA-1112-M1L, c/n 186, This aircraft was rebuilt as a Bf 109E with DB 601 engine and is on display in the Museum of Flight, Seattle, Washington. **Editor**

This Hispano HA-1109-K1L was rebuilt as a Bf 109G-2 with a DB 605 engine and is now on display as Yellow 4 in the Luftwaffenmuseum, Gatow, Berlin. **Constance Redgrave**

HA-1112-M1L c/n 133 C.4K-64 (N109FF), ex-USAFM, Military Aviation Museum, Virginia Beach, Virginia, being engined with DB 605.

Bf 109F-4 10212, ex-JG 5, Air Assets International, Lafayette, Colorado.

Bf 109F-4 10256, ex-11./JG 5, Air Assets International, Lafayette, Colorado.

Bf 109F-4 10276, ex-JG 5, Air Assets International, Lafayette, Colorado.

Bf 109G-2 13927, ex-6./JG 5 Yellow 6.

HA-1112-M1L c/n unkn C.4K-30, ex-471 Squadron 471-26, movie: Battle of Britain, Edwards Collection, Wilson Edwards, Big Spring, Texas.

HA-1112-M1L c/n 129 C.4K-61 (G-AWHE), movie: Battle of Britain, Edwards Collection, Wilson Edwards, Big Spring Texas.

HA-1112-M1L c/n 137 C.4K-116 (N6109), Quantico, Virginia.

HA-1112-M1L c/n 145 C.4K-105 (N6036), movie: Battle of Britain Red 4, ex-Edwards Collection, Richard Hansen, Batavia Illinois.

HA-1112-M1L c/n unkn C.4K-111, ex-471 Squadron 471-15, movie: Battle of Britain, Edwards Collection, Wilson Edwards, Big Spring, Texas.

HA-1112-M1L c/n 166 C.4K-106 (N90607), movie: Battle of Britain Yellow 8, Edwards Collection, Wilson Edwards, Big Spring Texas.

HA-1112-M1L c/n 187 C.4K-99 (N90604), ex-7 Squadron 7-77, movie: Battle of Britain Yellow 5, Edwards Collection, Wilson Edwards, Big Spring Texas.

HA-1112-M1L c/n 190 C.4K-126 (N90603), movie: Battle of Britain Red 9, Edwards Collection, Wilson Edwards, Big Spring, Texas.

HA-1112-M1L c/n 195 C.4K-135, movie: Battle of Britain, ex-Victory Air Museum, St Louis, Missouri.

HA-1112-M1L c/n 220 C.4K-152 (N4109G), movie: Battle of Britain White 5, Edwards Collection, Wilson Edwards, Big Spring, Texas.

HA-1112-M1L c/n 223 C.4K-154, movie: Battle of Britain, Edwards Collection, Wilson Edwards, Texas.

HA-1112-M1L c/n 178 C.4K-178, movie: Battle of Britain, ex-Victory Air Museum, The 1941 Historical Aircraft Group, rebuilt with DB 601N engine.

HA-1112-M4L c/n unkn C.4K-112, ex-7 Squadron 7-92, ex-40 Squadron 40-2, movie: Battle of Britain, Red 11, Wilson Edwards (N1109G) currently in storage with the Edwards Collection, Wilson Edwards, Texas.

NEXT ISSUE

Aviation Classics
www.aviationclassics.co.uk

The Northrop F-5 Freedom Fighter

The Turkish Stars Aerobatic Team fly eight Canadair built NF-5As and Bs, acquired from the Royal Netherlands Air Force. **Constance Redgrave**

ISSUE 19 will be on sale from February 22 priced just **£7.99**

The next issue of *Aviation Classics* moves forward into the 1960s with an iconic Cold War jet fighter that was to become one of the most successful and widely used aircraft of the period. The design began as the N-156 of 1959, a privately funded single seat light fighter concept from Northrop, and developed over the next 20 years into a variety of roles, serving with 36 air forces worldwide. Northrop also developed a two seat version from the same design, the T-38 Talon, which became the world's first supersonic trainer when it entered service in March 1961. Aside from the dedicated trainer aircraft, there was also a separate two seat variant known as the F-5B.

Although the US Air Force did not require a lightweight fighter, a small number of F-5s were purchased as training and aggressor aircraft, as well as 12 that were tested in combat conditions during the Vietnam War under as the Skoshi Tiger project. The two seat trainer was a different story, the US Air Force and Navy acquiring the majority of the 1187 built as advanced weapons trainers.

The majority of the early single seat fighters were supplied to US allies, with more than 800 being supplied to air forces as far apart as Norway and Taiwan. A complete upgrade to the aircraft resulted in the F-5E and two seat F-5F of 1972, as well as a new name, the Tiger II. The new aircraft proved equally popular with air forces world wide, with 1411 being built, many under licence in Korea, Switzerland and Taiwan. The fighter versions were to see combat service with the Ethiopian, Iranian, Kenyan, Moroccan, Saudi Arabian and Yemeni air forces between 1979 to the present day. Aside from the large number of operators across the globe, the lithe and nimble F-5 is most famous as the mount of a number of national aerobatic teams, including the Patrouille Suisse, USAF Thunderbirds, Iranian Golden Crowns and the Turkish Stars. *Aviation Classics* explores the complete history of this often overlooked but highly significant aircraft which was truly a fighter for the world.

For pre-ordering and subscription details call 01507 529529 or go online at www.aviationclassics.co.uk

On the *Aviation Classics* website you'll find historic aircraft and aviation heritage news highlights. There are also online articles and videos.

SAVE £12
SUBSCRIBE TODAY

The EADS Heritage Flight Messerschmitt Bf 109G-4 returning to its home base of Manching in Germany. **Joe Rimensberger**

Get 4 issues of *Aviation Classics* when you subscribe for just £20 a year (UK)

That's just **£5** per issue

MISSED AN ISSUE? As a subscriber you can purchase single issues for only £5. Call 01507 529529 and quote your subscriber number or visit www.aviationclassics.co.uk for more details

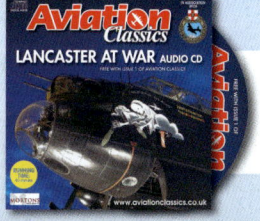

FREE audio CD with every subscription
While stocks last

📞 **01507 529529** 🖱 **www.classicmagazines.co.uk**

NEXT ISSUE

Aviation Classics
www.aviationclassics.co.uk

The Northrop F-5 Freedom Fighter

The Turkish Stars Aerobatic Team fly eight Canadair built NF-5As and Bs, acquired from the Royal Netherlands Air Force. **Constance Redgrave**

The next issue of *Aviation Classics* moves forward into the 1960s with an iconic Cold War jet fighter that was to become one of the most successful and widely used aircraft of the period. The design began as the N-156 of 1959, a privately funded single seat light fighter concept from Northrop, and developed over the next 20 years into a variety of roles, serving with 36 air forces worldwide. Northrop also developed a two seat version from the same design, the T-38 Talon, which became the world's first supersonic trainer when it entered service in March 1961. Aside from the dedicated trainer aircraft, there was also a separate two seat variant known as the F-5B.

Although the US Air Force did not require a lightweight fighter, a small number of F-5s were purchased as training and aggressor aircraft, as well as 12 that were tested in combat conditions during the Vietnam War under as the Skoshi Tiger project. The two seat trainer was a different story, the US Air Force and Navy acquiring the majority of the 1187 built as advanced weapons trainers.

The majority of the early single seat fighters were supplied to US allies, with more than 800 being supplied to air forces as far apart as Norway and Taiwan. A complete upgrade to the aircraft resulted in the F-5E and two seat F-5F of 1972, as well as a new name, the Tiger II. The new aircraft proved equally popular with air forces world wide, with 1411 being built, many under licence in Korea, Switzerland and Taiwan. The fighter versions were to see combat service with the Ethiopian, Iranian, Kenyan, Moroccan, Saudi Arabian and Yemeni air forces between 1979 to the present day. Aside from the large number of operators across the globe, the lithe and nimble F-5 is most famous as the mount of a number of national aerobatic teams, including the Patrouille Suisse, USAF Thunderbirds, Iranian Golden Crowns and the Turkish Stars. *Aviation Classics* explores the complete history of this often overlooked but highly significant aircraft which was truly a fighter for the world.

ISSUE 19 will be on sale from February 22 priced just **£7.99**

For pre-ordering and subscription details call 01507 529529 or go online at www.aviationclassics.co.uk

On the *Aviation Classics* website you'll find historic aircraft and aviation heritage news highlights. There are also online articles and videos.